W
MOMM
DIE

WATCH MOMMY DIE

MICHAEL BENSON

PINNACLE BOOKS
Kensington Publishing Corp.
http://www.kensingtonbooks.com

Some names have been changed to protect the privacy of individuals connected to this story.

PINNACLE BOOKS are published by

Kensington Publishing Corp.
119 West 40th Street
New York, NY 10018

All Kensington Titles, Imprints, and Distributed Lines are available at special quantity discounts for bulk purchases for sales promotions, premiums, fund-raising, and educational or institutional use. Special book excerpts or customized printings can also be created to fit specific needs. For details, write or phone the office of the Kensington special sales manager: Kensington Publishing Corp., 119 West 40th Street, New York, NY 10018, attn: Special Sales Department, Phone: 1-800-221-2647.

Pinnacle and the P logo Reg. U.S. Pat. & TM Off.

ISBN-13: 978-0-7860-2499-5
ISBN-10: 0-7860-2499-2

First printing: May 2011

10 9 8 7 6 5 4 3 2 1

Printed in the United States of America

To the strong survivors,
Elizabeth McLendon Buckner
and the daughter of Laura Ling.

ACKNOWLEDGMENTS

Many people contributed in some way, small or large, to this book. To those who requested anonymity, please know how grateful I am for your assistance. To the others, I would like to thank you here:

McKither Bodison, Warden, Lieber Correctional Institution; Michael C. "Mickey" Braswell, at East Tennessee State University; Kelly Lee Brosky, at the Horry County Office of Public Information; Elizabeth McLendon Buckner; Patti Burns, at the Georgetown County Library; forensic pathologist Dr. Kimberly A. Collins; Dr. Gordon Crews, Associate Professor, Marshall University; Kathleen "Kelly" Crolley and the Owl-O-Rest Factory Outlet furniture store in Surfside Beach, South Carolina; Sergeant Robert A. Cross, Richmond County Sheriff's Office; librarian extraordinaire Margaret Devereaux; my agent, Jake Elwell, Harold Ober Associates; the manager of International and Business Affairs at truTV, Laura Forti; Ann M. Fotiades, Unit Manager, CBS News Information Resources; Greg Froom, at the *South Carolina Lawyers Weekly;* Ginger Gaskins-Weiss, at the Office of the Berkeley County Attorney; Sergeant Jeff Gause, Horry County Police Department; South Carolina Department of Corrections Communications director Josh Gelinas; Laura Ling's tennis buddy, Janis Walker Gilmore; Kensington editor Gary Goldstein; Georgetown County public defender Reuben Goude; the J. Reuben Long Detention Center; the Honorable Deadra L. Jefferson; Margaret Knox, at the Office of General Counsel, SLED; Tracy Minarik, of BlueWaters Pottery, at the Center for Clay Arts, Little River, South Carolina; U.S. Marshal Thedus Mayo; Keith Moore;

Maria Montas, CBS News Archives; Captain Bill Pierce, at the Georgetown County Sheriff's Office; Tonya Root, of the *Sun News;* Stanko's high-school science teacher, Clarice Wenz; and Hillary Winburn, at the Conway Library.

AUTHOR'S NOTE

Although this is a true story, some names will be changed to protect the privacy of the innocent. Pseudonyms will be noted upon their first usage. When possible, the spoken word has been quoted verbatim. However, when that is not possible, conversations have been reconstructed as closely as possible to reality based on the recollections of those that spoke and heard the words. In places, there has been a slight editing of spoken words, but only to improve readability. The denotations and connotations of the words remain unaltered. In some cases, witnesses are credited with verbal quotes that in reality only occurred in written form. Some characters may be composites; and in one case, two characters have been made of one real-life person. The object is to avoid embarrassing anyone who, after all, did not ask to be included in the narrative.

PROLOGUE

"Nine-one-one, what is your emergency?"

Weak and dazed, a small female voice whimpered incoherently on the other end of the line. "Uh . . . uh . . . I . . ."

"May I help you?" the male dispatcher asked.

"I, uh . . ." For a moment, the voice sounded far away.

"Pardon me?"

A deep breath: "I'm at my house and I've been *raped*." She spit out the last word through clenched teeth.

"What's your address?"

"My mom is dead."

"Pardon?"

"My *mom* is *dead!*"

"Okay. What—what, what's your address?" the dispatcher stammered.

She recited her address. The operator asked her to check her mother: "See if she has a pulse."

"I can't. My hands are tied."

"Okay, just hang on." The tape picked up the sound of the dispatcher typing on a keyboard.

"Please hurry."

"Ma'am, ma'am, just stay on the phone with me. I've got people on the way, okay? . . . So who did this?"

"My mom's boyfriend."

"Your boyfriend?"

"My *mom's* boyfriend!"

"Your mom's boyfriend. What's his name?"

The victim now elongated her words and enunciated carefully: "Ste-phen Stan-ko." She started to cry. "I'm scared," she said. He had made her watch while he killed her mother.

"Calm down for a second, okay. I'm going to put you on with another dispatcher, okay?"

"Okay."

"Okay, hold on."

After a pause, a mature and calm female voice came on the line. "Hey," she said.

"Hi," the victim replied. "I'm bleeding from my ear."

"You're bleeding from your ear?"

"Oh God! Oh God!"

"Did he try to hurt you?"

"He raped me!"

"He raped you?"

"My hands are still tied!"

"You're still tied up?"

"Yeah!"

"Okay. We got men out there. They should be there shortly."

"Please hurry. Help me, help me, help me."

"Is he around, do you know?"

"No, he left. Oh God, this isn't supposed to happen to me. There's blood everywhere. I think he cut . . . he cut my neck."

"Did you ever think he might do something like this?"

"No, no. I want my mommy," she said.

"How old are you?"

"Fifteen. I tried to put up a fight. I tried! I tried!"

"Did he hit you or something?"

"Oh God, yes! Mommy—oh God—Mommy!"

The dispatcher kept the girl on the line until help arrived. The girl was letting out high-pitched cries of anguish, repeating again and again that her mother was dead.

"What's taking them so long?"

"They will be right there, honey."

"I want my mommy. Please help my mommy."

One of the first responders to the scene of horror was Charles "Chuck" Petrella, a young paramedic with the rescue squad. Petrella talked to Penny and stayed with her as she was ambulanced to the hospital, leaving her dead mother behind.

Petrella, a father himelf, was moved by Penny, and the next day came to visit her in the hospital. On his way, he stopped at the hospital gift shop and bought her a teddy bear, little knowing that one day she would clutch that teddy bear tightly even as she sat in a court of law delivering testimony that could send her attacker, the murderer of her mother, to death row.

PART I

MR. HYDE

South Carolina, July 2004. The South Carolina Lowcountry shore. Stephen Christopher Stanko was bespectacled, impeccably neat, thirty-six years old, mild-mannered, white—and only just out of prison. Fresh to the outside—having just served eight years of a ten-year sentence for kidnapping, fraud, and breach of trust—he squinted in the strong summer sunshine.

Sure, his morning-fresh freedom gave him a fish-out-of-water feeling—but not as bad as most ex-cons, he figured. He'd shed his prison skin and emerged from his squalid surroundings into the crisp air of freedom with that ol' Stanko sangfroid intact.

He had to pat himself on the back. He had chameleon skills, and could be just what anyone wanted him to be. Plus, he'd actually *accomplished* something in prison. That put him in—what?—the 99.9 percentile of ex-cons!

He entered prison a normal civilian and was released a *published author.*

With a pleasure that bordered on the autoerotic, he enjoyed stroking his own ego. Have to go away for a few years? *Boom,* start a career. He'd turned lemon into lemonade.

Most guys got out and had nothing better to look forward to than manual labor. He had bigger plans. Much bigger. He'd used prison as a tool for upward mobility. It was proof of what a genius he was. Not only had he created a product that would generate income, he'd done some serious planning as well. He knew how to get over in modern society.

Still, even on geniuses such as himself, prison took its toll. It cut away at a man like a thousand small torturous cuts. His confidence was rendered porous by prison. Deep down, gnawing like a rat on the inside of a bedroom wall, was his insecurity. He worried that he'd lost his touch, that years behind bars had institutionalized him.

Ah, but it was all coming back to him—life without bars. Easy as pulling a nickel out of a child's ear. All he had to do was conjure the cheery illusion of truthfulness and sincerity and he'd be sure to succeed. You had to know just how much of the truth to mix in, and he had the knack.

Great webs of deceit he could weave—and almost every dewy silver strand was based on a verifiable fact. Some people couldn't lie for five minutes without betraying themselves. Stanko could go for weeks.

While serving the last days of his sentence, he'd arranged for his first few days of freedom. To help him, he'd recruited the goodwill of a woman he called "Hummer," the mom of a guy in Stanko's cell block. When he first got out, he called Hummer and she "loaned" him money for a motel so he'd have a roof over his head.

Hummer came in handy—for a little while, anyway. He knew that she was not a bottomless well, however. Pretty soon he was going to have to rely on his charm for food and shelter.

Existing as an ex-con can be a tricky business. Stanko coped by speaking about it, but only in positive terms. It was a neurolinguistic technique, a sleight of speech, like hiding something in plain sight. He hoped if he spoke openly and matter-of-factly about prison, others would think it matter-of-fact.

The story of his crimes, as he told it, was always framed as the prelude to revelation and epiphany. Prison gave him a chance to find himself, to discover his true value. And that was considerable. Just ask his *publisher*.

When he chose to talk about "going away," Stanko liked to paint his criminal history as white-collar crapola. No big deal. A freakin' railroad job. He'd admit, maybe, that he was a bit of a bs artist. But there was nothing un-American about that—it was all part of getting ahead.

But he never mentioned his kidnapping conviction, the details of which could seep right into a person's nightmares. Anyone with a dollop of decency would deem them disturbing—and Stanko was hip enough to know he had to keep them secret.

And that part of his personality, the one that came out when he was angry and with a woman, must never emerge again. That was a rule. If he had a fatal flaw, that was it. Put that guy in the recesses of the mind and keep him there. When he did think about it, Stanko realized he was as a man stricken with lycanthropy, like the Wolfman, Lawrence Talbot, fearing the rise of the full moon would transform him into a bloodthirsty beast, like Dr. Jekyll, keeping Mr. Hyde on the down low. A monster that did very bad things—did them ecstatically—lived inside Stanko. Then it went away, leaving Stanko to endure the soul-crushing consequences.

Thinking about it made it worse for him. The idea was to sublimate the urge, push it deep, deep inside and hold it there. It was a constant struggle—like holding a balloon underwater.

An ex-con turned literati darling once described incarceration as living "in the belly of the beast." And when you were released—Stanko thought, pushing the metaphor—you came out the beast's ass. No bad men were cured in prison, Stanko knew. They just got worse, until they turned to complete shit.

Now, the Hummer ticket cashed in and spent—at least for the time being—Stanko headed for the Myrtle Beach area. Where better in the summer?

WELCOME TO THE GRAND STRAND the sign said.

During the first weeks of his freedom, he stayed in a number of rooms, all cheap—the landladies (there were never landlords) mostly unpaid. He looked for a job, but it was tough for a quality guy like himself to face the rejection. One look of suspicion or distaste from a prospective employer and his mood was shot the rest of the day. He got so mad.

He needed something to do with his days; so he began work on his research, maybe get an outline started for his latest literary creation. All he needed was a blank notebook, a cheap ballpoint, and a library with a *pretty librarian.*

THE LIBRARIAN AND HER DAUGHTER

Stephen Stanko took up his research at the Horry County Memorial Library–Socastee Branch. It was a good library, with many books on subjects that interested him. Happily for Stanko, it fit the second criteria as well. The librarian was gorgeous! A raven-haired beauty.

"I'm Stephen Stanko, the *author*," he said to her.

"Laura Ling, pleased to meet you," she replied. (Not to be confused with the Laura Ling who was the sister of TV personality Lisa Ling, who was held captive for a time in North Korea.)

Stanko asked her where she was from.

Dallas, Texas, born and raised, she said, her inflection emphasizing a musical Southwestern drawl. Stanko kept asking questions and she answered. She was born Laura Elizabeth Hudson. Her mother was Sue McKee Wilson Hudson. Dad, Earl Pierce Hudson, died too young. There was something they had in common, they both completely rocked high school. Laura was the BGOC—"big gal on campus"—at North Garland High. She had range. A member of the Beta Club ("Me too," Stanko said, telling the truth) and vice president of the student council, she was inducted into the National Honor Society and was a nominee for Miss North Garland. Good-looking, brains, and politically savvy, too—a triple-threat gal, laugh out loud.

After high school, Laura went to Texas A&M University, where, an honor roll student, she majored in English. She later earned a master's in library science at the University of South Carolina.

After school she married Chris Ling and had three children: two sons and the youngest, a pretty daughter, Penelope, who was called Penny (pseudonym). When they divorced, the boys lived with their dad, Ling moved into a place in Murrells Inlet, with her daughter, and she took a job as a reference librarian at the Socastee Public Library, near Myrtle Beach.

The library was modern and designed to please the eye, a one-story brick building, with its own parking lot and a semicircular driveway that allowed cars to drop library-goers right out front. Plus, a roof extended out over the driveway in front of the main entrance, so those entering and leaving weren't exposed to rain or intense sun.

Out front by the road was a brick structure that existed only as a mounting surface for the sign. At the top was the county emblem, which reminded passersby that this was THE INDEPENDENCE REPUBLIC. Below that were the street number and the name of the library. In front of the brick sign, a spotlight protruded from the finely manicured lawn, so the words remained legible after dark.

Inside, Ling proved herself a master librarian. For any serious researcher, Ling was perfect to befriend. It wasn't that her knowledge of any subject was exhaustive. She might not have known a fact, but she knew where to look it up. Her responsibilities at the library grew, and one of the extracurricular activities she signed up for was teaching senior citizens how to use a computer.

Upon first meeting, Laura Ling was attracted to the seemingly harmless Stephen Stanko. She found his intelligence and quiet confidence tremendously appealing. And he was good-looking to boot.

He didn't hide being an ex-con. *White-collar* crimes, he always added. He'd learned his lesson and changed his ways. Seen the light. Now he had a *cause*.

One of the first questions she asked him was "Author?" Yes, he replied enthusiastically. He'd written a book in prison, and it had been published—a fact that Laura Ling wasted no time verifying. There it was, on her computer screen. His book was a call for prison reform and modernized methods of rehabilitation. Ling was so impressed. As far as she knew, he was the first published author to walk into her library, which, after all, was a branch. Sure, he was an ex-con. That was *secondary*.

Yeah, one book published, Stanko boasted, but he'd written several. In addition to his scholarly work, he also had two novels and an autobiography in the can. He was shopping the autobiography around, figured that would be the next to be published.

He was a smart guy, maybe an intellectual, too smart to be a criminal. And now that he was free at last, he couldn't have seemed more rehabilitated.

She ordered a copy of his book for her library's shelves and told Stanko to consider her library *his* library. He had access to all of the books, not just in the branch, but in the entire system. If he wanted a book and couldn't find it on the shelf, they could go together to the county library system's online catalog. The library had subscription-based databases for research in newspapers, magazines, and journals published from the mid-1980s on. There was a free *New York Times* archive on the Web, but it only included before 1922 and after 1987. Otherwise, you had to pay a fee. After years of dealing with clumsy microfiche, the Horry County libraries now had the much-easier-to-use microfilm for its periodical archives. And, of course, he would have access to the Internet. He had come to the right place, she said. Socastee was a library where he could do *all* of his research and see a friendly face at the same time.

Through Ling, Stanko made another friend, seventy-four-year-old Henry Lee Turner. Turner had taken one of Ling's computer classes, held at the library. Later, when he had computer problems, he called Ling and she came over to his house to help him, bringing Stanko with her.

Ling was well loved by her colleagues. She went the extra mile to help people. Turner was an aging veteran, who lived in a mobile home and loved to fish. For a con man, they were the perfect marks.

Laura Ling urged Stephen Stanko to be ambitious. In September, he sent a proposal for a grant to the National Institute of Justice to work with underprivileged children. His idea was sort of a Scared Straight program, during which he would make those tough street kids aware that illegal behavior had extremely unpleasant consequences.

He never heard back. An ex-con who wanted to work with kids! How many red flags did that raise?

Ling learned about, but was untroubled by, the terms of Stanko's probation. He'd been released a year and a half early with the caveat that he leave his residence only for work or for church. Any other outing had to be approved in advance by his probation officer.

Laura eagerly introduced Stanko to her family, confident of the impression he would make. And she was right. They thought him fine. Victoria Loy, Laura's sister, remembered him as "pleasant and solicitous." She recalled an attentive man who focused on Laura and made her feel special. And he couldn't have seemed more normal. If there was anything off-putting about the new boyfriend, Victoria didn't pick up on it. She didn't know what he was like before prison, but he seemed like a real nice guy after it. And Victoria remembered how happy Laura was, and how warm and good it felt to see her that way. She had a new handsome boyfriend, with smarts and charm, a published author who looked good either in a suit or a golf shirt! *Whew.* Laura was happier than she had been in a long time—and that made her friends and relatives happy.

Laura's home was close to the corner of Murrells Inlet Road and Mary Lou Avenue, about three hundred yards, the length of a short par 4, from the water's edge. She brought Stanko home to meet her daughter during October 2004, on what happened to be pretty Penny's fifteenth birthday.

Penny remembered well the occasion of Stanko's first visit. She could tell he wanted the evening to go well. He was on his very best behavior—not that he wasn't always. But on this occasion, he was almost nervous, because his hopes were so high.

And, more important, as far as the teenager was concerned, her mother was *so* happy. She was beaming with joy, radiating happiness, when Stanko was at her side.

That made Penny happy—and she approved of

Stanko, too. He knew stuff, could make her laugh, and seemed like the "all-around great boyfriend."

Penny remembered saying some things that became really, really ironic, when she looked back on it. After Stanko's visit on her birthday, she had lightheartedly needled her mother.

"Gee, Mom, thanks for bringing home an ex-con," Penny had said. But she was just kidding. She thought Stephen seemed like "a great guy, without a great past."

The teenager heard Stephen talk about his future in such hopeful terms. He wanted a new start on life, a new beginning. Her mom, who normally enjoyed helping people, looked at that as "an opportunity." She wanted to help him begin anew.

After knowing her for two months, Stanko told Laura that he was being evicted from his apartment. Was it okay if he moved in with her? Laura said she'd have to get the approval of Penny.

Stanko said, "Of course," and the matter was presented to the teenager. Penny, finding joy in her mother's happiness, responded, "Sure, why not?"

Penny and Stanko even spent some quality alone time. He helped her build a birdhouse. Taught her how to drive a car with a stick shift. Everything was moving along nicely, Stanko thought.

The Lings lived in an oil-painting-worthy village of Murrells Inlet, another picture postcard from South Carolina's Lowcountry. Best known for its fishing, the village was a sensual delight. Scenic, for sure, but it also felt, smelled, and sounded good. In the mornings, there was the glorious cacophony of the feeding gulls in the inlet. You could watch them, diving into the water, poking their sharp little beaks into the pluff mud, the dark soft mud in the marshes—in search of tasty morsels. Murrells Inlet tasted good also. Its restaurants, thirty of them, were seafood places mostly, of course, but some ethnic entries as well to offer variety, and they were considered the best around. There was also a seafood market for do-it-yourself chefs. Visitors who wanted to go to sea and catch their meal could easily charter a boat from an appropriately briny captain—or rent a canoe or kayak and piddle-paddle at a leisurely pace in the inlet. Plus, there were potentially romantic strolls through Brookgreen Gardens, the world's largest outdoor sculpture garden, aromatherapy provided by the bountiful magnolias and azaleas. And, as was true of the entire Myrtle Beach area, there was plenty of golf. It was a great place to live—a great place to fall in love.

For Stephen Stanko, Murrells Inlet was indescribably beautiful. The contrast to the scenery he'd grown used to in prison was practically dazzling. Locals didn't necessarily see it as perfect, however. Compared to the beaches on the Atlantic Ocean, Murrells Inlet was swampy.

The Lings lived in a small L-shaped house. With light green siding and black shutters around white window frames, it looked like it could have been a mobile home bent at its center. It was situated so that its concave angle faced the road. There was a wooden porch and a set of steps at the front door, just left of center.

Stanko felt like he'd stepped in it—stepped into *paradise*. It wasn't just the locale, either. Like Humbert Humbert, the hero/villain of Nabokov's *Lolita*, he'd lip-smackingly insinuated himself into his own peculiar dream. Only two months after meeting Laura Ling, Stephen Stanko was cohabitating with her and her daughter.

OWL-O-REST

For some of the time after Stephen Stanko got out of prison, he had a job, but most of his energy was dedicated toward confidence games. In his heart of hearts, in his innermost psyche, he was a flimflam man. No getting around it.

On December 8, 2004, Stanko—as usual, well kempt and wearing a suit—walked into the Owl-O-Rest Factory Outlet furniture store in a small strip mall between a post office and a suntan place on 17 Business North, in Surfside Beach, South Carolina.

It was a family business, owned by a woman, her ex-husband, and her mom. The woman was Kathleen "Kelly" Crolley, who years later recalled, "The store was started by my stepfather in June of '83. I originally agreed to help him part-time, while completing college here at the beach. A year later, he passed away."

The establishment was modestly sized—7,500 square feet.

She was twenty-one at the time. Her mother had four children under eight—and one on the way. The store was no gold mine—not now, and definitely not then—

but Kelly played with the cards she was dealt and ran the store to the best of her ability. She made some changes. Now the store stocked a lot of coastal designs and also offered a lot of special orders for people. They worked with about 150 different vendors.

Crolley was one of four people working on the day Stanko came in. He was wearing business attire. Although he was polite enough, he wasn't relaxed and seemed in a hurry.

"If I was to order a gift for my wife, would it be delivered in time for Christmas?" he asked.

Crolley said it would. All he had to do was say the word and she would place the order immediately. The present would arrive in plenty of time.

"If it doesn't arrive on time, could you give me a photocopy out of a catalog? You know, so I'll have something to wrap and put under the tree."

Crolley remembered saying no problem. The man said he was in the market for a rolltop desk and another one, which would fit into an odd space.

"I think he said four feet. He decided on the one for sure and would think about the other," she recalled.

Stanko explained that he was building a house on Pawleys Island. As Crolley and Stanko looked at all kinds of desks, discussing the pros and cons of each, he answered his cell phone five times.

"He would walk around the corner, sometimes to accept the call and thank the other party for their contribution, and offer to meet them for lunch," Crolley recalled. He told them he hoped that he could find people to match their generosity.

She normally would not inquire about a customer's private conversation, but she couldn't help herself. She told him that she wasn't trying to be nosy, but she was curious. "You know, as to what was going on," Crolley said.

Stanko told Crolley he was a corporate attorney practicing in Texas, but he had taken off work for the past year to a year and a half to begin a charity: the Children's Cancer Research Foundation.

He was pleased to say it was doing very well. There was to be a big write-up the next day in the *Sun News,* with all the businesses that were sponsoring the charity. He was giving a plaque to all the businesses that helped. He said he'd raised about $500,000 so far.

His reason for starting the charity couldn't have been more personal. He had a thirteen-year-old niece stricken with cancer. At that very moment, he said, she was hospitalized at the Medical University of South Carolina.

"My baby girl was born prematurely there. She weighed one pound, twelve ounces, and everyone did a great job," Crolley said. During that tough time, she'd stayed at the Ronald McDonald House. She couldn't say enough good about the place, and she was pleased to say that today she had a healthy and happy little girl.

After that brief exchange, the seed planted, Stanko returned to shopping for a desk. There were more phone calls. Crolley left the customer with a couple of catalogs and went to talk to her ex-husband and mom.

"You think it would be okay for me to give one hundred dollars to a very good cause?" she asked them.

She told Stanko that they weren't able to contribute much, but that the store would like to participate. "He never asked me for a dime!" Crolley remembered, still flabbergasted by Stanko's acting ability.

He placed the order for one desk, still undecided about the second. As they were doing the paperwork, she noticed the delivery address seemed a little off.

"A lot of my customers are second-home owners or have just moved here and will frequently not know the

directions or exact address of their home, so I let it go—
but it was a flag," Crolley explained.

In retrospect—twenty-twenty hindsight—there were
other clues that not all was as it seemed. The desk was to
be a surprise, Stanko said, a Christmas gift for his wife,
so he had to talk with his secretary about how to work
out his deposit without the wife knowing about it.

Stanko said he would come back the next day to complete the deal. He wanted to sleep on it before he ordered the second desk.

Before he left, Crolley said, "Wait here, I want to give
some money for the cause, and the store does, too."

Stanko was pleased.

"What was the name of the charity again?" she asked.

"You could just make the checks out to me, Stephen
Stanko."

The red flags seemed so obvious to Crolley years later.

"I could do that, but we'll need a receipt from you for
the store—you know, for tax purposes."

She gave him an Owl-O-Rest check for one hundred
dollars, and one for twenty-five dollars from her. On the
receipt, Stanko put the name of the research foundation
and signed, *from Steve Stanko*.

After Stanko left the store with the checks, Crolley ran
the sequence of events over and over in her mind and
came to the conclusion there was something iffy about
that guy.

To be safe, she called the Better Business Bureau and
asked if they had any record of Stanko's charity in South
Carolina. They said they didn't.

After hanging up, she remembered that he'd said he
practiced corporate law in Texas. Maybe the charity was
registered down there, she thought.

Her next call was to the *Sun News*. The guy she talked
to said he had no knowledge of Stanko's charity, and

knew nothing of the big article scheduled for the next day. Afterward, Crolley suspected that she might not have talked to the right person.

When Stanko did not return the next day, as promised, Crolley still didn't write him off. She thought perhaps he had gotten busy with "all the commotion," the *Sun News* thing, and all of those plaques.

The following day, she called him. During the conversation, he said the *Sun News* event had gone well, and she had to admit that she'd been busy and hadn't gotten around to buying a copy of the newspaper.

She said she'd already ordered the rolltop, but he had to place the order that day in order to receive the second desk in time. He asked if he could give her his brother's credit card number.

Crolley said she couldn't do that without speaking directly with his brother. Stanko said okay, he would visit the store the next day with the cash.

"I never spoke with him again," she recalled.

Crolley kept an eye on the checks and found that the store check was cashed at a nearby bank. On the same day the check was cashed, a little video store beside the bank was robbed.

"My mom even went to the video store to inquire as to what the robber looked like, which was kind of awkward for her, but we were afraid there might have been a connection," Crolley said.

She never did get to the proper authorities to find out the information she was after.

"My personal check was held longer and I was actually concerned—not so much for personal safety, but more for identity theft."

She had a special watch put on her account and asked around if anyone else had heard of Stephen Stanko.

"I really feared he was bad news, but did not know

what to do about it. I wasn't even sure a crime had been committed, since he never asked for the money," Crolley explained.

Kelly Crolley's experience with Stephen Stanko was typical of those first months when he needed cash and was busy thinking up new confidence games.

He felt no twinge of guilt. A man had to do what he had to do. Getting a job was Mission: Impossible, so what else was he supposed to do?

He'd have to cast his spells on people.

He always scammed women, and he made thousands of dollars just with his ability to lie effectively. On some, he pulled the "collecting money for sick kids" bit.

For others, he said, "I'm a lawyer," and offered various legal services for a fee. When he scored, he'd hit a bar or a bookstore or a mall, and begin trolling for a new victim.

Professionally Stephen Stanko might have been struggling, but his personal life couldn't be beat. Those early days with Laura Ling—romancing, then cohabitating—were about the best times that there ever were, according to him.

He later said, with no apparent sense of irony, that he and Laura shared a love that was straight out of a Harlequin romance novel. It was an *unconditional* love. They loved each other without question. They never passed judgment.

Removing the rose-colored glasses, we find something less than nirvana in Murrells Inlet. In reality, Stanko sold Laura and Penny Ling a package of lies, and they bought it all.

He said he had an engineering degree from a military

college, that he'd worked as a paralegal. He also told them that he'd practiced law without a license—but that turned out to be the truth.

He kept busy doing things, always painting his activities with broad strokes of legitimacy and benevolence. He was charitable and political, always on the side of good.

Stanko suspected the authorities were keeping an eye on him, and he geared some schemes directly toward them. He wanted to send a clear message that he was trying to succeed, trying to be a positive force on society.

To accomplish this, he'd started a program to help juvenile delinquents return to the straight and narrow. Plus, his literary ambitions were rekindled. He couldn't divulge the details, he said, but he was working on a major literary work.

As time passed, from 2004 to 2005, Stanko wasn't feeling the upward mobility he had when he first got out of prison. His genius was rendered all but moot.

To those who bothered to observe carefully, Stanko's activities were a mask covering up his bleak reality. He was just another ex-con who couldn't get a job.

RESEARCH

During this time, Stephen Stanko did have at least one friend, who called him once a month or so to see how he was doing. It was Dr. Gordon Crews, one of the coauthors of Stanko's published book, *Living in Prison.*

The book's complete title and byline was *Living in Prison: A History of the Correctional System with an Insider's View* by Stephen Stanko, Wayne Gillespie, and Gordon A. Crews.

Stanko and Crews had had frequent phone conversations when Stanko was in prison. Then, like now, Stanko mostly griped. Stanko told Crews it was tough on the outside being an ex-con. Nobody wanted to hire the guy who was just out. Crews reminded him that he was a guy with a lot of skills, and to think positively.

Stanko hit Crews up for money. He tried to sell his future royalties from the book to Crews, who said he should be writing again. Just because he was a free man didn't mean he had to stop writing. He wasn't a prisoner/writer. He was a writer!

Stanko wanted to write another book, to use his extraordinary experience and scientific knowledge, not to mention intuition, to teach the world a precious lesson about some other topic that wasn't "living in prison."

Stanko gave some thought to the topic of his new yet-to-be-written book. He kicked around a few ideas and decided: serial killers. He'd always been interested in the subject. It would be cool to become an expert.

That decided, Stanko's trips to the Socastee library became purposeful. Multipurposed even. He read all day, and kept copious notes. And when he was taking a break, he was chatting—quietly, of course—with his girlfriend.

He thought about being comprehensive, to learn about every serial killer in history, their MOs, their body count, their signature. The book could be like an encyclopedia. It could work. There was that much public interest. There had even been serial killer trading cards a few years back.

Maybe he wouldn't make it comprehensive. For one thing, it had been done; for another, he figured the book would be better with a more narrow scope.

He would focus—look in minute detail—on the serial killers he found most fascinating. Six to ten killers for the whole book—the serial killers who appealed to Stanko more than the others.

Like many modern-day enthusiasts, Stanko observed serial killers with something that greater resembled admiration than disdain. There was a definite hierarchy, guys who stood out. Guys with superior bloodthirstiness and perversion. Members of the—drumroll—"Serial Killer Hall of Fame."

He had a notebook that he was filling with notes from the books he read in the library. He also spent a lot of time in periodicals. He printed news and magazine articles about hard-core crime from the library's microfilm archives and kept a scrapbook.

* * *

Which killers to include? Some were a lock.

Like "Zodiac," for example. ID unknown. Bastard got *away* with it. Terrorized millions for years. He was the original masked gunman prowling lovers' lanes in Northern California, shooting and stabbing young lovers during the late 1960s and early 1970s.

This was before the big Zodiac movie. All he knew, he learned from books. Stephen Stanko liked Zodiac a lot. He was psychologically terrifying, and he backed it up with death.

Plus, his terror campaign was visual. He had a Zodiac costume that he wore when he went out to perforate young white women—like every day was Halloween.

To some extent movies such as *Halloween* and *Friday the 13th* were based on Zodiac, who added the "masked homicidal maniac stalking teenagers" theme to the big picture of serial murders!

One of Zodiac's intended victims—the male half of a necking couple that the killer ambushed beside a lake— survived Zodiac's stabbing, although his girlfriend was murdered. He *saw* Zodiac, and lived to talk about it.

Zodiac's shirt, the survivor saw, had a circle with crosshairs over it, a symbol he had also used in his letters and other written communications. The killer wore a sack, square at the top, over his head, with eyeholes cut in it. As he was being stabbed, the survivor saw that Zodiac was wearing glasses inside his spooky hood.

In his letters, Zodiac made the cops and the press look stupid, jerking them around with an unbreakable code that he promised would, if deciphered, identify him.

Although some of Zodiac's codes were solved, the one with his name in it was not. He was taunting the cops, yanking them around. His letters described a bloodlust only appeased by murder, and a raging misogyny, all cloaked in a crude attempt at far-out 1969 hippie vernacular. Zodiac thought shooting chicks was the "ultimate trip."

Criminal profilers, professional and amateur alike, analyzed the many clues Zodiac supplied, and tried to figure out what kind of guy he was. Many theorized that the Zodiac had been a military man—perhaps a sailor.

Like Dad, Stanko thought.

Stanko had Zodiac pegged as not much of a stud. If he was any kind of lover boy, he'd have worked it so that he got a piece before he snuffed them. Stanko assumed a lot of these "gun does my talking" types suffered from erectile dysfunction.

At the scene of a cabdriver's murder in San Francisco, a bloody fingerprint, presumed to belong to Zodiac, was found. Over the years, there had been a handful of suspects in the Zodiac murders. Some didn't pan out, and some stuck around.

The best suspect was the late Arthur Leigh Allen, whose spending records revealed him to be frequently in Zodiac's vicinity. He also had proximity with several of the victims, and may have been an acquaintance with one of the victims. His handwriting looked like Zodiac's; he had a history of doing really sick things; and his demeanor, when he was questioned, was oddly defiant, very much the type of personality to use the mail to laugh at authority figures, while simultaneously terrifying all of Northern California. Some said the case against Allen was a construct of a true-crime writer, and, in reality, was much weaker than presented. Allen was said in a couple of books to have received a speeding ticket in the vicinity of one murder. This was declared untrue by a third source. Plus, his thumbprint didn't match the bloody one found at one of the murder scenes.

One thing that everyone could agree on, Stanko discovered, was that Zodiac—along with Charles Manson and the murder at Altamont—was part of that "death of the counterculture" gestalt, symbols of the end of an era, the 1960s—such a hopeful decade turned horrible by violence—giving way to the disastrous 1970s.

The killer not only wrote taunting letters to police and press, sometimes using code, but he established his bona fides in a shiveringly creepy fashion, enclosing in the envelopes bloodstained cloth torn from a victim's shirt.

Maybe, some theorized, Zodiac was more than one guy. Did a conspiracy theory fit? Maybe the one writing the letters was never the one shooting the gun. Paranoids noted that the case resembled a military mind-control experiment that had gotten out of hand.

There were a lot of theories—some almost solid, others wacko—and the Zodiac letters continued for years. One guy thought that he turned into the "Unabomber." Zodiac claimed for years in his writing that he was still killing people; after the initial burst of murders, no more bodies could positively be linked to him.

In some ways, Stanko thought, the Zodiac killer was the most legendary of the serial killers.

Stephen Stanko also exhaustively researched "Son of Sam," aka David Berkowitz. Son of Sam was a derivation of the Zodiac theme a few years later. He also shot teenagers and young adults in the nighttime.

Unlike Zodiac who prowled the plentiful desolation of Northern California, Son of Sam patrolled the side streets of New York City. He found victims on front stoops, walking down the sidewalk, and (like Zodiac) necking in parked cars.

Son of Sam always used the same gun: a fearsome .44 bulldog. He shot couples or females alone. Never males alone. Because of the girth of his bullets, he cruelly maimed the victims he didn't kill.

Like Zodiac, Son of Sam wrote taunting letters to the police and press. But the East Coast version was an upgrade in a way. His prose was written by a deviant poet, exhibiting a well-honed terroristic craft. Stanko was a writer and noticed the difference right away.

The similarities in the messages of mayhem were compelling as well. The chilling taunts of the Zodiac and the Rimbaud-like prose-poetry of Son of Sam bubbled up from the same misogynistic vat.

Berkowitz was caught and arrested, and the police said he was the Son of Sam. But, just as some people believed Zodiac was a team effort, there was a compelling theory that Berkowitz did not act alone. Perhaps Son of Sam, which referred to itself as a group in the letters, was a Devil-worshipping cult, holding meetings in a cave in a park north of the city, a club of death, in which the same .44 was passed around so that every satanic member had an opportunity to kill with it. The killing only stopped when one of them was caught, and he took the rap for everybody.

A writer searched Westchester County in search of this cult and found evidence that it existed—in a park, in a cave decorated with satanic symbolism.

The theories grew wackier. One suggested that the Sam kills were filmed from a van always in the vicinity, those snuff films going for top dollar to the pervs who paid for that junk.

How good could those films be? Stanko wondered—if they did exist. They were shooting at night from a distance. To get any kicks out of the kills, you'd need a camera getting close-ups inside the cars where the carnage was.

At first, Berkowitz confessed to all thirteen shootings. He had a loony tunes tale to tell: Sam was a cranky neighbor who worshipped the Devil, drank blood, and sent messages to Berkowitz via the incessant barking of his dog, Harvey. Berkowitz said he acted alone, and cops, eager to wrap up the nightmare, were eager to believe him.

Later, Berkowitz said he'd only done a couple of the shootings, that others had pulled the .44's trigger as well. Then he had his throat slashed in prison and claimed to have "found God."

Stephen Stanko discovered Ted Bundy–land, a vast continent of research on the crown prince of serial killers. There were people who thought Bundy was the most fascinating serial killer of all time. He combined the looks and charm of a swinging bachelor with an unquenchable thirst to kill as many pretty young girls as he could.

Now here was a guy that Stanko could identify with. A chick magnet/snuff artist. Bundy helped launch the career of the legendary true-crime writer Ann Rule, who worked beside him and never sensed the evil.

Bundy was a 1970s serial killer, and the fun part here was the way Bundy continued to lie about and cover up his murders, even as the evidence mounted against him, and his charm and powers of persuasion were such that he always had allies right up until the end.

Although most experts believed Bundy killed at least thirty-five people, when Bundy finally confessed, he admitted to only thirty. He was a rapist, a necrophiliac, and a postmortem surgeon.

After seducing his always lovely victims into a private moment, he took them by surprise—either coming up from behind or sometimes accosting them as they slept—and rapidly bludgeoned them into unconsciousness.

On some occasions, the bludgeoning itself turned out to be fatal; but in some other cases, after they were knocked out, he would become intimate and manually strangle them.

Bundy did not give up his freedom easily. After one of his arrests, he escaped by jumping out a second-story courthouse window. Hurting his ankle in the fall, he limped around free for a short while.

He was a nomadic killer. He killed in the American Northwest, on the salt flats, and in the Rocky Mountains. He killed in Florida, and it was there that he was caught the last time and eventually was pushed into the electric chair. Predictably, he had gone to his execution kicking and screaming.

Stanko thought Bundy's modus operandi was worthy of extra thought. Hit 'em over the head, knock them out or make them groggy, and *then* get intimate. There would be a lot less potentially harmful rasslin' that way.

One of the newest serial killers who was Hall of Fame worthy was "BTK," another writer of taunting letters. BTK was an acronym for bind, torture, and kill. He did his thing in Wichita, Kansas.

BTK was different, because although FBI profilers would have called it impossible, he ran off a string of murders that terrified Kansas, stopped, and then came back a generation later to create a second nightmare for that city.

The BTK case had some things going for it, in a fetishistic way. Lots of bondage. Dude was into rope— exquisite restraint. Military men knew their knots!

His first kills occurred in a spree: He wiped out most of a family, stringently binding them before asphyxiating them slowly. Found dead were the dad, the mom, and little brother on the main floor, and little sister hanging from the rafters of the basement, her toes only inches above the floor, pants pulled down and smeared with semen. The older siblings came home from school that day and found themselves alone in the world.

That pervy stuff was one thing, but Stephen Stanko really latched onto him because BTK had literary aspirations. The killer wrote letters and sent creepy drawings. He illustrated one of his crime scenes in a graphic and horribly accurate way—like Zodiac and Son of Sam might've if they'd had artistic skills. His most troubling drawing was accurate right down to the placement of the furniture in the victim's bedroom, to the position of the victim's eyeglasses on top of her dresser.

For almost thirty years, no one had a clue who BTK could be. Might be your next-door neighbor. His career was like a movie sequel. He BTK'd a bunch of victims, hibernated for years, and then came back.

Another reason Stanko liked this case was because it made the straights of Wichita—the cops and the press and the political leaders—seem really stupid. Law enforcement became so desperate, it did silly things.

Those knuckleheads had heard of subliminal advertising, like when movie theaters had inserted single frames of Coke and popcorn during a movie, and supposedly sales went up. It was supposed to work on the subconscious without the conscious mind even knowing it. Like Keystone Kops, the police rigged a TV show about BTK—they knew BTK would be watching.

During the program, which would review in detail all of BTK's kills and communications, they would subliminally insert a symbol the killer used in his letters, sort of a BTK logo that hadn't been made public. That was accompanied by a photo of a telephone and a drawing of an Indian chief. Out of that, the killer was supposed to subconsciously understand the message: "BTK, call the chief," as in the chief of police. BTK did not call.

But he did eventually get caught, a generation later. Dennis Rader did himself in by purposefully leaving clue after clue, until, unaware of the sophistication of cyber sleuthing, his computer gave him up.

Some days when Stephen Stanko came into the library, he studied not a serial killer but a famous murder, such as the murder of Beth Short in 1947 Hollywood, better known as the "Black Dahlia" murder.

This was a good one because there were photos. Beth Short was a rather lazy black-haired starlet who came from New England to Hollywood to be a star. Instead, she ended up floating around Southern California, accepting donations from various escorts.

The last stranger she found herself with tortured her for days, carving her flesh and slicing a Sardonicus-like smile into her cheeks. That brutally inflicted rictus came last, and she drowned in her own blood.

Her remains were drained of blood by her killer. She was surgically sliced in two at the waist and placed in a vacant lot in the Leimert Park section of Los Angeles.

Stanko stared at the photos of the pale and mutilated form lying obscenely like a broken manikin only a few inches from the sidewalk. The photos were in black and white, and you could feel the evil juju coming off them. They hearkened back to the days of film noir, dark movies he'd seen as a kid—all fedoras, bullet bras, and shadow.

What must it have been like to be there and see that bisected nude body? It was almost too intense to think about.

The shelves of the library were rich with Black Dahlia books, everybody and their mother thought they knew who had killed the Black Dahlia. At least two unrelated people claimed it was their father. But no one knew who it was. He—or they—got away with it. Like Zodiac, wreaking havoc in the world, and walking.

As Stephen Stanko researched killer after killer, one of his favorites—one he would return to, again and again, re-reading passages that he was already familiar with—was the prolific Gary Ridgway, aka "The Green River Killer." He killed so many.

There were different ways to rank the serial killers, but number of victims was the most scientific, and Ridgway was right up there. When he finally confessed, in 2001, he recalled murdering at least forty-eight women.

The murders took place in the 1980s and 1990s. Ridgway killed both white and black women—when the assumption of the time was that heterosexual serial killers usually stuck to the opposite sex, but the same race. Not Ridgway. He was an equal-opportunity killer, choking his victims sometimes with his arm and sometimes using a ligature.

He committed his crimes near Seattle and Tacoma, Washington, and earned his nickname by using the Green River as his initial dump site. The disposal ground, Stanko figured, was probably a matter of convenience rather than aesthetics—"down by the river" being a place where a fellow could have some privacy. Although he did spread his kills out over two decades, the great majority of them occurred in quick succession from 1982 to 1984.

Unlike a lot of serial killers, Ridgway wasn't very bright, with a two-digit IQ. Stanko certainly couldn't identify with that. Stanko was a flippin' genius.

Ridgway committed his first violent act at sixteen and stabbed a six-year-old boy. Stanko read about Ridgway's troubled mind. "I'd always wondered what it felt like to kill someone," Ridgway said of his youth, and Stanko could feel him, man.

Ridgway had served in Vietnam, aboard a navy patrol boat. Like Arthur Shawcross ("The Genesee River Killer") in Rochester, New York, he graduated from harming children to murdering women down on their luck, prostitutes and runaways.

He would use the same dump site repeatedly before moving; so when remains were found, bunches of remains were found. His dump sites were so secluded, however, that those remains were usually skeletal by the time they were discovered. The victims were left naked and sometimes posed in positions designed to degrade them further.

Because of Ridgway's venue, the Great Northwest, some of the detectives working his case had also been involved in the search for Ted Bundy. In fact, after Bundy was captured, detectives interviewed him in hopes he might be able to shed some light on the Green River case. Bundy gave it the old college try, but his expertise was unhelpful.

During the long investigation, Ridgway was arrested twice, both times on prostitution-related charges. Following his first arrest, he was considered a suspect in the Green River killings, but he was crossed off the list after passing a polygraph examination with flying colors. Murderers with severe personality disorders, police had learned, sometimes could fool a lie detector because they lacked shame and guilt, and didn't feel the normal stress when lying.

In 1987, police took hair and saliva samples from Ridgway; so, when DNA technology developed, these samples were used to match Ridgway with semen found on Green River victims. He was arrested in 2001 and, at first, charged with twenty killings. By the time he was convicted in court, twenty-eight more victims had been added to his kill list.

Stephen Stanko was a straight guy, but his all-time favorite serial killer was gay: Jeffrey Dahmer. Maybe the gay aspect enhanced the grisliness of Dahmer's tale for Stanko, but maybe not. Maybe it was just the fact that Dahmer was so completely sick in so many ways, he was number one, the ultimate nightmare.

And he did it in Milwaukee, Wisconsin—the most *normal* of cities.

On the night of May 27, 1991, in Milwaukee, a naked fourteen-year-old Asian boy burst out through the front door of a house and began to scream in the street. In quick pursuit was a blond young man named Dahmer.

The cops showed up, and the frightened teenager said the man was trying to kill him. The blond man told the police that he was sorry for the fuss, but this was just a "lovers' quarrel."

The cops sided with the older man, and the boy was dragged back inside the house. Cops reported the incident as *Intoxicated Asian, naked male. Was returned to his sober boyfriend.* When cops did see the fourteen-year-old again, he had been dissected, his severed skull on display in Dahmer's home.

Dahmer was caught. His home was searched by the crime lab. The discovered evidence thrust Dahmer to the top of the all-time greatest serial killer list.

They found evidence of cannibalism. He stored parts of his victims in vats. There wasn't just a homosexual angle, but a racial angle as well, with the great majority of the white killer's victims being poor and members of a minority.

He was saving parts. Who knew what all Dahmer was

doing with those body parts? Eating some, sure—but the guy was probably playful, too.

The arrest came down on July 22, 1991. Dahmer was tried and convicted, and sentenced to almost one thousand years in prison. He didn't serve nearly that many, however, as he was killed by a fellow inmate in November 1994.

When Stephen Stanko wasn't researching other criminals, he enjoyed getting access to the library computer and looking up himself. He was listed as an author, and people anywhere could order his book online.

Very cool. While Googling himself, he learned that he was not the only famous Steve Stanko. There was a muscle-bound guy who had been Mr. Universe in 1947. He was, in fact, a legend of bodybuilding's "golden era."

Somewhere along the line, as Stephen Stanko learned about Zodiac and Son of Sam, BTK and Bundy, Ridgway, Dahlia and Dahmer—all for the book he was going to write, of course—his interest shifted.

According to the Georgetown County Sheriff, A. Lane Cribb, who later read Stanko's serial killer notes, there came a time when Stanko no longer focused on what serial killers were like. He began to wonder what it would be like to *be* a serial killer. He'd already had some experience. Like BTK, he knew how good it felt to tie up a woman. But he'd yet to cross that line between here and the beyond. Cribb came to believe Stanko had feverishly pondered becoming a sex killer, a destroyer of innocence, a sadistic betrayer of everything vulnerable, a breaker of the ultimate taboo—he had pondered becoming a child-raping, knife-across-the-throat snuff artist.

STAND-UP

Ah, but that was the *serious* side of the man. That was only one facet of Stanko's personality. He could write anything. Even *humor*. He spent a lot of time while in prison thinking about what a funny guy he was. He knew it was a tough row to hoe, but he thought he might take a crack at being a stand-up comic. He would be the ex-con comic. Tim Allen had pulled it off, and Stanko figured himself funnier than that guy. He would be the first to expose the outside world to some *real* prison humor! There was nothing like a long stretch behind bars to bring out the yuks.

Now, out and about, he kept a separate notebook—separate from the serial killer stuff—that consisted of his "comedy routine." When he thought of a joke, he'd put it in there. The routine got out of order after a while, and the pages were filled with arrows and inserts scribbled up and down the margins.

He could hear himself doing it, hear roaring laughter from a packed house. . . .

[Reacting to applause] *Thank you, thank you. Okay, my name is Steve Stanko* [pause] *and before you begin making fun of my name, let me say that I was recently released from an eight-and-a-half-year stint in prison, and this is kind of therapy for me.*

Thinking twice now about poking fun at "Stanko" now, aren't you?

It's always funny, when I make that announcement, to watch the reactions in the audience. The men that think they are tough sit up and poke their chest out. The less aggressive seem to get shorter. I wasn't sure at first what that was from. And then, one club-owner told me that they had to pop one guy off his seat [make an oral popping noise] *like a plunger.*

And, of course, gay men smile, and their faces light up. Sorry guys [turn around, shake butt and wag finger] *this is an exit hole only! See me after the show, though, and I will give you some names and inmate numbers that you can write.*

The women, on the other hand, are another story. That all depends on the man they are with. The proper woman will cower closer to their date . . . spouse . . . escort. No, just kidding. But they still look me up and down with that questioning face. [Wiggle eyebrows, give audience a wicked smile.]

Rougher, country, "red neck" women usually start calling me forward or winking. After going out with a few of them, I realized that all they wanted was information about their families and exes. "Did you know my daddy? . . . brother? God-damn husband? Is he okay? Queer? . . . Dead?"

No, really, none of you have anything to be afraid of. I didn't kill, rape, attack, mutilate or do any of the really "cool" crimes. I was one of those [dripping with sarcasm] *really*

*bad guys: Breach of trust with fraudulent intent . . . 673
counts, of course.*

*If any of my victims are in the audience, this gig doesn't
pay squat, so leave me alone after the show. Ten years for
that—go figure, ha ha.*

*Prison is strange. It is and it's not what the media makes
it out to be. It can be tough. I mean, the first day I was given
a total body shave, a delousing, a wire-brush scrub, stuck
with two needles and told I would probably get a rectal exam.*

*Yeah, at the end of the day I just looked at my cell-mate
and said, "Do you think they will let me out of the cell tomorrow?" He just kinda smiled and said, "I hope not!"*

*The first thing I had to do once in prison was learn the
language of the convicts. Everyone knows what a rat or a
snitch is, and of course shanks and shivs are homemade—
excuse me, cellmade—weapons.*

*But there is also the "deck", a pack of cigarettes, "buck"
which is inmate-made wine. Oh yeah, good stuff, not Dom
Perignon but Dumb Parthenon, when it hits you will buck
like an idiot in a Roman arena.*

*One of my favorite prison slang words is "sack," a quan-
tity of marijuana so small that it is folded and folded into a
piece of one-inch square paper until it is about the size of a
pinkie nail. Costs five bucks.*

*And then there's the "sit-up." No, that is not how you trick
inmates into indecent carnal acts. . . .*

And on and on it went. Stanko thought he was a riot.
When he wasn't studying serial killers, he was watching
stand-up comedy on TV, checking out the tricks they
used, the timing of it. He was *so* going to be a star.

Then the unexpected happened. He got a real job.
During the first months of 2005, Stanko worked as a
salesman at Stucco Supply in Myrtle Beach.

But the job didn't last. He was fired on April Fools'

Day by the general manager, Jeff Kendall. Stanko was hired to be a salesman, but he didn't make enough sales—so he was served the pink slip.

On the surface, one might think Stanko a natural at sales. Instead, he daydreamed, perhaps plotting the future, not maximizing the present.

Perhaps Stanko's preoccupation with manipulating people proved to be a detriment. That was counterintuitive, but maybe Stanko actually found himself unable, or just unwilling, to work for a living; so hungry was he to scam and to con, to exploit the fact that others had consciences.

According to one "dear friend" of Laura Ling's, it was that first week in April, after Stephen Stanko lost his job, that Stanko "totally took over" the Socastee library. She said he turned the place into his own personal office, where he pretended to be a lawyer and conned old ladies out of their money. She spoke to Laura about it, told her there was something dead about Stanko's eyes that gave her the chills. Laura said, "Mind your own business"—and she did.

For Laura, Stanko was now a liability both at work and at home. He was spending her money faster than she could make it. She was a librarian, not an heiress, and on the verge of receiving an eviction notice. Something had to give. It was time she read Stanko the riot act.

BOILING OVER:
APRIL 8, 2005

Stephen Stanko's own urge to kill, and kill again, boiled over on Friday, April 8, 2005, sometime after midnight. He'd completed his self-taught course in serial killers and he'd given himself a grade of A. Now, with his real job kaput, his obsession with murder blended with a growing rage. His rickety dam of self-control cracked, then gave way, releasing a torrent of turpitude.

He stressed badly. He needed money. Being fired turned out to be a greater blow to his ego than he would have expected. Rejection of any kind pumped up Stanko's pressure cooker.

According to his story, Stanko and Laura Ling had an argument. She slapped him and a lit cigarette in his mouth flew between his glasses and his face, burning him.

That was it. *Mr. Hyde, come on down!* Let the bondage begin. Stanko bound Ling's wrists together behind her back. He was too jacked and did a sloppy job.

BTK would have laughed.

* * *

Stephen Stanko then turned his attention to Ling's teenage daughter, who was in her room asleep in bed. When he entered her bedroom, he flicked on the lights. Penny woke up.

Penny's mind tried to register what she was seeing. At first, it simply didn't compute. Stephen was in her room, with a knife in his hand. He'd gotten home about nine o'clock that night and everything was normal. She'd gone to sleep at about eleven-fifteen, and all was still peaceful. Now it was an hour and a quarter later, and Stephen was next to her bed with a knife in his hand. At first, he just stared at her, and she hoped it was a dream. It didn't register. Maybe he had secretly called a fire drill or something.

After a couple of seconds, Stanko said, "Scream, and I will kill you both."

He was referring to her mom. Mom was in trouble. She had to get to her. Stanko produced more neckties and was about to bind her wrists at the small of her back when she wriggled free.

Penny ran down the hall and looked in her mother's room. Mom was on the bed, moaning and kicking.

That was the last thing the daughter remembered for a while, as Stanko hit her over the head with a blunt object and knocked her out. When she woke up, she saw him beating her mother. The punches became frenzied. Stanko dished out a vicious beating that continued until his hand was bleeding and he couldn't punch anymore.

Stanko refocused his attention on Penny. He ripped off Penny's clothes and got on top of her. She tried to struggle, but there would be no more escaping.

The blow to the head sapped her will and he was too

strong. She felt the blade of the knife upon her neck. As she was raped, she heard her mother beside them moaning.

When the act was complete, he positioned the daughter so she could watch as he returned his attention to Laura Ling. Stanko still kept his weight on Penny so she couldn't move. He flipped Laura onto her stomach and, with Penny watching in horror, choked Laura until she was dead. She fought hard. She heard her mother making choking noises. Then the noises stopped, and that was it.

Penny forced herself to look away. She closed her eyes really tight and tried to make it go away. She didn't want this to be the last image she had of her mom.

She tried to replace the nightmare with pleasant memories of her mom. How beautiful she was—how smart and funny. She was a warm and inviting person, the kind of person everyone wanted to be friends with. She was—oh God, now she was *gone*.

At some point, he pushed Laura off the bed and she lay still on the floor between the bed and the wall. Stanko got up and looked down at his lifeless girlfriend. He then looked down at Penny; his eyes still filled with raging ire, he said something truly bizarre.

"Look what you did to her!" he screamed at the girl. "And I loved her!"

The killer flipped the teenager over, forcing her into a prostrate position. He lifted Penny's head, and, producing a knife, twice slit her throat.

Stephen Stanko took a shower, and when he re-dressed, he felt in vain for a pulse in Laura Ling and her daughter. He later claimed he felt suicidal at that moment, but his actions suggest he was a man with plans for a future.

Believing Laura and Penny dead, he tarried: calmly removing a gold bracelet from Ling's lifeless wrist, then packing a bag. He emptied out her purse and pocketed her car keys. He went into her wallet and took all of the cash and her ATM card. Only then did he leave the house.

As was true of many famous murderers, Stanko had turned violent, not under a full moon, but under the slenderest silvery sliver—on the eve of the new moon. Those were the darkest nights of the month, and killers on the run liked their nights dark.

His first stop was Ling's bank, where he used her card to empty her account of seven hundred dollars. A surveillance camera captured him, his face composed, as he made the transaction at the drive-through machine.

Penny was not dead, however. Why Stanko couldn't find her pulse is one of the mysteries—and miracles—of this story. She regained consciousness and even made it to a phone. Bound, with blood still flowing from her neck wounds, Penny called 911.

She later explained that she had no idea how she had the strength to get to the phone or how she dialed the three numbers and hit send. Next thing she knew, there was an operator talking into her ear and she was explaining that she had just been raped and she feared her mother was dead.

"When he left, he took my mom's car keys," Penny said.

"What kind of car does your mother drive?"

"It's a red Mustang." She further ID'd the car for police, so the manhunt could start immediately. The conversation between Penny and dispatch lasted for sixteen minutes, until first responders arrived at the scene on Murrells Inlet Road, at about 3:00 A.M.

They found a scene of unspeakable horror, the teenager beaten and bleeding from her neck. Blood spattered on the wall. Laura Ling, still in her red plaid pajamas, on the bedroom floor, her body facedown and wedged between the bed and the dresser.

Her hands were bound behind her back with a gray-and-black necktie, so tightly that the medical examiner later discovered ligature marks where the silk dug into the flesh.

As Penny had feared, Laura Ling was dead. The men asked Penny about the man who killed her. She told them everything she knew. It was Stephen Stanko, the author, the ex-con, her mom's live-in boyfriend.

He was an out-of-work writer working on a book. He was an ex-con who wrote a book about prison. He always seemed like a nice guy, and he just snapped. Penny had no idea why.

The wounds to Penny's neck were serious but not life-threatening. He had slit her throat, just as she said, twice, one above the other. The deepest cut came at the insert point of the bottom slash, where his knife caused a puncture wound that resembled a horizontal tra-cheotomy incision.

In Penny's room, on the bed on its side, next to a stuffed toy zebra, was a white lacey purse on its side. Beside it was a pile of its contents. The purse was Laura's. The killer had spilled it out, looking for the keys to the Mustang.

When the ambulance arrived, Penny was taken away. Her mother was left behind. Laura's body needed to be photographed and examined thoroughly by detectives before it could be removed to the morgue for autopsy.

At the hospital, after her neck was stitched up, Penny was visited by a female cop, with a rape kit. Penny said she was pretty sure she remembered exactly what Stanko did and didn't do to her, but oral and anal swabs were taken, nonetheless, in addition to the vaginal swabs.

Penny closed her eyes and endured the procedure, hoping beyond hope that she was allowing the cop to gather DNA evidence that would put her attacker away.

* * *

Georgetown County sheriff A. Lane Cribb had been in law enforcement since 1973, thirty-two years. He attended Horry-Georgetown Technical College, Limestone College, and the University of Alabama, where he received a bachelor's degree in business administration. His first job as an officer of public safety was with the South Carolina Alcoholic Beverage Control bureau.

Cribb worked as a criminal investigator with the Florence County Sheriff's Office (FCSO) and then returned to Georgetown County in the same capacity. He was first elected Georgetown County sheriff in 1992, and had been reelected three times.

He loved to learn more about being a cop, and had graduated from courses at the Carolina Command College, National Center for Rural Law Enforcement (NCRLE), and the South Carolina Criminal Justice Academy.

He was also a joiner of clubs and fraternal societies. He was an Elk and a Mason. Plus, he was a member of the National Sheriffs' Association (NSA) and was a past president of the South Carolina Sheriffs' Association (SCSA).

Within minutes of Penny's 911 call, an all-points bulletin (APB)was on the air, and Sheriff Cribb was heading a manhunt that would make newspaper headlines across the United States. Stanko was described in the police "be on the lookout" (BOLO) as six-foot-three and 192 pounds, with medium-length dark hair and glasses with silver aviator frames. He might be headed toward North Carolina, the bulletin stated. Sheriff Cribb secured a warrant for Stanko's arrest, accusing him of murder, criminal sexual misconduct, and car theft.

CRIME SCENE

From the Georgetown County Sheriff's Office (GCSO), the lieutenant in charge of criminal investigations, William Pierce, arrived at the Ling home. He worked in plainclothes, always a neatly tailored suit. With his burly physique, shaved head, and trimmed goatee, he had the aura of a stern, single-minded pursuer of justice.

Pierce started with the sheriff's office in August 1990 as a reserve deputy, and became a deputy sheriff assigned to the Uniform Patrol Division two years later. In 1997, he was assigned to the Criminal Investigation Division to cover Waccamaw Neck and Pawleys Island. In 2002, he went to school in Atlanta to become a polygraph operator. After an internship with the South Carolina Law Enforcement Division, (SLED), Pierce conducted lie detector examinations all across South Carolina.

Since 2003, when he was promoted to lieutenant, he had investigated crimes in addition to his polygraph duties. But none of his experience could prepare him for the Ling murder scene. It was worse than anything he could have imagined. He knew immediately that they were after a monster. The carnage was something that a civilized human being would be incapable of doing.

Not knowing for sure that the living witness would survive, Lieutenant Pierce examined the scene as if forensic evidence against the killer would be essential.

The emergency people had somewhat contaminated the scene in their understandable urgency to treat the seriously wounded Penny, but other than that, the home was as the killer left it.

Laura's body was still on the floor between the bed and the wall, her hands were still bound together behind her back with a pair of silk neckties. Near the body was a small lamp, with a glass globe that had been broken during the violence. On the lamp shade were what appeared to be bloodstains. Pierce also found droplets of blood in the hallway, and in the bathroom.

The entire lamp was bagged as evidence. Swabs were made of each discovered blood droplet. All of the evidence was sent to Senior Agent Bruce S. Gantt Jr., at the SLED crime lab, who would determine to whom the blood belonged and how it probably got there. All in all, swabs were made from blood found in Laura Ling's bedroom, and the hallway wall, as well as in the bathroom, especially on the medicine cabinet.

Driving Laura Ling's red Ford Mustang, her savings in his wallet, Stephen Stanko drove northeast on Route 17, switching to a northwesterly heading in Forestbrook on a major thoroughfare alternately called Black Skimmer Trail, the Edward E. Burroughs Highway, and Route 501. He got off at Singleton Ridge Road, in Conway, South Carolina.

He pulled into the driveway of Henry Lee Turner, his old buddy from the library, on Kimberly Drive in Conway.

Turner lived in a white "single-wide" mobile home on a cul-de-sac in the Coastal Village Mobile Home Park. The mobile home had bluish green shutters and wooden stairs at the side and back doors.

Stanko had been there several times before, once with Laura when Henry was having computer woes. It was about six-thirty in the morning. Turner was asleep, but he got up to answer the door.

Stanko said, "My dad just died."

"I'm sorry to hear that, Steve," Turner said.

"I just—I just need someone to talk to."

"Well, come right on in."

Turner attempted to console him. Stanko agreed to get them breakfast and borrowed Turner's keys so he could drive Turner's truck to McDonald's and purchase food.

Not everyone on the Coastal Village street was asleep. John Marvin Cooper, who lived next door on Kimberly Drive, was up and having his coffee when he heard a car pull into Henry Turner's driveway. He looked out the window and saw a red Mustang, and a guy with glasses getting out. He didn't think much of it. He'd seen the man with the glasses visiting Henry before.

It was sometime between seven forty-five and eight o'clock when the man, who he could now see was wearing a baseball cap and a shirt with some sort of purple logo on the front, exited Turner's house, got into Turner's 1996 black Mazda pickup, and left. Cooper thought that was odd. Cooper left for work at eight-fifteen; as he did, he waved at Turner. He wasn't curious enough to ask why the bespectacled visitor was driving Turner's truck. Didn't seem like any of his business.

It would turn out to be important that while Stephen Stanko was out getting breakfast, Turner called his son

Roger on the phone. Turner told his son that Stanko was upset about his father's death and was going to be staying with him for a while.

Minutes after Cooper left for work, Stanko returned in Turner's truck, carrying a bag of McDonald's.

After eating, and while Turner was in the bathroom shaving in front of the medicine cabinet's mirror, Stanko pulled out a gun and, using a pillow as a silencer, shot Turner dead, once each in the chest and back.

The pillow had kept the shots quiet, so Stanko went about his next task deliberately, thoroughly. He searched Turner's home for things that might have value to him on his trek toward freedom, or his trek toward oblivion. Whatever it turned out to be, there'd be a trail of death.

Stanko stole another gun and some more money. Now armed, and even more financially flush, he left Laura Ling's car in the cul-de-sac outside Turner's house and drove away in Turner's 1996 Mazda B2300 two-wheel-drive extended-cab pickup truck. To make the truck easy to identify, it had a Shriners tag on the front and two Shriners decals on the back.

At nine-thirty Friday morning, Stephen Stanko called the Socastee library and talked to John Gaumer, Laura Ling's boss. He identified himself. He was, after all, in that library all the time and was known there.

"Laura's probably not going to make it into work today. She's not feeling very well this morning," Stanko said.

"What are her symptoms?" Gaumer asked.

"Copious vomit," Stanko said. "We're thinking it's something she ate."

Gaumer said he was sorry to hear that and hoped she felt better. Stanko thanked him and hung up.

FIRST RESPONDERS

At nine o'clock Friday night, Henry Lee Turner's neighbor John Marvin Cooper finished his shift and came home. He and his family did their normal thing. He did notice that the red Mustang was still in Turner's driveway, and the truck was gone.

"I just assumed he (Turner) was out," Cooper later said.

The Coopers went to bed at about eleven-thirty, but didn't have a restful night.

At 11:05 P.M., Myrtle Beach police officer Robert Kelly Todd Jr. was home on Temperance Drive and had just started watching the news when there was an urgent pounding on his door. Todd answered it, and standing there was a nervous and upset Roger Turner.

Turner said that he'd been watching the news, too, and they flashed a "Fugitive Alert" for Stephen Stanko. On TV, they said the guy had already killed two people. (Either the newscast incorrectly reported that Penny Ling had died or Roger misheard.) Roger said that was the same guy who was staying with his dad.

To further amp up Turner's anxiety, his dad was supposed to have come to a cookout earlier that evening and he never showed up. He'd tried to call his father's landline and his cell, but no answer, and both answering machines were full.

Turner said he didn't know what to do and asked Todd for help. Todd said he would call the Horry County police to see what he could find out, and after that, they'd drive over to Henry Turner's home to see what was up.

Turner told Todd where his dad lived, and Todd suggested they meet up at the McDonald's near there and then go to the house together. Roger Turner said okay and left, heading for McDonald's.

Todd placed the call. At first, he tried to talk to guys from the Horry County police with whom he'd worked. Frustratingly, none of his friends were on duty, so he asked to be put in touch with the road supervisor, who turned out to be Sergeant Jimmy Edwards.

Todd explained that he was a Myrtle Beach cop and asked the dispatcher to have Edwards give him a call. Edwards called back, and Todd told him about Roger Turner's worries. Todd said he would do a drive-by to see if it looked like anyone was home. Todd drove to the McDonald's, picked up the waiting Roger Turner, and cruised slowly past Henry Lee Turner's home.

"Look in the driveway. There's the Mustang Stanko stole," Turner said.

Todd turned his car around and parked so that they could see if someone was leaving the house. He called Sergeant Edwards and said he believed he'd found the stolen Mustang.

"Can you read the plates?" Edwards asked.

"Yes," Todd replied, and read off the numbers.

Edwards quickly verified that this was indeed Laura Ling's automobile. The verification was made at 12:25 A.M., Saturday, April 9. "I'll be right there," Edwards said, and soon joined Todd and Turner outside.

They approached the house and looked behind it. A look of horror crossed Roger Turner's face. "My father's pickup truck is gone," he said.

Edwards told Todd to get the man's son out of the area, so Todd drove Turner back to the McDonald's. There they were joined by a lieutenant. The three sat in the restaurant until word came.

The first responder to the interior crime scene was Officer Thomas McMillan, of the Horry County Police Department's (HCPD's) Special Emergency Response Team (SERT).

All McMillan knew as he stood outside the mobile home was that Turner's son had called in, saying his dad was missing, that he'd missed a family meal, and something was wrong. That, plus the stolen car out front, was enough to give him a solid notion of what he would find inside.

Through Roger Turner, the anxious son, keys were located. McMillan entered the mobile home from the left side door. He called out and got an eerie silence in return. The officer could feel the heaviness to the silence—the utter stillness that so often surrounded death.

He began his search at the Kimberly Drive end. Standing with his back to the street, he was in a narrow hallway, with a closet to his right and a bed on his left.

McMillan moved to the left, along a wall. In the plasterboard wall, there was what appeared to be a bullet hole. There was no telling how old it was, but still it was a further harbinger of the dreadful. He stepped lightly past the foot of the bed to get to the doorway that led to the rest of the home.

In front of him now was the living room, which comprised about half of the total square footage. To his left was a bathroom. It was clearly a bachelor pad, more disheveled than filthy, with stacks of things covering just about every surface space.

There was a pool table, and even that was being used as surface space for piled-up papers and magazines. There was a couch, along the right-hand wall, and a chair with a pair of side tables.

At the far end of the living room, he looked to his left into a tiny kitchen. There was an empty bottle of beer here. A full six-pack there, a couple of cigarettes in an ashtray. There'd been a little party going on.

McMillan looked to his right, and there was a doorway leading to the bathroom/bedroom suite that made up the far end of the mobile home.

The door was closed. The SERT officer knocked hard and called out one last time, using his command voice. No response. McMillan stepped back and kicked the surprisingly flimsy bedroom door open and right off its hinges.

With a bang, the door fell flat—damn near striking the body lying on the floor.

McMillan stepped through the doorway at the far end of the living room when he saw the body, which he presumed to be that of Henry Lee Turner. It lay just beyond the fallen door. The body's head, facedown, was pointed toward the Kimberly Drive end of the home, and the feet were in the doorway to the victim's private bathroom.

The victim was wearing a purple polo shirt, blue jeans, and black athletic shoes. Looking past the body, McMillan saw Turner's bed, and, beside it, his personal computer on a small table. Behind the investigator was Turner's dresser, with a large mirror mounted on top of it.

McMillan looked in every space in the home. That meant he had to step over the body and into a small bathroom, where blood droplets were visible to the naked eye. There was no one hiding.

The SERT officer advised that the home was clear, and there was one apparently deceased victim inside. It was 3:33 A.M. Only then did he concentrate his attention on the body, which was facedown, bullet hole in the back. McMillan was now joined by EMT officer Walter Gable.

McMillan also discovered a pillow, with gun residue on one side and blood on the other. Placing the pillow between the body and the muzzle, the killer had used it to serve as a makeshift silencer. It must have worked, because none of the neighbors—some of whom were only a matter of feet away—had heard the shots.

The victim's pants pockets had been pulled inside out. There was an electric razor, still plugged in, lying on the floor near the body. Photo ID found at the scene proved the body to be that of Henry Lee Turner, as suspected, born on April 16, 1930. He'd been a little more than a week shy of turning seventy-five.

The cards were of plastic and laminated paper. They included Turner's driver's license, which said he was five-six, 185. Also there were Turner's five Visa cards, his AAA club card, Social Security card, uniformed services ID, a concealed-weapons permit, a card establishing him as a VIP customer at Food Lion, and his VA and Medicare cards. Lastly, a business card for a local lawyer who specialized in motorcycle accidents.

Judging from the extra bullet hole found in the wall, it appeared the killer had fired a test shot, perhaps to see if his pillow/silencer was effective. Turner was in his private bathroom. The killer fired the test shot from as far from Turner as he could get without going outside. If the pillow idea didn't work, the killer could say, *Oops, I was playing with your gun and it went off. Sorry about the hole in your wall. I'll pay to have that fixed.*

But the pillow did work and the test shot was adequately silenced. Turner was shaving when his killer entered the back suite of rooms, with gun drawn, and fired.

Crime scene specialists arrived on the scene and began processing it for evidence. The hole in the wall was probed and, after some digging, yielded a .38 Special bullet.

In the back bedroom where the body was found an officer wearing gloves went through Turner's dresser. In one drawer was found two spent .38 cartridge cases.

The killer had picked up his ejected shells and had "hidden" them in a dresser drawer. Why bother? Didn't the killer know how thoroughly the scene of a homicide was searched? Didn't he care?

At 4:34 A.M., Sergeant Jeff Gause arrived and observed the interior of the mobile home in detail. Gause took many photos of each space within the structure, and he later used these to draw a schematic of the space, like a simple pencil layout of the house, showing not just the location of each room, but each piece of furniture as well.

By that time, the crime lab people were busy. There were eleven blood swabs taken from various locations near Turner's body—in the bathroom on the cabinet door, tub, air vent, and floor, and three locations on Turner's bedroom floor. These would be taken to the lab and subjected to DNA testing.

Five minutes after Gause, HCPD detective Anne Pitts arrived. She "caught" this one and became the Turner murder's lead investigator.

Dr. Dan Bellamy, the deputy coroner, arrived and pronounced Turner dead. The body was lifted and it was discovered that he had a bullet hole in his chest as well.

There were no exit wounds.

He was shot once in the chest, one in the back. The order of the shots would remain a point of contention, even among the experts.

Dr. Bellamy took the body's temperature and estimated the time of death as approximately nine o'clock on the morning of April 8. That done, the body was taken out and delivered to the morgue to await autopsy.

Within hours of Penny Ling's 911 call, long before they knew of Turner's murder, police officers from neighboring Horry County Street Crimes Unit #2 were at headquarters for a special briefing. They were informed of the Ling crimes in Georgetown County. There was a connection with a Horry County library, so their job was to interview the county's library employees to see if anyone had seen or heard from Stephen Stanko. Two officers were sent to Conway, and another pair to handle Murrells Inlet, Garden City, Surfside Beach, and Myrtle Beach. Their efforts were cut short that night, however, when a Myrtle Beach cop called and said he was with Turner's son, and he thought that the red Mustang they were looking for was parked out in front of Turner's house. So Street Crimes Unit #2 regrouped at a McDonald's on Singleton Ridge Road and Route 544, just south of Turner's home.

After the SERT team discovered Turner's body, Unit #2 was assigned to evacuate neighbors of the crime scene, until it could be secured.

The Coopers, Turner's next-door neighbors, had been asleep for less than two hours when they woke up to a phone call from Horry County dispatch, informing them that an officer was at their back door. The officer explained the importance of the red Mustang and ordered the Coopers to evacuate.

"Why?" Cooper asked.

"To be out of harm's way," the officer replied.

Cooper told the officer that he had some knowledge of Stanko's movements and was instructed to come to police HQ the next morning and give a complete statement.

Unit #2 also woke up Jeff Humes, another Kimberly Drive neighbor. Even as he was scrambling to evacuate, Humes managed to tell the officer that the last time he saw Henry Turner was the previous Tuesday afternoon, when Turner offered to sell Humes his truck. Asked about the red Mustang, Humes said he'd seen it in Turner's driveway "off and on for the past year or so."

In one Kimberly Drive home, cops found Tamara Florence and Thomas Grant (pseudonyms), who were particularly annoyed at being roused in the middle of the night for evacuation. (At four-thirty that morning, the pair were taken to HQ to give a written statement, but were not in a cooperative mood. Although they did give their interviewer their landline and cell phone numbers, they refused to say anything about anything until they got a full night's sleep. Their written statement was only two words long: *Sleeping today*.)

Next door to Florence and Grant, police talked to Jamila Woodberry, who said she was at work and missed everything.

Police had better luck at the home of Rosa Yaccobashi, who said she'd seen the red Mustang repeatedly in front of Turner's home "for the last few weeks." She'd seen that guy they were looking for on several occasions, just sitting in the yard talking to Turner. Police asked Yaccobashi when was the last time she saw Turner.

"Few days ago," she said. "He was out on his Harley."

"Anybody else come visit him?"

"Yes, there was another gentleman that stayed with Henry. Big, tall guy, maybe sixty. They rode motorcycles together."

Not long after police arrived at the Ling scene, Sheriff Cribb ordered a WANTED poster be created for Stanko, one that included his 1996 mug shot and a photo of Laura Ling's Mustang. The poster gave a description of Stanko, a description of the car, and said he was wanted for murder and criminal sexual conduct.

A day later, when Turner's body was discovered, the poster was updated. The photo of the Mustang was replaced with one of the Mazda, and the line *Armed and dangerous, Con man* was added.

Detective Troy Allen Large was armed with the McDonald's receipt they'd found, and he had located an eyewitness who saw the wanted man returning with a bag of McDonald's. Using the receipt, which was stamped with the time, as well as the date, Detective Large was able to access and seize surveillance video from the store that showed the killer navigating the fast-food restaurant's drive-through.

THE BLUE MARLIN

Behind the wheel of the black pickup, Stephen Stanko left the cul-de-sac in which Turner had lived and headed west—378 to Interstate 20, into the city of Columbia. He'd had a busy night and could really go for a beer. He began looking for an appropriate place to eat and have a drink or two. He stopped at a bar-restaurant on Lincoln Street, not far from the state capitol or the University of South Carolina campus, a steak house called the Blue Marlin.

It was the kind of place that bragged about the quality of its food: *Blue Marlin produced a cuisine that captured perfectly the strange and perhaps mystical concoctions of the Low Country.* The story went that the menu evolved from the days of the plantation owners, when the owners, up till then fed with bland European-type fare, smelled and were enticed by the spicy aromas coming out of the Low Country. As their peoples possessed kindred spirits, the Blue Marlin also worked some Louisiana Delta into their cuisine, a strong Cajun and Creole influence.

Perfect, Stanko thought. He could eat and sit in at the bar for a couple—shoot the breeze. He had a wallet full of Turner and Ling's cash and was eager to spread it around a little. He was a big man—and big men made the party happen. Finally he had some noticeable affluence, and he could affect a lifestyle he felt was owed to him, a style long overdue. He changed his shirt before going in. He sat at the bar and drank steadily. Repeatedly he bought a round for the house, and quickly became a popular guy. How could one act less like a killer on the run? Though he was even then the subject of a nationwide manhunt, he did not hide. He was boisterous and social. When*ever* Steve is here, it's happy hour!

One of the people Stephen Stanko met at the Blue Marlin was Erin Hardwick, from Lexington, South Carolina. He said his name was Steve and bought her and her friends drinks. Round after round. They wondered where he got all the throwing-around money—and someone asked him

"I'm in commercial real-estate development," Steve responded. "I just closed a deal. We're building a commercial high-rise building, right here in Columbia."

He added that he owned, or co-owned, a lucrative smattering of Hooters franchises.

"In South Carolina?" she asked.

"Throughout the Southeast," he replied.

Everyone noticed that he had an injured hand. When they asked him how he did it, he offered a variety of stories. His first tale was that his car broke down and he punched it in anger. To Hardwick, he said he'd participated in the Cooper River Bridge Run a week before and had taken a spill near the end of the race. Later, he switched again, saying he punched a guy who was hitting on his date.

Observing this activity from a more objective point of

view was Jane Turner, no relation to Henry, who was a friend of Erin Hardwick's. Turner was at the Blue Marlin with her date. She remembered Stanko bragging that he was a real estate agent from New York who was in South Carolina to "close a big deal." His exaggerations increased as the night progressed. She remembered him doing shots and flashing money. When Turner and her date left, she recalled feeling that leaving Erin in the bar with *that man* might not be the best idea. But Hardwick assured her she'd be fine, and Turner did leave.

Since the Blue Marlin was a steak house more than a saloon, it closed earlier than the taverns of the region. Stanko had been running a tab since a certain point. He asked the bartender what he owed.

"One-eighty," the youthful bartender Ryan Coleman answered. Coleman remembered Stanko bragging that he was the vice president of some company or another. Whatever, the guy had a wallet full of Benjamins. Stanko gave him three $100 bills and told him to keep the change.

Since everyone was having such a good time, largely on account of Stanko, it was way too early for the party to end. Taking several Blue Marlin customers and the bartender with him, festivities traveled a somewhat meandering path to another local tavern.

Coleman went along with the party, but it wasn't because he liked the guy. He didn't. When one of Coleman's friends implied that Stanko was full of shit, Stanko obnoxiously threw a handful of cash in the air—"Making it rain," he called it—and turned the air blue with a torrent of profanity. Coleman felt almost compelled to go along. With $120 of Stanko's money in his pocket, he was on the hook to buy a couple of rounds, at least.

Erin Hardwick stayed with the party till the end, and before they parted, Stanko gave her his e-mail address.

Well fortified with alcohol, Stanko got in the pickup and hit the road.

Stanko listened to the car radio as he resumed his flight westward on Interstate 20. A sportscaster talked about the Masters golf tournament under way that weekend in Augusta, Georgia. That is, if weather allowed. The town was hustling and bustling with bored golf enthusiasts. The rain caused play to stop on several occasions. The first round had started on Thursday, but had to be completed on Friday. The second round began on Friday, but most of the players were still out on the course when rain halted play once again. There was plenty of downtime and business was great in Augusta's drinking establishments. There was talk of more rain, so there was no telling if the tournament, one of the most prestigious on the Professional Golfers' Association (PGA) tour, would be completed by Sunday, as scheduled. That meant a *bonus* night of partying for those so inclined. A Monday finish was very possible.

Everyone considered Tiger Woods to be the favorite to win, but he hadn't gotten off to a great start. The early tee times produced the lowest scores, because those golfers completed their round before the weather became too bad. Tiger had a later tee time and shot his round in the thick of it. After the first round, he was seven strokes behind the leader, a relatively unknown Chris DiMarco.

This was *perfect,* Stanko thought.

The Masters oozed class out of its pores. It was played on the Augusta National Golf Club golf course, a fairy-tale beautiful setting for golf. The winner received a green jacket—along with a truckload of money, of course. Augusta had undulating greens and water features spanned by arching bridges. There was no rough (long grass), only pine straw. With azaleas and magnolias in bloom, the Masters tournament was, for those attending or watching on TV, a rite of spring.

TV announcers were not allowed to refer to "the crowd." Too vulgar. Spectators at the Masters formed "the gallery." They were the most affluent and polite fans in golf, perhaps in all of sports.

The gallery had a code of ethics, just as the golfers did. If a woman left her folding chair next to the green with her purse on her seat, she could be certain both chair and purse would be there when she returned.

For a gathering such as this, the cost of security was surprisingly light. The great bulk of that security was outside, carefully scrutinizing admission. Positively and absolutely no riffraff. Once members of the gallery entered Augusta National, they were secure.

That kind of setup made Stephen Stanko eager. He could drink, meet people, maybe a woman, and plan out his next move. The Augusta locals would be oblivious to a white man with spectacles wearing a golf shirt and khaki pants. Stanko pulled Henry Lee Turner's Mazda onto the exit ramp for Augusta National and trolled for locations.

SEARCHING

A warrant to search Henry Lee Turner's home was requested by Investigator Scott Bogart, and granted by a judge, allowing law enforcement to go over the entire house with a fine-tooth comb.

The warrant also allowed the police to search Turner's small yard and the items in it. Police were particularly eager to search the tan-colored "pop-up" camper parked behind the home, and the red Mustang in the driveway. As it turned out, the search of the camper would bear little fruit. The Mustang was another story. . . .

Things stood just as they had when Roger Turner first noticed, with horror, that his dad's truck was missing. The only difference was that the entire lot on the cul-de-sac had been sealed off with police tape to prevent curiosity seekers from accidentally contaminating potential evidence.

The search warrant was purposefully open-ended, allowing crime scene specialists to search for and collect just about anything, including biological and trace evidence that might be pertinent to the murder.

Cell phones and computer equipment were subject to seizure—although an additional search warrant would be necessary to search for information stored *within* those phones and computer hardware.

Police were obliged to seize and process any and all "firearms, shell casings, parts of firearms, projectiles, and live bullets" that might be found.

Investigators Bogart and Pitts performed the search. Among the items seized and processed were an Enterprise Car Rental notepad; a green beer bottle; two cigarette butts; assorted papers and books; a glass mug, with flowers painted on it; a six-pack, with two bottles missing, of a beer called Yuengling Lager; a silver camera; credit cards; two nickels; an Old Timer knife; two spent .38-caliber casings; the bloody pillow silencer; a .22-caliber rifle; a twelve-gauge shotgun; sixteen blood swabs, taken from various spots near to where Turner's body was found; the victim's electric razor; a lead projectile resembling a bullet (the test shot); and a Dell personal computer.

From the Mustang, police found a briefcase with assorted papers belonging to Stephen Stanko, including the college-ruled notebook in which Stanko had written his "comedy routine." (During the course of the investigation, several cops would read the so-called comedic material. None laughed.)

There was also a black folder, manila folders, a cup, bag, and receipt from a Bojangles' fast-food restaurant, a gray vehicle floor mat, and two blood swabs taken from the steering wheel and the gear shift.

The warrant ordered, as they all do, that a complete inventory of items gathered at the scene be made and presented back to the court. That list was compiled by Bogart and Pitts and returned to the court by the middle of the afternoon of April 9.

* * *

On Saturday morning, April 9, Laura Ling's remains were autopsied at the Medical University of South Carolina. Dr. Kim A. Collins, out of the Wake Forest University School of Medicine, Department of Pathology, noted aloud that the deceased had suffered a puncture wound to the throat. She had been severely beaten about the face and strangled.

There was one bruise on Ling's face that was of particular evidentiary value. It had a well-defined and unusual shape, and appeared to have been made by a ring, which, if located, might help link the killer and his victim.

During the autopsy, Dr. Collins located and described every wound on Ling's body. It was a lengthy process. The killer had been prolific with his punishment, and there were many wounds to chart.

That same morning, Henry Lee Turner's remains were autopsied, in the same hospital as Ling's. Dr. Kim Collins was in attendance for both postmortem procedures.

Before the surgery, X-rays were taken of his upper body. These pictures would prove to be vivid evidence of the lead slugs inside Henry Lee Turner's chest.

It turned out that under his blue jeans, purple polo shirt, and black athletic shoes, Turner had been wearing what the coroner referred to as "patriotic boxers" and white socks. Full dentures were still in the victim's mouth, and a bloody white handkerchief was found in one of his pants pockets.

There was an old adage about crime scenes: A killer always takes away part of his victim, and the victim always takes part of his killer. The search for trace and biological evidence linking killer with victim was exhaustive. Fingernail clippings were taken from each hand. The blood-stained bullets were removed.

Dr. Collins believed Turner had been shot first in the chest, then in the back.

Following the autopsy, the victim's clothes and dentures were bagged as evidence, items to be scrutinized further by county and state forensic scientists. That evidence—plus the bullets, and a gun residue kit—was officially passed from the Medical University of South Carolina to the Horry County Police Department, at 8:40 P.M. on Saturday. The receiving officer was Detective Neil B. Livingston.

Back in Murrells Inlet, law enforcement was going over Laura Ling's home carefully, looking for useful information. Police discovered a file cabinet filled with the killer's paperwork. In the cabinet were his files on serial killers, the product of his hours of real research in the Socastee library. Every file was carefully examined.

In addition to his writings, they found hundreds of clipped magazine and newspaper articles about notorious killers, a scrapbook of deviant violence.

The two largest files were on two killers Stanko obviously found special: Gary Ridgway, the Green River Killer, and Jeffrey Dahmer, the notorious cannibal.

Sheriff Cribb examined the clippings and read Stanko's copious notes. Cribb was the first to wonder if what Stanko was really doing in the Socastee library was learning how to *become* a serial killer.

"We found a lot of information about serial killers," Cribb said. "He just seems real interested in serial killers, and now he's starting out, heading that way."

THE MASTERS

Viewing the world through the windshield of a pickup truck, Stephen Stanko carried out his game plan. The sign said: WELCOME TO AUGUSTA, GEORGIA: HOME OF THE MASTERS. He visited a series of local bars, drinking and mingling with golf fans.

At the first bar, he expressed an interest in going to the tournament and watching Tiger smack it around. Forget about it, he was told. There was no point in going anywhere near the golf course because the event was sold out, and sneaking on was about as easy as robbing Fort Knox.

One of the bars Stanko visited was Rhinehart's Oyster Bar on Washington Road. A seafood restaurant, there was nothing fancy about it. Rhinehart's ambience was "beyond casual." The restaurant's logo/spokesman, "Buford Pickens," wore overalls.

Maybe Stanko pretended to drink more than he did, to maintain a maximum manipulative advantage over his newfound drinking buddies. Or, perhaps because of his adrenaline level, he was partially immune to the effects of alcohol.

It was at Rhinehart's that Stanko met a woman named Dana Laurie Putnam. She thought she noticed him first, but soon they made fervent eye contact and . . . *sparks!*

Her hair was black, like Laura Ling's. But this woman's hair was curly and had been shaped in an upswept fashion at the beauty parlor. This, accompanied by a kind, pleasant face, and a gracefully long neck, made her look both elegant and cute as the dickens at the same time.

Pleased to meetchu. She explained her name was pronounced Dan-uh, not Day-nuh, as was sometimes the case. She fell in at his side and remained there for the rest of the night. He said his name was Stephen with a *P-H.* Stephen Christopher—like the medal. They became fast friends. She said she was just a few days past her thirtieth birthday, and she and her friends were celebrating.

Stanko said he wasn't out looking for bimbos. He'd been there, done that. He was looking for a woman he could *respect*—respect and *admire.* Truth was, everyone who knew Putnam respected and admired her; but coming from this guy, it sounded special.

As was true of all of the women Stanko was attracted to, Putnam had brains. She worked at the Southeastern Natural Sciences Academy—an environmentalist working to save the Earth a little bit at a time through education, research, and general consciousness-raising.

As had been the case in Columbia, the party was mobile. They moved from Rhinehart's to Surrey Tavern, located at the Surrey Center, a fifty-two-store shopping mall on the north side of Highland Avenue at Wheeler Road in Augusta. Again, Stanko bought a lot of drinks.

As Dana later recalled, "He pulled out a roll of money and asked me to dance."

Stanko dropped his "came to see the golf" ploy. He told Putnam that he was a restaurateur visiting her lovely city on business.

"What sort of restaurants?" Dana asked.

"Chain restaurant franchises," he replied. "Hooters and Checkers."

"Where do you live?"

He said he lived in Myrtle Beach but was planning a move to Georgia.

"Oh, whereabouts?"

"Here, in Augusta. I love it here. I've even taken out a post office box until I find a place to stay."

They had a long talk, during which he told more lies. He said that he gave "shag lessons" (referring to the dance, but perhaps aware of the double entendre) and in the summertime worked as a lifeguard. And he kept spending money, buying round after round of drinks. Putnam thought Stanko was blotto drunk, and told him he was too drunk to drive.

"What'll I do?" he asked.

"I'll drive you home. You can sleep on my couch," she said trustfully, and that was what happened. Putnam wasn't completely trusting, however. When she went to bed, she locked her bedroom door.

SUNDAY

Dana Putnam woke up on Sunday morning, and her new friend was gone. She thought perhaps that was that. But he called. He had walked to get his truck, which he'd abandoned near the previous night's last bar.

Relieved that she herself had not been abandoned, Dana invited Stephen Christopher to accompany her, along with her parents, to services at the First Baptist Church of Augusta.

As it so happened, the First Baptist Church accommodated shut-ins by broadcasting their Sunday services on local cable television. A recording of that Sunday's telecast verified Putnam's story. There they were—he, in a suit, and she, with her distinctive hairdo, in the very back pew on the right.

Dana's father, Charles Putnam, quizzed the man who'd suddenly appeared in his daughter's life. Stanko repeated his stories about Hooters. Now he added that he had a collection of upscale automobiles.

"Where did you go to school?" Charles Putnam asked.

"The Citadel," Stanko said. "I have an engineering degree."

Dana told her grandmother, Pauline Putnam Hicks, that this Stephen Christopher fellow was one of the nicest guys she ever met. Despite the fact that he was practically a stranger, Dana never considered that he might be other than he seemed.

In fact, she was sweet on him, and his manner toward her became increasingly romantic. After church, he took her to a fancy restaurant, where he gave her a gold bracelet—the very bracelet he'd pulled off Laura Ling's lifeless wrist.

"I could fall for you. I could fall in love with you," he said, looking deep into her eyes.

The local Sunday newspaper ran Henry Lee Turner's obituary, with a drawing of an American flag beneath his bold-type name, signifying that he was a veteran of the armed forces.

Without the slightest hint of violence, the obituary copy said that Turner had passed away unexpectedly at home on April 8. It said he was born in Hyman, South Carolina, a son of the late Asbury Jackson Turner and Letha Alma Turner.

In addition to his parents, he was predeceased by his brother, A. J. "Junior" Turner. He had retired as a master sergeant from the U.S. Air Force after twenty years of service. He was a Mason, a member of the Omar Shrine Temple and the Jester Court #113.

Turner was survived by his three children, Debbie Turner Gallogly, of Roswell, Georgia; Rodney D. Turner and his wife, Allison, of Lilburn, Georgia; Roger A. Turner and his wife, Juanita, of Myrtle Beach; six grandchildren, as well as his sister, Betty Dempsey, and her husband, Jack, of Bonneau, South Carolina.

As per his wishes, his funeral would be held privately

at sea, with arrangements made by Grand Strand Funeral Home and Crematory, of Myrtle Beach.

Turner's daughter, Debbie, told a reporter that her father was a very trusting person. "He loved inviting people into his home for meals," she said.

By Sunday, students living at Coastal Carolina University (CCU) were very nervous. The school was in Conway. Henry Lee Turner was murdered less than a mile south of campus, and just down the street from the school's off-campus apartments.

Just turn on any radio, on any local station, and the message was practically immediate. There was a killer on the road. He raped, murdered, and then murdered again.

Last known location: Conway.

Police were asking the public not to panic, but rather to "heighten their threat level." Folks were to be on the lookout for anyone suspicious. They were to keep their doors locked. Obviously, picking up hitchhikers—a dangerous activity on a normal day—was particularly foolish now.

Female students in particular were frightened and worried that this serial "sex killer on the loose" might take advantage of their convenient college campus.

Ted Bundy and "the Gainesville Ripper" loved to kill Southeastern coeds. Maybe this deadly pervert planned to dine from that same malevolent menu.

It bordered on overkill when authorities posted flyers around the campus and school housing "notifying" students of the already infamous rape and murders.

"A bunch of us are really worried," said one wide-eyed Coastal student. "I live off campus at University Place, sort of right here where it happened, but I feel safe because we have our security force here."

And the school's security force, working hand in hand with all of the region's law enforcement agencies, *was* on the ball. Every time a student looked around campus, police were there, keeping an eye on things.

Rumors were flying like dandelion seeds. Some were true; some were sort of true; some were bogus. Stephen Stanko was an ex-con who went nuts after losing his job, raped a fifteen-year-old girl, and went on a berserk killing spree. Rumor had it, two more bodies had been discovered, one on Highway 90, another on 22—and that the killer murdered someone in Wampee. He was last seen in Little River.

As it turned out, there *was* a new double murder, but the radio said it stemmed from an unrelated home invasion. Folks were skeptical about that—police were just trying to avoid a panic.

In home after home, the shotgun was loaded and set against the wall near the front door. Neighbors bragged to neighbors about how armed and ready they were—then laughed about how great it was to live in the South. God help the traveling salesman who transported his wares from town to town in a black truck. His best bet was to pull off at a roadhouse and drink. There was talk of closing all schools.

The Horry County police were trying to sew up locations where Stanko might have left incriminating evidence. They entered the library where Ling worked, spoke briefly to the man in charge, and then sealed off Ling's office. Crime scene technicians were called to go over Ling's workspace. On the cops' way out, they confiscated the library's copy of Stanko's book, *Living in Prison*.

They'd rarely had such a busy day. In addition to processing their murder scene and searching for a killer on the run, they had to deal with protection for those who feared they might be next. An officer was sent to stay with Turner's girlfriend, Cecilia Kotsipias, who lived in Charlotte, North Carolina.

A lot of info was coming in by phone, and all of it had to be sifted for credibility and usefulness.

Some potentially interesting info came from Jeff Kendall, Stanko's boss at Stucco Supply. He'd fired Stanko a week before and had to call him on Tuesday to order him to stop telling people he still worked there.

Kendall was still patting himself on the back for hiring Stanko. Not everyone would take on an ex-con. Kendall was the one who had given him a chance. Didn't work out—but at least he'd *tried*. He recalled Stanko as a "smooth talker"—wording that found its way onto Stanko's wanted poster next to "dangerous" and "con man"—as a guy who'd shown no hesitation or shame when talking aloud about prison. If he didn't talk about prison, he couldn't brag about his book, and that was where Stanko's monologues frequently led.

Sunday was the day that Tiger Woods made one of the great shots in golf history. In the morning, Tiger finished his third round three strokes ahead of DiMarco. During the afternoon, the fourth, and final, round was a head-to-head matchup between the two.

Surprisingly, DiMarco didn't fold and remained in the chase, even regaining the lead. On the sixteenth hole, however, Tiger hit "the Shot," pitching from the rough to the top of a hill on the green. Gravity took over and the ball changed directions ninety degrees, taking a sharp right-hand turn, and rolled downhill toward the hole. The ball paused dramatically at the lip of the cup. To the delight of the golf ball's manufacturer, the Nike swoosh was clearly visible on the TV close-up, just before the ball plopped into the hole.

Verne Lundquist, who was calling the action for CBS-TV, said, "Here it comes. . . . Oh, my goodness! Oh wow! In your life, have you seen anything like that?" TV audiences saw Tiger victoriously punching the air.

After seventy-two holes, Woods and DiMarco were tied, and Woods won with a birdie on the first hole of a sudden-death play-off. Like most of America, Stephen Stanko watched the action on TV.

That day, Horry County police received a call from a very tiny voice that said she had known the wanted man, and she thought maybe her story would help somehow.

So responding officers went to visit Harriet Cunning-ham (pseudonym), who turned out to be an elderly widow living in an assisted-living apartment complex.

"You know Stephen Stanko?" one responding officer asked.

"Oh yes, I am his client," Cunningham said.

"When did you last see him?"

"I had him over for dinner, the night before the murders."

"Client? What was your relationship, Mrs. Cun-ningham?"

"Steve was helping me to get the check the Veterans Administration owed me, a check for more than two hundred thousand dollars," she explained.

It was a service for which she'd paid a $1,300 fee. The big check, she said, was owed her because she was the widow of a war vet. She knew her rights. It had been "on its way" for three weeks. The big ol' check had been scheduled to arrive via FedEx on April 10, but it hadn't arrived. When she heard about the horrible murders on

TV, she became fearful that Stephen had stolen the check and was using the money to go on the lam. She called her sister in Georgia and then called 911. She feared that maybe he would come back and make her endorse the check over to him. She needed protection. The responding officers tried to reassure her. They were fairly certain that there was no check, and Mrs. Cunningham had been the victim of a simple con.

Following the interview with Mrs. Cunningham, a press release from the HCPD, released on April 11, said: *As a result of our initial investigation, we believe that Stanko has targeted senior citizens in the past in an effort to scam them out of money.*

MONDAY

On Monday morning, April 11, Dana Putnam went to work on Telfair Street in Augusta. Stephen Stanko visited her there, and brought her a single yellow rose. He told her he was leaving the Augusta area on Tuesday morning, but that he would be back, and he would call her frequently while he was away.

He said he wanted to be with her for a very long time, and this startled her. It wasn't that she doubted his sincerity. She just thought it too fast.

She met him less than forty-eight hours before and he was getting serious.

Still, she didn't discourage him, and they parted with stars twinkling in their eyes. After he was gone, Dana called her mother, Janice Putnam, and told her all about it.

That same morning, Erin Hardwick—the woman Stephen Stanko had befriended at the Blue Marlin restaurant and bar in Columbia, South Carolina, on Friday night, the first night of his flight—followed her morning routine and turned on the *Today* show. At first, it was just Tiger, Tiger, Tiger, then—

Holy . . . !

Hardwick stared at the TV screen with unblinking eyes. Her heart leapt and she could feel a swirl of butterflies in her stomach. They were showing a photo of Steve. It was *him*.

She couldn't wait to tell somebody. When she got to work that morning, she was full of the news. The guy she met Friday night was wanted for rape and murder!

Hardwick reported her encounter to the police; she told them that he talked to everyone in the bar and was making friends left and right. Another piece of the Stanko puzzle fell into place. The pieces were assembling, all right. Trouble was, the picture wasn't clarifying.

Stanko was a curious one, a criminologist's fascination. He was social yet deadly. It was like the Southeast had been revisited by Ted Bundy. The killer's combination of social skills and depraved behavior was very rare.

That's why he was attracting so much attention from the press. Stanko was likely a psychopath who could maintain a rapidly fluctuating social life, attracting men and women into his circle of cash and alcohol (and sometimes romance), even when fleeing for what he must have known was his life.

Michael Polakowski, an associate professor of criminology and criminal justice at the University of Arizona, looked at the pattern of facts emerging regarding Stanko and said, "This guy is unique, especially given the timeline. To develop all these relationships is pretty extraordinary."

In the meantime, also Monday morning, Horry County judge Brad D. Mayers signed an arrest warrant stating there were reasonable grounds to believe Stephen Christopher Stanko had murdered Henry Lee Turner.

While that was going on, Melanie Huggins, Clerk of Court for Horry County, was signing three subpoenae, all requested by Investigator Scott Bogart.

The first was to be served on the Internet service known as America Online, and required AOL to provide "any and all" information for the account named oneknight68.

That info was to include all e-mails, e-mail addresses, location, or IP addresses. The IP stood for Internet Protocol, a unique number assigned to every device connected to the Internet.

The subpoena explained that the e-mail address belonged to Stephen Stanko, who was a fugitive from justice, and that the info was only being sought to facilitate in Stanko's apprehension.

If, during their search, AOL discovered that Stanko had other e-mail accounts, they were obliged to turn over all info regarding those as well.

The second subpoena was addressed to Horry Telephone Cooperative, ordering pretty much the same scope of info, only this time regarding the e-mail account called scstanko@sccoast.net.

And the third was to Google Mail (Gmail) in Mountain View, California, regarding the e-mail account known as sc.stanko@gmail.com.

In another courtroom, a similar process was under way granting a search warrant to Detective Chuck Powell, allowing him to seize and search Henry Lee Turner's cell phone, in particular info identifying incoming and outgoing calls on that phone between April 5 and April 11. The info should also include the dates and times local phone towers were accessed by the phone between those same dates.

* * *

Georgetown County sheriff's deputies revisited the Socastee library on the afternoon of April 11. Library employees Tracy Carey and John Gaumer each signed a "Voluntary Consent to Search" form, which allowed Georgetown County sheriff's deputies to search the library thoroughly without a warrant.

Investigator Tracy M. Lewis seized Laura Ling's Gateway computer—screen, keyboard, mouse, and printer—in hopes there would be information in there, a hint as to where Stephen Stanko was headed.

Library employees expressed anxiety that Stanko was going to come back. After all, the library was like a second home to him. A deputy was assigned to guard the library door.

Seizure of the computers at the Ling crime scene required a search warrant, and this was granted that same day by Chief Magistrate Isaac L. Pyatt Sr. to Georgetown County investigator Tom Digsby.

To justify the warrant, the affidavit said: *During the search of the home it was discovered that the suspect was a published author and that he did research and corresponded with others on computers.*

Several computers were located in the home, the affidavit said, some in the room that appeared to be the suspect's "office." The computer found in the home's community area also had Stanko as one of the listed profiles:

The victim of the sexual assault advised investigators that the CompuDirect computer was the suspect's primary computer but he did use all of them at times. It is common for those who use computers to store information on them and to use them to correspond with others via e-mail or in chat rooms.

Therefore, it was reasonable to expect that the hard

drive would contain information that would be helpful to the murder/sexual assault investigation, and might be *helpful in locating the suspect.*

On the afternoon of April 11, columnist Steve Huff, formerly of the Court TV website, and now with his own blog, was among the first to make a connection between the newsworthy manhunt under way in the Southeast and the published book that listed Stephen Stanko as a coauthor.

Living in Prison, Huff noted, was written by two college profs and an inmate. Stanko provided the experience, while Gillespie and Crews offered historical and systemic context.

Different chapters in the book were written by different authors, and who wrote what was clearly marked. Huff had no problem determining what Stanko had and hadn't written.

In one passage, Stanko wondered if a nation's morality could be judged by how it treated its prisoners. Stanko wrote that the United States was number one in the world in prison population, and that the subject of the American corrections system was polarizing and frequently sparked heated debate.

Huff did some research online and learned that the book received a handful of reviews after its release in 2004. Critics agreed that the best part was Stanko's input, as he vividly personalized the prisoner experience.

The book seemingly offered a strong voice to activists seeking prison reform, but was a less than satisfying read for anyone seeking entertainment. Every strand of prose was braided with self-pity.

Great pains were taken to establish each prison indignity and humiliation. Maybe the self-centered nature of

Stanko's writing was of little concern to those whose tub he thumped, but to Joe Six-pack it seemed like a lot of whiny verbiage—e.g., his living space was six and a half by eleven; he had to defecate in front of his cell mates, who were larger and of a different race. For twenty-three hours a day, there was no way to get *away* from his cell mates, except on weekends when it was *twenty-four* hours a day. And cell mates wouldn't leave him alone. All that stress and psychological punishment built up inside a man. A prisoner could release that pressure only through communication and interaction with cell mates. And it didn't always go well. One fight, and a cell could become a "battlefield."

Just as bad was the neglect that prisoners endured from their captors. One night, Stanko broke his pencil and had to wait four days for a new one. He worked his way through the system. Every time they moved him from one prison to the next, he was shackled all over again, to men imprisoned for similar crimes. Even if he qualified for one job, they gave him another, according to *their* needs rather than his. Most guys pulled cafeteria and yard duty.

A lot of blah-blah-blah for an argument that could be rebutted so simply: Prisoners aren't supposed to *like* prison. In fact, the idea is to make the prisoner as miserable as possible so he won't want to come back.

"Be thankful you *have* an f'ing toilet" was the effective, and largely unspoken, rebuttal to *Living in Prison*'s theme.

As all of this was going down, following the case on television was Penny Ling, who was lying on a hospital bed, a clean white bandage covering her stitched throat.

It occurred to her that Stephen Stanko wasn't acting like a man who was hunted. He was going to bars, partying with gusto with people who moments before had been strangers.

Maybe, she thought, he wasn't in a hurry because he didn't know about the quantity of publicity he was receiving. Maybe he hadn't seen a newspaper, hadn't watched the news. The types of places he was hanging out in usually had sports on the TV.

Maybe he thought she was dead, Penny wondered. Maybe he was taking his sweet time running away because he didn't know he'd left a living witness.

The joke was on him!

STANKO SIGHTINGS

While talking heads blabbed about Stephen Stanko, providing twenty-four-hour news channels with lots of time-consuming, if not repetitive, programming, the message that a killer was on the loose was getting through, loud and clear. Every black pickup struck fear into the heart of the Lowcountry.

Police across South Carolina girded their collective loins, realizing that manhunt-oriented wild-goose chases were going to blend with the usual busy array of complaints: suspicious behavior, domestic disputes, drunks, crank phone calls, vandalism, and false alarms.

Midafternoon on April 11, a man called and said he was a former employer of Stanko's and now his home's burglar alarm was going off. He was afraid it was Stanko "comin' to get" him. A thorough search turned up no Stanko, no burglar of any kind, and what triggered the alarm remained forever undetermined.

Sarah Rock, of Myrtle Beach, called the cops saying she saw Stanko that morning at the Hardee's in Charleston, the one on Coleman Boulevard, and he was wearing a green T-shirt with BIKE OBERFEST on the front.

Some callers were bonkers; others serious and real—but unhelpful. A Myrtle Beach woman called and said, "Stanko used to live" with her. That statement sounded provocative, but it turned out the woman meant she was a landlady and had rented Stanko a room some months earlier. She had no idea where he was, or had been since he moved out. If they found him, they should try and collect the back rent he owed.

Roger N. Goode (pseudonym), of Best Buy in Myrtle Beach, called Horry County police and said that Stanko had been in his store looking for a job. Goode heard he was an ex-con, politely declined, and recommended he see human resources at the Best Buy in Fayetteville, where maybe there was an opening. This looked to the responding officers like an excellent lead, until Goode said this happened in October of 2004, six months earlier.

At four o'clock on the afternoon of April 11, a fisherman called the Myrtle Beach Police Department (MBPD) and said he'd seen the "wanted person" getting out of a black pickup. The truck was now parked in the Holiday Inn parking lot across the way. He was calling from the Fifth Avenue South beach access, just east of the Whispering Pines Golf Course and the Myrtle Beach International Airport.

The fisherman said he'd watched as the guy got out of the truck and began to walk south along the beach. He was a white guy, wearing a white tank top, blue jeans, and sandals.

Several officers reported to the scene immediately. There were two black pickups in the hotel lot, one a Ford, one a Nissan, not a Mazda to be seen. Simultaneous to this, officers searched the beach, south of the parking lot, and came back empty.

The cops found the fisherman and took his pertinent info. He was Thomas Hunt (pseudonym) and he lived in an apartment on Mitchell Street. In his brief written report of the incident, Officer Timothy J. Taylor wrote that the complainant appeared *drunk and mistaken*.

Hysterical phone calls came in from out of town as well. A driver on the Ohio Turnpike thought he saw Stephen Stanko, too. The witness's name was Mike Conrad and he saw the subject late on the afternoon of April 11 at Turnpike Milepost 100, not far from Clyde, Ohio.

Taking the call for the Ohio State Highway Patrol was Trooper E. A. Weaver. Conrad told Weaver he'd gotten a pretty good look at the guy's vehicle. No, no, it wasn't a black pickup.

"It was a black Eagle Talon, with rust on its front," Conrad said. It wasn't the vehicle the suspect was presumed to be driving, but who knew? He could have switched.

Conrad got suspicious when the guy did a really weird thing, a criminal thing. He parked his vehicle, got out, removed a New York license plate from the rear, and replaced it with another plate. He couldn't see what kind of plate it was. The guy got back in his vehicle and was last seen "hauling ass" southbound on the Ohio Turnpike.

The subject, Conrad said, was wearing a camouflage jacket, gray jeans, and appeared disheveled. He wore glasses, had brown hair. That was all he remembered.

Weaver asked why Conrad hadn't called right away (several hours had passed since the witness saw the subject changing his license plate). Conrad apologized, saying he went home and put on CNN. He wanted to get a look at the killer's photo on TV one more time so he could be sure.

At five-thirty on the afternoon of April 11, someone resembling Stephen Stanko was spotted driving erratically across South Carolina. A witness named John Fickling was returning to Columbia, South Carolina, from a visit to Sunset Beach, North Carolina, just north of North Myrtle Beach. Sitting beside him was his fiancée, Teri. The subject was driving a black pickup truck, and Fickling first noticed him when he saw him in his rearview mirror, repeatedly trying to pass the car behind him. Fickling's first thought was that the guy was nuts and to give him a wide berth.

Asked to give the precise-as-possible location of the sighting, Fickling said that he and the subject both had just turned off Highway 410 onto Highway 417. The witness explained that he liked to keep to the back roads rather than Interstate 20 because he didn't like all that traffic. At one point, while stopped by a disabled car and a tow truck on the road, with the pickup behind him, Fickling took a closer look. The man in a hurry was in a black Mazda. He was 99 percent sure it was a Mazda. The truck was not willing to wait out the light and pulled onto the shoulder to pass Fickling on the right and roar away. At that point, he noticed there were two people in the truck. Fickling apologized for not getting the license plate number.

On April 11, Investigator Anne Pitts called the Boca Raton Police Department (BRPD) and spoke to Officer B. C. Allen. Pitts said they'd gotten a call up there in

Horry County from a Boca Raton resident who reported seeing Stephen Stanko in Spanish River Park.

The eyewitness was Caroline Smith (pseudonym), twenty-six years old, who lived in an apartment on North Ocean Boulevard, right by the ocean. Smith said the previous day, at five-thirty in the afternoon, she was on the beach, right across the street from where she lived, when she was approached by a white male. This was at the public beach access to the park, and the guy was walking north.

She described the subject as approximately six feet to six-three. Average build. Light brown hair, no glasses, clean shaven, pitted complexion, wearing a white button-down shirt, beige shorts, carrying a bottle of sunscreen and a small black case resembling a shave kit.

The man asked her if she had the time and tried to strike up a conversation with her about the difficulty he'd had finding a parking place. Told her he worked in a funeral home. Said his name was David.

Smith found the man's behavior odd and became increasingly uncomfortable. There were few people on the beach at that hour. "I made an excuse to leave, and I did," Smith told Pitts.

On the morning of April 11, Smith was visiting foxnews.com when she saw Stephen Stanko's photo. She thought he resembled the man on the beach. She couldn't be sure. Similar age, but no glasses. She also thought his hair was lighter brown. But she thought it was worth making a phone call. No, she had no idea what kind of vehicle the man on the beach drove. She didn't see, and he didn't mention. And no, the man on the beach had no apparent injuries.

Pitts informed the Boca cops that they had to take every sighting seriously, and there was reason to think Stanko had headed south. There had been other sightings, Pitts said, in the Jacksonville area, near Middleburg. In reaction to the report, Boca police released a BOLO for Stanko and the black Mazda pickup.

Boca police followed up on the sighting by checking out the public beach access area off North Ocean Boulevard. Nearby was the Sea Ranch Club of Boca. Police asked if their surveillance cameras might have recorded something useful. The club replied that no such surveillance footage existed, and their private security staff provided only "limited patrols" of the club's exterior. Boca police canvassed the area but found no one who recalled seeing Smith's chatty stranger.

April 11 had brought many false leads, and as it turned out, April 12 was just as bad. Stephen Stanko look-alikes were coming out of the woodwork. One of the first calls of the day came from the father of a Florida woman who had been chased by a man outside a Miami Beach club. The father told police his daughter subsequently saw Stanko's picture on TV. She turned "white as a sheet and freaked out." She was sure it was the man who chased her. Of course, he was long gone now.

At Coastal Carolina University, campus hysteria hummed along unabated. Kathryn Donohue, a CCU student who waitressed at Ruby Tuesday, reported that at about seven o'clock the previous evening she'd seen Stephen Stanko. After her shift was through, she saw his picture on a campus flyer and she was certain it was the same guy.

"He was with another person," she told campus police, a person who was *ambiguous* in terms of gender. *Androgynous.* At first, the waitress thought the person was a man, based on the dress, actions, haircut. When she got up close, she could see that it was actually a woman.

It was the female who paid the check. With a credit card. The man and woman didn't talk to each other during their meal, and spent most of the time looking out the window as if they were waiting for someone.

The credit card provided a lead by which police could establish that the man with the he-she friend was not the guy.

Stephen Stanko was nowhere near CCU, Miami Beach, Boca Raton, Jacksonville, Columbia, Clyde—or Myrtle Beach. He wasn't in any of the places witnesses said he was.

CNN, MSNBC, and Fox News kept showing Stanko's photo, dwelling on the perverse and sadistic details of the Ling crimes. The result was predictable, and for a time, Stanko was spotted even more often than Elvis.

So where was he? Despite the media saturation, the real Stanko was playing a real-life game of "Where's Waldo?" blending like a chameleon into a crowd of similitude.

With that much notoriety, the law enforcement agencies directly involved (Georgetown County, Horry County) were being inundated with not only tips from people eager to be an eyewitness, but offers of help from the outside.

One volunteer, who repeatedly e-mailed the Horry County Sheriff's Office (HCSO) during the manhunt, was a fellow by the name of Johnny Johnson (pseudonym), who claimed to be a private investigator who had been doing "pro bono" intelligence work for the law enforcement agencies of the world ever since 9/11. The guy had found a handful of e-mail addresses that, he said, belonged to Laura Ling. He recommended that Ling's Internet activity be investigated for clues that might help the manhunt. Cyber investigators followed up on the lead and found the following entry on one membership website that read: Hello, my name is Laura Ling. I'm 43 years old from USA. I speak English. My marital status is divorced. Nothing uncommon there from a middle-aged single woman. And no help at all with the manhunt.

Stephen Stanko's coauthor Gordon Crews told WBTW-TV in Florence, South Carolina, that if he knew Stanko, the man would *not* be taken alive.

"I don't see him giving up," Crews said. "I don't see an easy resolution to this at all."

TV news smelled the fear and played to it. A psychologist explained how spree criminals on the run were like terrorists.

"Domestic terrorists," he said.

Sure, a couple of lives had been lost, but the greatest product of the killer's spree was mass fear. You couldn't blame TV, the psychologist said. People had the right to know.

Throughout the Southeast, Tuesday morning, April 12, 2005, would have been a good time to rob a bank. Police forces were preoccupied with the manhunt, and everything else could wait.

The tension in the Lowcountry seeped not just into CCU, but into the region's public schools as well. Beth Selander, the principal at Seaside Elementary on Woodland Drive in Garden City Beach, sent a mass e-mail to her students' parents, stating that there had been a double homicide that was being investigated by local police, and that there were several rumors about other incidents that the principal, in her position to know, knew were only rumors and had no basis in fact.

She sent her employees a checklist of safety reminders. Number one set the terse tone:

1) Lock all exterior doors to your school and position someone at the front door to monitor entrance into the building.

The list said children should not go outside for the remainder of the day, and promised that when school was over, security would check the entire building before leaving for the night.

She asked all parents to do their part in dealing with these nervous times—to take every precaution to keep their children safe, yes, but also to help their children feel more secure, and to reduce anxiety rather than fuel rumors.

ARREST

Dana Putnam was still in a pretty good mood regarding the weekend's turn of events on Tuesday morning, when the phone rang. It was her mother with sobering information.

Mom said she'd just read an article in the morning paper. The article was on page 5B, and Dana should look at it right away. It was about a man named Stephen Stanko who had murdered two and severely injured a third, a teenage girl whom he'd also raped.

The Feds got involved because he committed his crimes in South Carolina and had perhaps fled the state. The Feds had a $10,000 reward out for the guy.

The article said the guy was a braggart who loved to talk about being an ex-con and how it had turned him into an advocate for prison reform. Dana felt the hair on her arms stand on end. Her mother continued.

In the newspaper article, the police were candid about their lack of information. They didn't have a clue where he was headed. In the article, Horry County police lieutenant Andy Christenson said, "He could be anywhere in the United States."

That meant he sure as hell could be in Augusta, Georgia, Dana's mom thought.

In the paper, Lieutenant Christenson noted that Stanko had relatives in Fayetteville, North Carolina, but there was no indication that he was heading there. Those relatives had been contacted and had no knowledge of his whereabouts.

Wherever he was, the cop added, he was *very* dangerous. The article discussed the fact that Stanko had done eight-plus years in prison, and that he really did author a published book.

The report revealed Stanko's recent work record, which was less than stellar. He didn't seem to have the attention span to hold down a steady job. He was driving a stolen pickup truck, and they gave the year and make.

But the clincher was the photo that accompanied the article. "That's your Stephen Christopher," Dana's mom said.

Dana didn't argue. The weekend had been too good to be true, so it only made sense that it wasn't. She took a deep breath and drove to the Richmond County Sheriff's Office (RCSO), where she told Sheriff Ronnie Strength her story.

Police tapped her cell phone so they could monitor Stanko's calls. Within hours, Putnam received a call from Stanko asking if he could spend the night on her couch again.

"Hey, gorgeous," Stanko said. "Let me ask you something: How the heck do I get you off my mind? I miss you. It's almost a *physical* missing you."

As she set up a date with him, police electronics experts were busy using the signal from Stanko's cell phone to determine his location. They discovered he was in a West Augusta restaurant.

A police drive-by read the plate number and verified

that the stolen Mazda was parked outside the restaurant, which was part of a large shopping mall.

By the time Stanko left the restaurant and walked to the truck, law enforcement was there in force and ready for him.

At three o'clock on Tuesday afternoon, Stephen Stanko had entered a mall restaurant called the Atlanta Bread Company. He sat at a small wooden table near the front of the shop and ordered a grilled chicken sandwich and a soft drink.

The mall, in Northwest Augusta, was called Augusta Exchange. It was built on eighty-seven acres of farmland and opened in 1997. Its most notable features were a Target store and a twenty-screen movie complex, which included IMAX.

The Atlanta Bread Company was a chain restaurant with the slogan "Come for the food, stay for the culture." The restaurant started out in 1993 as a single café in Sandy Springs, a suburb of Atlanta. Ten years later, there were more than one hundred of them in twenty-three states.

Waiting tables inside the restaurant was restaurant supervisor, twenty-four-year-old Chris Ainsworth, who remembered Stanko as polite and dressed well.

"He looked like a nice guy. He seemed calm, like nothing was wrong," Ainsworth later said.

Seventeen-year-old assistant store manager Marcie Crown said that she didn't recognize Stanko, even though his picture had been on television. His hair looked darker in person than it did on TV, she explained. He was dressed normally—gray jacket over a yellow dress shirt, jeans, a light blue vest, and a tie.

"He did not look dangerous at all," Crown commented. "It's very freaky."

As Stanko was eating, the call came in that the stolen truck had been found. That news lit up law enforcement. After a few days of chasing ghosts, a license plate number was something real. This was *it.*

Within minutes, the mall was surrounded with deputy U.S. Marshals from the Southeast Regional Fugitive Task Force, along with members of the Richmond County Sheriff's Office.

When Stanko came out, at approximately 3:25 P.M., exiting the mall through the Mattress Depot, he was promptly and efficiently arrested.

An eyewitness to the arrest was twenty-one-year-old Jeremy Nave, who worked at the Atlanta Bread Company and was arriving at the shopping mall in his car as Stanko was exiting on foot.

"I saw a guy dressed in a suit," Nave recalled. "He looked like he was coming from the Hallmark store. I stopped and let him cross the street. He walked toward his truck. Next thing, I turn around and see him on the ground, with two guys dressed in bulletproof vests standing over him. When I saw U.S. Marshals, county deputies, and the FBI, I figured it was a drug bust."

Inspector James Ergas, of the U.S. Marshals, involved in the arrest, said it didn't appear Stanko knew the jig was up, until the handcuffs were snapped on.

Officers patted him down and found a knife. He was handcuffed and whisked away. Stanko was charged with "unlawful flight to avoid prosecution." During his brief stint in a Georgia jail, Stanko was separated from the rest of the jail population, according to Richmond County sheriff Ronnie Strength.

Fox News reported at 3:58 P.M., about a half hour following the arrest, that Stanko was in custody.

* * *

Inspector James Ergas and Deputy Kenneth Shugars, also of the U.S. Marshal's Service, questioned the suspect.

"Any aliases?"

"Yeah. 'Stephen Knight.' 'Chris Knight.'" Then a joke: if they were named Stanko, they'd have aliases, too.

Beyond that, Stephen Stanko denied anything and everything. Whatever it was, he didn't do it. What was he doing in Mattress Depot? He was applying for a job.

Stanko told Deputy Shugars that he was in Augusta to see the Masters, but he hadn't gotten in. He stayed for the fun of it, because there was a 24/7 cocktail party under way.

Stanko repeated some of the lies he had told over the course of his flight. He told the federal officers about the restaurant franchises he owned. He said he drove a Jaguar, but it was in the shop.

He was asked about his injured hand, and he said he got that in a bar fight in Columbia, South Carolina. On the drive to the courthouse, Ergas said, Stanko was "very quiet, very sullen."

Stanko briefly appeared before a federal magistrate judge in Georgia regarding the charges of criminal flight. An arrest warrant from Georgetown County in South Carolina for the murder of Laura Ling, countersigned by Judge William P. Moeller, was presented.

In response, there was also an extradition hearing. Judge John Baxter signed a "Waiver of Extradition" form allowing Stanko's return to South Carolina to face the music without further ceremony.

Back at the Augusta parking lot, Sergeant Scott Peebles, of the Richmond County Sheriff's Office, was busy in the shopping mall's parking lot getting Henry Lee Turner's pickup truck ready for a thorough inspection from the men and women of the county crime lab.

He called Edwards Paint & Body Works, which regularly towed for law enforcement. Edwards agreed to come put the Mazda on the back of a long flatbed truck.

At 3:53 P.M., less than a half hour after Stanko was arrested, Sergeant Peebles notified Investigator James "Jim" Gordon, at the county Vehicle Processing Bay (VPB), that he had arranged for the truck to be moved.

The truck was transported to the VPB and arrived at quarter after four. Gordon took down all of the truck's pertinent info: it was a 1996 Mazda special edition B2300, with an extended cab. It was black with purple side stripes. He also wrote down the truck's South Carolina tag number and VIN.

Gordon noted that the truck arrived with all windows up and all doors locked. No key was with the vehicle. In the bed was a cooler, blue with a white top.

He secured the vehicle.

The crime lab people wouldn't be able to sink their teeth into that truck until a search warrant was acquired. No hurry. Neither the evidence nor the suspect was going anywhere soon.

HEMBREE

In Georgetown and Horry Counties, the machinery was already working toward prosecuting Stephen Stanko for the murders. The two counties shared a single chief prosecuting attorney. He was Solicitor J. Gregory Hembree. In another state, Hembree would have been known as the district attorney.

"'Solicitor' is just an archaic term we use here in South Carolina, because that's the way we are," Hembree explained with good cheer.

On Tuesday evening, Hembree was standing in shorts, watching his ten-year-old son's baseball practice, when his cell went off. It was Captain Bill Pierce, of the Georgetown County Sheriff's Office. They had arrested a suspect in Augusta, Georgia, and were already in the process of moving him to Georgetown County.

Pierce said, "Stanko says he might want to talk to you. Where are you?"

"I'm on my way is where I am," Hembree said—and that was it for baseball practice. He grabbed his son, drove home, executed a quick wardrobe change, then drove to the GCSO. When Stanko got there, Hembree was waiting for him.

As a matter of practice, Gregory Hembree did not interrogate suspects. That put him in a position to be a potential witness. He had, however, from time to time, had suspects who wanted an in-person meeting with the prosecutor. Motives varied. Hembree usually accepted the invitation. He wanted to "be available to facilitate the conversation with law enforcement." At those meetings, there was no interrogation. The solicitor left the questioning to the sheriff's office. When Solicitor Hembree met with Stephen Stanko, he would allow Stanko to do most of the talking.

Now Hembree and Stanko sat in a small interview room.

"Mr. Stanko, I understand you want to speak to me. What is it you want to say?" Hembree asked.

Stanko told the solicitor that he wasn't sure what he was going to do. There was a chance that he wasn't even going to combat the charges against him. He said he knew his was a death penalty case. Maybe, he suggested, he would just accept the fact that he should be executed.

"He didn't admit to anything," Hembree recalled. "I felt baited." There was an attempt, it seemed, to recruit Hembree over to his side, to help out good ol' Stephen Stanko.

Stanko seemed to be saying, *Come on, Greg, we're a couple of white guys here in South Carolina, let's cut a deal.* It was offensive.

The killer thought he was being charming. Hembree saw it as typical "jailhouse manipulation." Guys in desperate situations tended to be conniving.

It was Stanko's intelligence that separated him from

the pack, though. Coming into the meeting, Hembree knew that Stanko had a prior, and that he had a history of scamming people. But he hadn't been briefed on Stanko's intelligence.

At the meeting, Stanko was concerned with how he was going to be portrayed in the media. He was image conscious and considered the style and texture of his infamy, which he misconstrued as fame.

Perhaps there was a small sense of accomplishment in Stanko's demeanor. Maybe it was like Sheriff Cribb said. Maybe he'd studied to be a killer and had pulled it off. Now he wanted to help shape the media coverage—spin the story to his advantage so he could take his well-deserved place in the "Killers Hall of Fame."

Bottom line: Stanko was willing to take responsibility, as long as the solicitor made him look good in the press. Hembree, of course, made no such promise.

Convicting Stanko, Hembree felt, would be easy, even without a confession. By stealing his victims' vehicles, he left a track of bread crumbs for police to follow.

The solicitor patiently allowed Stanko to speak his piece, and then told him that if he had anything he wanted to share, to tell it to the sheriff. Hembree got up and left.

The meeting lasted less than five minutes.

Gregory Hembree already saw signs of psychopathy in Stephen Stanko. There had been a time when shrinks thought of that particular personality disorder in terms of what was missing. The psychopath was a person lacking components of his psyche—for instance, empathy, fear, remorse. But lately some shrinks had begun to ponder facets of personality *not* missing but rather in overabundance.

Sadism.

Hunger for control.

A relentless craving for reward.

Like a dope fiend needing his next spike, psychopaths need their next reward—sex, money, fame, whatever, a *trophy* of some sort—often an unreasonable expectation considering the deviance of their behavior.

So psychopaths took what they could get. As long as Stephen Stanko was incarcerated because of his violent rampage, he might as well soothe himself with thoughts of fame and image.

Maybe he'd make the celeb news. Maybe paparazzi were scheming to get a photo of him.

The new theories regarding acute personality disorders weren't all just psychobabble, either. Vanderbilt University scientists had discovered chemically testable differences between psychopaths and others. One was the variance in levels of dopamine, a naturally produced chemical that contributed to a person's motivation and pleasure.

Those scientists concluded that the elevated level of dopamine was not an additional symptom to the personality abnormalities already known, but rather *responsible* for the personality changes.

Gregory Hembree suspected from the outset that Stanko would opt for an insanity defense, based on his personality disorder. What choice did he really have?

There were doctors out there who would testify for a fee that psychopaths were criminally insane because they lacked the impulse control to prevent themselves from committing crimes.

That was okay with the solicitor, who considered it a desperate defense, one that never worked. The legal standard for insanity was whether the accused understood the difference between right and wrong. Psychopaths sure did understand the difference. They just didn't care.

A jury would have to accept new legal standards for insanity to buy that pitch—and that was not likely to happen. Not archaic ol' South Carolina.

One could argue that it was foolish to equate impulse control with criminal insanity. Those with strong impulse control didn't as a rule commit crimes. You'd have to empty the prisons if you accepted "I couldn't help it" as a legally valid excuse.

TALKING HEADS

Stephen Stanko's narcissism no doubt made him feel glorified by his fame, his *stardom*. He thought like a public relations agent. Hmm, he pondered, how to envelop himself in an aura of benevolence.

With a snap of his fingers, he thought about using his celebrity for the cause of *good*. He would dedicate his public profile to lowering the crime rate through prison reform! Excellent plan, a perfect continuation of the social visionary he'd been all along.

It was all the fault of the system—the prison system, the system of assimilating ex-cons into society—and he was going to *prove* it. He would have a trial and he would use it as a sounding board, as a soapbox, for the very same message he'd delivered in his book.

He would exploit his celebrity to the maximum, pedal to the metal, and that was no delusion! In the days after Laura Ling and Henry Lee Turner died, he *really was* the most famous criminal in America.

* * *

Stephen Stanko was national news. On the evening of his arrest, a segment on Stanko was featured on *Anderson Cooper 360°*, a news program on CNN.

Cooper's choice as an expert witness was Jane Elizabeth "Liz" McLendon Buckner, Stanko's ex-girlfriend and 1996 victim. At the top of the show, Anderson Cooper teased the segment on the killer's capture, concisely summing up Stanko as a "smooth talker, a published author—with a *dark* secret."

Liz was getting to be a media veteran. Her media tour, which would turn her into a staple on cable news, began when a local TV news reporter located her. She was put on the air live and told to address Stephen Stanko, who very well might be out there watching the coverage of himself on TV. She looked into the camera and asked Stephen to give himself up before anyone else got hurt. She asked him to think about his niece whom he adored, and think of how he would feel if someone hurt her. She had been good on TV, and now the national cable networks wanted her as well. For a while, she said yes to everyone.

In retrospect, the direct plea to Stephen Stanko on local news, Channel 2, would seem ridiculous to Liz. She appealed to the conscience of a man who lacked one.

"It was a waste of time," Liz said. "He wasn't paying attention to anything at that point."

Now Stanko was behind bars, and Liz could talk about events in the past tense. There was a terror to Stanko's spree, as long as it was ongoing, that was gone now that he was caught. Liz could start to heal again from the old wounds torn open anew by recent events.

On this night, she would share the Anderson Cooper show with a feature on breast implants (what you need to know before going under the knife); a plan to legalize

alley cat hunting in Wisconsin, where there was overpop-
ulation; dolphins stranded on the Florida Coast; and a
surefire way to self-determine the level of your racial
bias. It was going to be a full show.

Cooper started with the "breaking news," and that was
Stanko. He explained that Stanko looked "anything but
like a fugitive" when apprehended "a few moments ago
in Georgia." He looked like a successful businessman.

Cooper introduced an unspooling pre-recorded segment. An unnamed "friend" of Stanko's was quoted as
saying Stanko had pledged that he'd never go back to
prison. After eight years in, he'd only been out nine
months.

There was a description of the Ling and Turner murders, and an emphasis on his savage rape of a fifteen-
year-old girl. He'd been caught because he twice stole
the motor vehicle of his victims, making him traceable.

South Carolina lieutenant Andy Christenson was
shown making a public statement, obviously recorded
before Stanko's arrest. He warned that desperate people
did desperate things, that people should be "vigilant and
cautious." People should not take matters "into their
own hands." Christenson said the public was being
fooled by this guy. "He is very convincing," the cop said.
Folks should be looking for a fellow with the gift of gab,
a smooth guy.

Cooper said the killer not only dressed well, but he
was a published author as well, a book called *Living in
Prison*. He was released early because he could convince
others his life of crime was finished.

When Liz came on, Cooper explained that she had
been, during the early 1990s, Stanko's girlfriend for four
years. She discussed the "very, very wicked way he had of
twisting things around." She said he lied—he lied well—
that he was articulate and intelligent. She bought the

package, enough to dedicate four years to him. Most of that time "she didn't suspect him at all."

Cooper commented that Stanko had a classic socio-pathic personality. He was "surrounded by mirrors," a chameleon, whoever he needed to be depending on the situation. His manipulation of others was constant.

"He could make you believe something that you knew for a fact was not the truth," Liz explained. When, after forever, she began to catch on, Steve did an inadequate job of backpedaling, which she could see through. "He tried to convince me that it was not what I suspected," she said, but by that time, she knew better.

Cooper asked Liz if she had been scared when she learned Stanko was out of prison and on the run.

"Very," she said. Truth was, she was frightened from the moment he was released. She had no reason to think he would try to find her, but one never knew.

When she learned of his violent rampage, she became terrified. "He does have a personal vendetta against people who he think wronged him, and I'm sure I was on that list, somewhere along the way," Liz explained.

Cooper finished his Stanko segment with an interview of Stanko's coauthor Dr. Gordon Crews, who said he'd found Stanko to be an easy guy to work with. Dr. Crews described reading the first draft of Stanko's book, and being impressed with the prisoner's philosophy and ar-ticulation. He said he found Stanko's writing fascinating and "signed on immediately" to be a part of the project.

Of course, taking into consideration subsequent events, Crews felt he should revise all of his previous opinions. For the past few days, Crews had been learn-ing new things about Stanko—bizarre, incredible things. Crews had Stanko characterized in his mind as a model prisoner who was toiling to let the outside world know what it was like on the inside. The book, as Crews saw it, was a cry for reform, and Stanko was the lead crusader.

It never—seriously, *never*—occurred to Crews that Stanko would return to his violent ways once out. It was mind-blowing. How wrong could a guy be?

He'd seen Stanko as depressed, yes. Violent, no.

"You could tell that depression was setting in," Crews said, "because he kept describing himself as, you know, kind of getting slapped down constantly. Nobody wanted a convicted felon working at Best Buy with them. The last time I spoke with him, he was very depressed, on the verge of giving up."

Crews said he had a great deal of sympathy for Liz Buckner, because he knew how convincing Stanko could be, and couldn't blame her at all for falling under his spell. He was glad, in retrospect, that nothing confrontational had occurred during the writing of the book. Knowing what he knew now about the crimes that sent Stanko to prison the first time, he could see the pattern repeating itself. He would put on a façade designed to accomplish whatever it was that he wanted to accomplish—whether it had to do with acquiring money or sex, a job or a relationship. If he was confronted with his lies, confronted strongly, he resorted to violence.

(Crews and Liz later appeared on the same segment of the Greta Van Susteren show on Fox News. Although she regretted it later, Liz was given an opportunity to address Crews and she really blasted him. She wanted to know how a person who had committed the crimes that Stephen had committed against her could be allowed to use that experience to make a profit. In retrospect, she was railing against the system, but Crews took the brunt of it. And she did later feel bad about her misdirected anger.)

After finishing with Anderson Cooper, Gordon Crews stuck around and appeared later in the evening on the same network, this time being interviewed by "former prosecutor turned media wolverine" Nancy Grace, who implied he was a vulture for trying to make a buck off Stephen Stanko's previous crimes, a criticism Crews couldn't help but liken to the pot calling the kettle black.

He told Grace that his becoming Stanko's coauthor was the publisher's idea, since Stanko was an inmate and Crews a scholar. He said he put in three and a half years on the project that became *Living in Prison*, both writing his own section while helping to hone Stanko's already-impressive prose.

Crews said that Stanko was brimming over with confidence and enjoyed painting himself as a new breed of writer. Like Truman Capote or Hunter Thompson, he was going to create a genre of writing.

It sounded maybe like Crews was describing someone perfect, but no, Stanko's faults were always in evidence as well. The professor thought the inmate had a lot of talent, but he sometimes came on too strong. He had none of the humility one might expect to see in an individual who'd spent years behind bars.

Grace asked if, during the entire time the professor and the inmate worked together, had Stanko ever discussed the details regarding his kidnapping charge. Crews replied that Stanko had not. Looking back on it, Crews said, Stanko's range of topics when they communicated was extremely narrow.

If Stanko referred to his crime at all, he called it

"white-collar," combined with a "domestic dispute," just one of those spouse things that got out of hand. He'd been stressed because of work and they had a fight. Certainly nothing worthy of a ten-year sentence.

Grace wasn't impressed with Crews's naïveté.

PEOPLE ARE MEAN

In all spectacular murder cases, there were many players, and the media and public underwent a natural process of separating the good guys from the bad guys. In this case, a misperception had placed Dana Putnam in some people's eyes on the list of bad guys. The reason? She had aided and abetted and heaven-knows-what-elsed the killer.

The negative blowback took Dana's supporters by surprise. Those who loved her—and there were many—were stunned by this interpretation of the facts. She had the misfortune of being in the thick of a sensational news story. Public figures had long understood that it was a mistake to read about yourself on the Internet, or listen to call-in radio shows when you are the topic, but Putnam was unprepared for the reckless criticism of strangers.

In hindsight, she should have known there would be a negative reaction—some people had their minds in the gutter. When that reaction came, the loudest barks wouldn't necessarily come from the smartest dogs.

Putnam was criticized for taking a liking to the guy she met at her birthday party, for being nice to him and giving him a place to stay at the tail end of a long night of drinking. She hadn't seen through the con man's con, and for this, she was to be held accountable? People were just *mean*.

Her friends—as well as clear-thinking strangers—saw Dana correctly as one of the heroes of the story. After all, she was the person who supplied the information that led to Stephen Stanko's arrest.

Plus, her kindness ended his flight and kept him in one place. Her actions, keeping Stanko calm and focused on a "strangers in the night" romance, might even have prevented additional violence.

Back when Dana was still answering questions, she was asked how she felt. She said it made her feel good, *great*, that the world was now a safer place.

"I feel like God had chosen me to bring him down," she explained.

Good feeling or no, Dana despised notoriety. She did not like her name on the front pages of newspapers in this, or any other, context. She stopped answering reporters' questions, which she felt would only fuel the publicity fire.

By April 13, public criticism had gotten so bad that Janice Putnam agreed to speak to the press and address the unexpected controversy.

Spitting fire, the mother said, "My daughter may not want to talk about what happened, but I do." Janice said it hurt her soul to see and hear her daughter's character sullied and rubbed in the dirt. "They are just slamming her, instead of praising her for getting this guy off the street," she said. People thought that Dana knew the guy was a psycho sicko and was nice to him, anyway, and that wasn't even close to what had happened. The guy was a con artist. Didn't they get that? Her daughter was conned—conned by a master. "It is just so upsetting with everybody making it seem like she is a scumbag and hangs out at lounges. And she is not that way at all." It was the people who called those radio talk shows who were the worst, spouting slanders against her daughter without knowing any of the facts, without knowing their butts from holes in the ground.

At least, the police had been nice. In Augusta, law enforcement authorities had gone on the record to say they believed Dana to be a hero and recommended that she receive the $10,000 reward that the Feds had put up.

Janice knew that, no matter how public opinion went—and she could only hope that people would start being nice—Dana's ordeal was far from over. She couldn't just close her eyes and make it all go away. Someday there was going to be a trial, and it was going to start all over again. Dana would no doubt have to testify, and there would be cross-examination during which she would be asked heaven-knows-what. She *didn't* invite him home to have some sort of illicit affair. She was trying to prevent a tragedy by getting an intoxicated man off the roads. How was she supposed to know he was a creep?

She assured everyone who might hear or see her words that she and her daughter were in complete agreement that they wanted "this man" put away.

"He was a real con artist," Janice said, adding that it would be a few weeks before her daughter learned if she qualified for the $10,000 reward.

Dana's father, Charles Putnam, also leapt to her defense, publicly stating that his daughter was merely "doing what a good citizen would do."

Greg Rickabaugh, of the *Augusta Chronicle*, called the federal police to find out the status of that reward money. He was told by Deputy Kenneth Shugars that Dana Putnam had been asked to fill out paperwork. Until that was done, the Washington office couldn't determine if she qualified.

EXTRANEOUS
MATERIAL

Solicitor Gregory Hembree was a thorough researcher. He tried to read every document pertaining to the case, but he had not read Stephen Stanko's journals in their entirety. He'd read enough to get the gist, and he would be shocked if there was anything in there that he would not have anticipated.

The comedy act that Stanko wrote was lame, based on a bizarre premise that free people and prisoners have basically the same feelings and concerns.

There was the serial killer research, which was pretty interesting preceding, as it did, a murder spree. Then there was the anti–law enforcement stuff in which Stanko was being persecuted unjustly. It all got to be *the same,* and he stopped reading. Stanko was always the hero, and that turned the veteran prosecutor's stomach a little bit.

Hembree decided not to use the serial killer stuff in his case. What he'd read made it seem like the work of an intelligent but amateur criminologist. There was nothing overt to indicate premeditation. Maybe he had whacked Laura and Penny over the head in imitation of Ted Bundy, and maybe he had used knots to bind his victims, which he'd learned from BTK, but he didn't put it in writing. Plus, there was no indication in Stanko's crime spree that he had learned any expertise, or any lesson at all, from his hours of researching serial killers.

When the time came, Stephen Stanko had been a hotheaded killer—disorganized, even—not the cool customer he might have hoped to be. For all of his intelligence, he had not been that clever—leaving a living witness, botching his bondage first try, and fleeing in a thoroughly traceable manner.

Also, the solicitor was thinking only in terms of the evidence he needed to get the lethal needle in the monster's arm. The serial killer material and the comedy act were extraneous to the case he intended to prove beyond a reasonable doubt. Stanko's actions vividly spoke for themselves.

Hembree thought the manhunt went well. Because Penny Ling survived, the BOLO went out many hours earlier than Stanko thought it would. That was the key. If only police had included Henry Lee Turner on their list of people who needed immediate protection, he might still be alive. But it wasn't anyone's fault. There were too many directions for Stanko to go. He had ripped off and angered many people.

In many cases when a killer was on the run, police could assume that he would contact someone he knew, a friend or family member. But this killer had forged new relationships so quickly, he didn't need to return to the familiar, and could head anywhere. There were a lot of potential targets that deserved protection before Turner.

Financial woes were only part of the problem, the

prosecutor understood. When you looked at Liz and Laura side by side, you saw the pattern. Hembree was convinced that in both cases some sort of rejection by a woman started the violence. It was a typical personality trait for criminal men: the inability to take no for an answer.

Gregory Hembree also took a look at Stephen Stanko's family, to see if there were any indicators of what might have caused him to kill. But he saw no clear answers. He'd dealt with people from really messed-up homes, mind-bogglingly messed up, and Stanko's upbringing couldn't compare. Stanko's youth was normal.

The solicitor grew up in a military household himself and heard no stories about Stanko's youth that wouldn't have described accurately a whole generation of well-adjusted Americans.

"Some families make the Stankos look like *Leave It to Beaver*," Hembree said, evoking a wholesome 1960s TV show. Stanko's dad was ex-navy, kind of old school, ran a tight ship, but that might describe a million households in America.

"Shoot, we've had whole generations of people growing up with their daddies like that," Hembree said.

A million dads are noncommunicative to a degree, or have some difficulty expressing affection, but their children do not turn into murderers. Maybe William Stanko's expectations for his sons were a little high.

"But it wasn't like he was beating the crap out of his children or anything," Hembree said.

Hembree checked out Stanko's siblings. None of them turned out a train wreck. They were pretty normal, with normal ups and down and range of success. The solicitor could see the house-fire death of Stanko's older brother as a contributing factor to his personality disorder, but he couldn't see it making him a killer.

Stanko's worst crimes were all misogynistic, not logically caused by a male sibling's death. It was more likely that Stanko saw his entire existence as spin control.

He killed to let the world know he had the capacity to kill, the cojones to take a life.

He hurt women to let all women know that when he was in a relationship, he was the one in charge. The master. King of the Castle. He saw himself as a rich and slick intellectual. When he looked in the mirror, he saw a handsome superior man, merciless and impeccable.

At about three-thirty on the afternoon of April 13, state court judge Richard A. Slaby signed a search warrant allowing law enforcement to have at Henry Lee Turner's truck in search of evidence. There was, the judge ruled, reasonable cause to believe evidence in a double homicide might be hidden somewhere in the Mazda. The warrant allowed police and crime scene personnel to search for biological and trace evidence, including—but not limited to—blood, hair and fibers, any sharp objects that could be used as a weapon, any firearms, parts of firearms, ammunition, or firearm-related items.

Police could also look for any "documents, receipts, or personal effects" that would link Stanko to the death of Henry Turner or Laura Ling. The warrant made special note of a missing piece of jewelry, the shape of which matched a bruise that had been found on Laura Ling's body.

The warrant required that an itemized list of the evidence found and seized be made and presented back to the judge for review within ten days.

* * *

Goldfinch Funeral Home prepared Laura Ling's remains for eternal rest. The work was done at their Beach Chapel, one of three funeral homes along the coast run by George H. Goldfinch Jr., this one on Pawleys Island, on the other side of Brookgreen Gardens State Park from Murrells Inlet.

Visitation was kept short, held on April 13, from six to eight in the evening. Goldfinch put an obituary up on its website, which was almost identical to the one that ran in the local paper. It noted that Ling's birth and death dates were July 10, 1961 to April 8, 2005. It gave her education and work history, details of the planned services in her honor, and listed her survivors as her sons and daughter, her mother and her sisters, Catherine Hatfield, of McKinney, Texas, and Victoria Loy, of Tulsa, Oklahoma. A nephew, McLean Hatfield, of McKinney, Texas, and Laura's ex-husband Chris Ling, of Kill Devil Hills, North Carolina, were also mentioned. It concluded: Memorials may be made to Socastee Public Library.

On April 14, Ling's remains were transported by hearse from the Beach Chapel to the Precious Blood of Christ Church, a somewhat progressive Roman Catholic church on Waverly Road, also on Pawleys Island. A mass of Christian burial was held; after which Ling's remains were transported to Northwest Dallas to the Hillcrest Mausoleum & Memorial Park. Another ceremony was held at an A-framed pavilion/pier that protruded into a man-made lake. Ling's remains were then entombed.

A page on the Goldfinch website was set up for people to share their remembrances and feelings regarding Laura Ling. Many of the entries were from people Ling knew in Texas who fondly recalled the laughter she brought. One entry came from one of Ling's former students from the days when she taught Sunday school in Texas.

But not all of the writing was from the Lone Star State. Janis Walker Gilmore, of Pawleys Island, was Laura Ling's tennis buddy, who recalled that she volleyed as she did everything, "flat out." Janis and Laura were not just casual tennis players who volleyed for exercise. They played United States Tennis Association (USTA) team tennis together for a couple of years.

Janis remembered Penny hanging around the courts waiting for her mother to finish, sometimes killing time by reading the latest Harry Potter book.

Laura was incredibly bright and funny. She once said to me, "You have it all—the big house, the husband, the nice kids, the money—I'd like to hate you, but you're just too damned nice!" That was Laura, Janis recalled.

Linda O'Quinn, a schoolmate of Laura Ling's during her master's program at the University of South Carolina, recalled that Ling was as beautiful on the inside as on the outside.

Simultaneous to the South Carolina services for Laura Ling, on April 14, was a hearing in the Georgetown County Courthouse, with Stephen Stanko in attendance. Part of Georgetown's Historic District, that courthouse was one of the oldest in the country, built in 1824 to replace the wooden one that burned in 1819. Designed with security in mind, the walls were six feet deep. Along the front were six impressive pillars and a balustrade.

Stanko waived his right to a bond hearing, and was held without bail. The judge signed an arrest warrant for a charge of armed robbery. The affidavit explained that there was reasonable cause to believe Stanko stole

Turner's vehicle, cell phone, and two of Turner's guns after the murder. After all, Stanko had been walking toward Turner's truck when he was arrested in Augusta.

The solicitor, already thinking in terms of the death penalty, wanted to pile on as many charges as possible, just to be safe.

THE MAZDA

At quarter past five on Thursday afternoon, the search warrant for the Mazda, signed by Judge Richard A. Slaby, made its way to the Richmond County Sheriff's Office VPB, where the truck waited. A copy of the search warrant was made and placed on the vehicle's dashboard.

An hour later, Investigators James Gordon and Shannon Mitchell began executing the warrant, starting with an inventory of the vehicle's contents. Photographs were taken of the truck from every angle.

One never knew what would turn out to be important later, so the photographic coverage of the truck was complete. Gordon noted that the vehicle had no easily discernible damage to its exterior.

There was no ignition key, so investigators had to break into the car. The interior was gray—gray cloth seats and gray carpeting. The floorboards were covered with red mats, which were removed and bagged as evidence. You could learn a lot about a suspect by what came off the bottom of his feet.

A closer examination of the cabin's interior revealed

an unknown brown substance on the inside of the driver's-side window. A quick McPhail's Reagent Hemident (MRH) test, involving a reagent and a sterile Q-tip, was positive for blood. A swab of that blood sample was made and taken as evidence.

The odometer read 107,019. The trip meter read 240.1 miles—a precise measure of the suspect's meandering flight.

The investigators opened up the cooler in the bed and found inside, resting in a couple of inches of water, nine unopened Coors Light beer cans and an unopened can of Pepsi. Also in there was a metal flask, with a logo for Canadian Club imprinted on it. In the flask was an "unknown fruitlike alcoholic beverage."

An inventory of the glove box taught investigators more about the victim than his alleged killer. That compartment held the vehicle registration, in the name of Henry Lee Turner, a small notepad with handwritten notes and numbers scribbled in it, a screwdriver kit, a green Dick's Sporting Goods lanyard, four packs of crackers—such as you might get at a restaurant when ordering soup, all unopened—a cell phone charger, flashlight, some miscellaneous auto parts and tools, a gift card to Henry Turner, a rusty and dusty pocket jackknife, multiple unused straws, and a combination padlock.

Sitting up on the dashboard was a pair of bifocal glasses in a soft black case. Beneath the steering wheel, on the driver's-side floorboard, along with the red mat, was a child's shirt, white with black trim, unknown stains, and the words ZOEY BETH.

On the passenger-side floorboard, police discovered a Krystal fast-food restaurant bag, with three empty burger boxes and no receipt, three unopened Miller Lite beer bottles in a six-pack container, a key ring with no keys but with a Ford Mustang electronic door/trunk lock fob, a yellow folding knife, and a leather pouch containing a Marlboro Country Store bottle opener.

Also down under the passenger seat was a generic plastic grocery bag containing a Kmart receipt printed at nine-fifteen in the morning on April 11 at a store in Martinez, Georgia. The receipt indicated the purchase of a Nokia cell phone. Also in the bag was a brochure from a piano store and the business card of the store's proprietor. There was an empty Mountain Dew soda pop bottle in the bag, and an empty Burger King Styrofoam coffee cup. The bottle and the cup were both swabbed at their lips, and that evidence saved for future possible DNA testing. There was an empty pack of cigarettes, a discount brand, a business card from a jewelry and repair shop, with a handwritten name across it, and a receipt from Amelia's Buds & Blooms, dated April 11, for a "single rose BV." Another receipt was from Harrington Sports, Inc., also dated April 11, for the purchase of three shirts. The customer, as written on the receipt, was the "Kristopher Family." Also down there on the floor was a pair of fingernail clippers, a plastic Honey Bun wrapper, three ink pens, candy, a business card for a sewing and vacuum cleaner store and a matchbook from Golden Egg Pancake House.

It would need to be determined what items belonged to Turner and what to Stanko.

Sitting on top of the passenger seat was an Ozark Trail carry bag, with a towel on top of it. This had to be the suspect's bag. He'd packed clean pullover shirts, pants (waist 36), socks, and boxer shorts. Also jammed in there were travel-size toiletries—toothbrush, electric razor, shampoo, etc. Stephen Stanko's first-aid kit consisted of an open box of twenty Band-Aids, assorted sizes. The box was open and a couple of the Band-Aids, size unknown, were missing. Also in there were a spare set of keys to the truck.

Sitting on the seat next to the luggage was a brochure for Hot Spring portable spas, and the receipt from the Krystal run, which had been made at twelve-thirty on the afternoon of April 12, only a few hours before he was arrested.

The investigators shifted their attention to the cabin's center console and found a Taurus .357 Magnum revolver, stainless steel, with brown grips, a two-letter six-digit serial number, six cartridges in the cylinder—five Winchester .38 Specials, and an RP .38 Special.

Among the items found in the center console near the gun were Henry Lee Turner's checkbook, a pack of Jolt Caffeine-Energy Gum, which looked to the investigator identical to Chiclets, and a notebook labeled *Classified Colors.* Upon further examination, they found the name *Laura Ling* written on the inside of the front cover. Bingo.

The console contained a pair of silver-rimmed eyeglasses. There was something odd about them, solder at the joints, which upon further inspection revealed itself to be a home repair.

Under the glasses was Stanko's 1986 Goose Creek High School class ring. Gordon and Mitchell knew about the unusually shaped mark on the victim Laura Ling's face. Might have been caused by a piece of jewelry. The grooves on the ring were filled up with an unknown substance. The ring was quickly bagged and given top priority.

Buried at the bottom of the console was a private investigator badge, with *Henry Turner* inscribed on it. The investigators wondered if Stanko knew it was there. A flimflam man with any kind of official-looking badge was a dangerous animal. That badge, in Stephen Stanko's possession, could have translated into deadly control.

Uninteresting items (napkins, a spark plug, Neosporin ointment) were pulled from the side compartments on both driver's and passenger side. Neatly over the top of the passenger seat was another change of clothes, dress shirt, dress pants. In the cargo area behind the seats, police found, among other items, more clean clothes for Stanko, and a lot of Turner's stuff, already there when Stanko stole the vehicle.

The evidence kept coming now. There was a fifty-cartridge box of Winchester .38 Specials, with five missing. Next to the ammunition was a green duffel bag, with what appeared to be blood splattered on it. Inside the bag was a receipt, for 8:00 P.M. on April 9, from a Hooters gift shop, where Stanko bought a new shirt. It was a business expense, an addition to his wardrobe for his role as owner of several Hooters franchises.

There was a dark suit coat and, under that, a brown-handled folding knife, with brown stains on it. Those stains were tested on the spot and came up positive for blood.

A metal card holder contained Stephen C. Stanko's business cards which read: PARALEGAL AND EXOTIC DANCER. This guy was a piece of work.

When every item in the truck had been logged in, and those deemed pertinent bagged for evidence, the investigators processed the truck for latent prints and biological evidence.

There were, in and on the truck, eleven spots of blood—and they field-tested those stains using McPhail's Reagent, brand name Hemident. Blood swabs were made from all eleven areas, and these were individually packaged and sealed.

Gut feeling was that the spots would turn out to belong to the suspect, as they were consistent with the driver of the truck touching things while bleeding from a wounded hand.

Ten latent prints were developed from the truck, and each was transferred to a card, where the precise location of the print was noted. When the processing of the truck was completed, thirty-two items had been seized in compliance with the search warrant and bagged for evidence. The rest was photographed and left in the truck.

That thirty-two number was misleading as some of those "items" were actually a sealed bag with multiple items inside, items investigators felt would not cross-contaminate their neighbors. The thirty-two seized items were turned over by Investigators Gordon and Mitchell to Investigator DeWayne M. Piper, who delivered them to the Crime Scene Unit office for further analysis and, eventually, safe storage.

Gordon performed the "further analysis" on the Taurus .357 himself. The revolver and the six cartridges were processed for latent prints, using high-intensity light and the state-of-the-art Reflected Ultraviolet Imaging System (RUVIS). The gun and cartridges were placed inside a cyanoacrylate-fuming chamber, exposed to the special light, and yielded two prints.

Police ran a quick check on the gun and found that it had been purchased by Juanita Turner on February 22, 1999, from a pawnshop in North Myrtle Beach. The woman was identified as the victim's daughter-in-law, wife of son Roger. The murder weapon, police learned, was one of four weapons purchased by the thirty-three-year-old Juanita, between 1995 and 1999. The other three were a .38 revolver, a 45mm derringer, and a .22 automatic.

In response to the subpoena requested by Horry County detective Scott Bogart, on April 15, Hilary Ware, of Google's commercial litigation counsel, sent a list of

Stanko's e-mail activity during the pertinent time period. She included with the list a bill for twenty-five dollars to cover costs. Horry County paid the bill, but, unfortunately, they found the e-mail activity unhelpful.

At three in the afternoon on Monday, April 18, six days after Stephen Stanko's arrest, Investigator DeWayne Piper called Anne Pitts, lead investigator in Horry County. Piper was concerned about matters of jurisdiction. Stanko had committed his murders in different counties in one state, and had been arrested in a third county in a second state. Pitts said that it was all right for him to turn everything over to Georgetown County, where the Laura Ling murder occurred, and investigators there would determine what belonged to which agencies.

Pitts had a question in return: "When you were searching the truck, did you find a lockbox or any will-related paperwork?" Piper said they had not. Pitts said she would be back in touch to discuss returning the truck to the Turner family, and that those arrangements had not yet been made.

In the meantime, Jim Gordon compared the prints found on the gun, and another print found on a phone card, to record inked prints from Stephen Stanko. He was able to get a positive match (ten-plus matching points) between the phone card print and Stanko's left index finger. But, unfortunately, Gordon was not able to match any prints from the revolver.

After the arrest, Georgetown and Horry Counties largely worked independently. The Ling murder and the

Turner murder were investigated and would eventually be tried separately.

At first, each had been in possession of evidence that best served the other's investigation; so, with paperwork carefully chronicling the chain of possession, a swap was made. Georgetown County gave Horry County Turner's checkbook and the other contents of the Mazda, and, in return, received Laura Ling's Mustang and its contents, which for a few days had been parked and sealed off at a garage known as Squeaky's Towing.

On Tuesday morning, April 19, Jim Gordon was back on the phone with Anne Pitts, who asked if a motorcycle key had been found in the truck. It had. She asked that it be returned with the vehicle, as the Turner family needed it. No problem.

On Friday, April 22, DeWayne Piper received a phone call from Debbie Gallogly, Henry Turner's daughter. She said that in her official capacity as executor of her dad's estate, she wished to reclaim his pickup truck, and would be leaving soon to get it.

Piper called Pitts to verify that Gallogly was the correct person to get the truck. Pitts said she was. A few hours later, Piper officially turned the Mazda and its access key over to Turner's daughter, along with a copy of the property receipts, itemizing what police were keeping as evidence, and a copy of the executed search warrant.

On May 10, 2005, the U.S. Marshal's Service gave the $10,000 reward to Dana Putnam. Accepting the reward, Dana said she was going to share the money with Penny Ling, who'd so bravely called 911, despite having her throat slit twice.

LAB RESULTS

On June 24, 2005, Senior Agent Bruce S. Gantt Jr. released his horrifying findings regarding some of the blood evidence discovered at the Ling scene.

Gantt concluded that he had thoroughly examined the small lamp with the broken glass globe found in the vicinity of Laura Ling's body. The brown stains on the lamp were indeed blood, and that the blood was most heavily concentrated at the lamp's base. Some were consistent in "size, shape, and distribution" with "medium-velocity impact stains," commonly associated with a blunt-force–trauma incident. Others were comprised of "expirated blood," such as that blown out of the nose, mouth, or wound with blood pressure supplying the propelling force.

Gantt had also examined a piece of luggage that had been found in the Mazda in Augusta. It was a tan canvas suitcase with a fabric-style exterior. The bag, Gantt determined, had spattered bloodstains on the inside, but not on the outside. The best theory here was that the suitcase had been in the vicinity of Laura Ling as Stanko beat her, with the lid open, so the blood spatter only struck the inside. Later, Stanko had brought the suitcase with him as he fled, first placing it in the red Mustang, and then moving it into the Mazda, thus providing a perfect chain of evidence linking the Ling crime scene with the scene of the arrest hundreds of miles away.

Three days later, Anne Pitts, in Horry County, received a report from the SLED trace-evidence department signed by Senior Agent Jennifer M. Stoner, who had also performed tests on a gunshot residue (GSR) kit used on Henry Turner's remains. The kit indicated that small quantities of metals were detected on the palm and back of the victim's left hand.

Although gunshot residue was most often found on the hands of the shooter—where primer, powder, and other projectile material was deposited by the discharge of a firearm, it could be found on the *victim,* near the point of entry for point-blank shots, or sometimes on the hands of victims who assumed a defensive posture as the shots were fired.

The evidence in this case had been removed from Henry Lee Turner's body, using the adhesive disc-type sampling collection method, and later examined through a scanning electron microscope.

After the tests were completed, Senior Agent Stoner concluded that the metal "may be associated with gunshot residue."

May be associated? Not that Pitts had to worry about proving Turner was shot, or that Stanko had shot him, but the picture of Henry Lee Turner holding his hands out to protect himself, perhaps to beg for mercy, Pitts thought, was very vivid and might be just the thing to creep inside the mind of an uncertain juror.

* * *

On July 18, 2005, Anne Pitts received the SLED report from the firearms department signed by SLED senior agent F. Dan DeFreese. This report said nine items had been tested, the first four all found in Henry Turner's pickup truck at the scene of Stanko's arrest: the Taurus .357 revolver, the unfired .38 Special cartridge bearing the headstamp RP, five unfired cartridges (which as a group counted as one item) of the same caliber stamped Winchester, and the fifty-round ammunition box.

Items five and six were the bullets removed from Henry Turner's body, seven was a bullet investigator pulled from the wall of Turner's mobile home, and the last two were the spent .38 Special RP cartridges found in the victim's dresser drawer.

After receiving the items from the Richmond County crime lab, SLED's first order of business was to determine if the gun was in working order.

The revolver was test-fired and found to be functional. The bullets fired during the test were recovered and compared microscopically with the two bullets found in the corpse and one dug from Turner's wall.

The wall bullet was too mangled for a useful comparison, and the official report was that the bullets found in Turner's chest *could have been fired* by the revolver found in Turner's truck, *or by another similar firearm.*

Pitts found the wishy-washy wording disappointing. She would have preferred that ballistics conclusively matched the bullets to the gun *to the exclusion of all other guns.*

Not that Pitts worried about the strength of the case, but she hated anything that a defense attorney might be able to latch onto.

The SLED report continued that *debris consistent with blood or body tissue* was found on the chest bullets. Not a shocker there. Also on those bullets was *fibrous debris* resembling *synthetic textile fibers*. This material was separated, air-dried, and rebagged to be transferred to the appropriate lab. The firearms people didn't do blood and fibers, and vice versa. The wall bullet also had a foreign substance, but nothing of any curiosity, just the plaster and drywall type material one would expect.

The report concluded by saying the test-fired bullets had been submitted for entry into the Integrated Ballistics Identification System (IBIS). If the bullets matched any connected with other crimes, Horry County police would be notified.

But there were no matches. As far as the cops could tell, Henry Lee Turner was the only person ever shot with that revolver.

The next day, July 19, the SLED DNA analysis team delivered their report to Detective Pitts. The blood found on various surfaces in Turner's bathroom and on the floor of his bedroom had undergone short tandem repeat (STR) DNA analysis and, disappointingly, all were DNA matches with the blood of the victim. It would have been great if the killer had bled at the murder scene, too. Sometimes they did. Victims fought back.

On July 22, forensic technician Patti B. Ruff in the SLED Evidence Processing Department, who had tested items of evidence from the Ling scene for blood and semen, filed her report, which had been reviewed and approved by her supervisor, Lieutenant Emily B. Reinhart. Among the items that tested positive for biological evidence were a candle, a black bra, pajama bottoms, a sleeveless top, a pink suit coat, with a matching shirt, a beige suit coat, a comforter, and a quilt. Items that tested negative included a silk necktie, a pair of white panties, leather belt, bath towel, and one pink and one white bra.

She also tested the Goose Creek High School ring and verified that the material in the grooves was dried blood.

Although Stephen Stanko's two murder trials would eventually take place years apart, the grand jury hearings for the Laura Ling and Henry Lee Turner murders took place on back-to-back days in August 2005. The indictments for the Ling crimes were submitted in Georgetown County by the Fifteenth Circuit Solicitor's Office on August 24. Indictments for the Turner murder were submitted to a Horry County grand jury on August 25.

Late that summer, in September, Joe Harper, a subrogation specialist at the Armed Forces Insurance Exchange (AFIE), wrote a letter to Horry County sheriff Phillip E. Thompson explaining that AFIE insured the victim, and was cutting a check, to go to Henry Lee Turner's estate, for $4,296.91. The money was to cover the costs of cleaning up and fixing the mobile home after the murder. The check was made out to the executor, daughter Debbie Gallogly. More than three grand of that money went to pay the bill of Crime Scene Services (CSS), of Monroe, North Carolina, cleaners of crime scenes. For that fee, CSS removed blood, body fluids, and fingerprint dust from the walls and floor of Turner's back bathroom and bedroom. They disinfected the entire home, always a good idea when there has been a death. The bedroom door was repaired. The CSS workers wore protective gear—masks, gloves, and boots—as they removed, transported, and disposed of "five boxes of biohazard." The bedroom and bathroom carpet and pad were replaced and the walls of those rooms were freshly sheetrocked and painted. Using estate money, Gallogly also repaired the bullet hole at the other end of the mobile home caused by Stephen Stanko's test shot.

For those in charge of making sense of Stephen Stanko's actions, the dust had officially settled and it was time to figure out what had just happened.

Who was Stanko?

What made him tick?

Why did he switch from a charming good-natured flimflam man into a homicidal maniac?

Had there been a harbinger? What caused the switch?

Was it organic or inorganic, nature or nurture?

PART II

GOOSE CREEK

Stephen Christopher Stanko was born January 13, 1968, on the island of Cuba, son of William Stanko, a master chief in the U.S. Navy stationed at Guantánamo Bay.

When William was transferred, his family moved with him, and Stephen grew up in a Roman Catholic household in Goose Creek, South Carolina, with two brothers and two sisters. The community was home to the Naval Weapons Station and Strategic Weapons Facility, where his dad worked.

At first, the Stankos lived in the Menriv section of Goose Creek, where the navy's housing development was located. Later, they upgraded to a ranch-style redbrick home, with a finely manicured lawn, on pretty Kenilworth Road.

Goose Creek, part of the urbanized northern suburbs of Charleston, was a small city with a population just under 30,000; yet its footprint crossed a county line. Part of the city was in Berkeley County, part in Charleston County. It had only officially been a city since 1961, but the area had been unofficially called Goose Creek, because of the area stream with that name, since at least the mid-1700s. Just to the east, on the other side of North Rhett Avenue, was the weapons station, and beyond that, the Francis Marion National Forest.

William ran a tight ship. Everyone obeyed, including their mom, Joan. The atmosphere in the home was sometimes hard for outsiders to deal with. There was a perceived weightiness to the Stanko aura. Hard for some to breathe, hard to relax in the Stanko house.

Stephen had one older brother, William Jr., a younger brother, Jeff, and sisters Peggy and Cynthia. The Stanko siblings coexisted under difficult circumstances in a very cold environment. One of Stephen's relatives once referred to that abject home as "like suicide." It was volatile. The siblings, it's been said, felt trapped, no escape.

According to one friend, Stephen felt that his dad preferred his older brother, Billy. William Jr. had been eight years old when Stephen was born. Stephen was the second brother, and he believed he got short shrift. Yet, Billy was considered a little bit wild by Stanko standards. Rode a motorcycle. Who knows what else?

When Stephen was fifteen years old, Billy died in a house fire, maybe arson, in St. George, a small town near Interstate 95 in Dorchester County. Billy Stanko was twenty-three when he died, and the Stanko home grew even heavier, now heavy with sadness.

Before then, Stephen had been a "golden boy," the kid who had everything going for him. With the exception of the typical adolescent faux pas, when he tried to grow a mustache before he was ready, his appearance was always impeccable.

He was Stephen "all-American" Stanko, and he appeared luminous back then, born with his own inner light. Teachers' eyes twinkled when they discussed him.

He was *brilliant*.

That boy was going to be something someday. He was even athletic, played football and baseball. Go Gators. The boy could do anything he wanted to do with his life, his coaches bragged.

Despite his active lifestyle, his youth was basically injury free. One time he'd been knocked cold when hit in the forehead by a beer bottle, but that was about it.

And what Stephen wanted was what his father wanted: admission into the Air Force Academy, where he hoped to become an aeronautic engineer, designing and building state-of-the-art military aircraft.

Befitting a boy who seldom lost, Stanko carried a quiet confidence with his perfect posture. But all of that changed after his brother's death. If Stephen thought he would step into the position of number one son in his father's eyes after Billy was gone, he was deeply disappointed. Dad turned his back on him, wouldn't have anything to do with him, like he *blamed* him.

Stephen's inner light flickered and dimmed.

In 1985, when he was a high-school junior, Stanko took the SAT college admission exam. He scored a 500 in verbal and 620 in math, not spectacular, putting him in about the eighty-fifth percentile. He asked for the results to be sent to four colleges: the Air Force Academy, Clemson, University of South Carolina, and Furman.

Stephen was a senior at Goose Creek High when his already fading self-luminescence extinguished forever. A slender envelope from the Air Force Academy arrived. Inside, a brief note: he had *not* been accepted.

Stephen had been certain that the Air Force Academy was his destiny—so much so that he had turned down scholarships at other schools in anticipation of his acceptance. Then the balloon popped.

About-face. He would later wonder, with bewilderment, how he had gone from the mountaintop to free fall so suddenly. How—if he was supposed to be a genius—could he do such stupid things?

According to Stanko, this was the time in his life when he became "lost," his moral compass spinning. His life plummeted at a frightening pace. Instead of going to a prestigious institute of learning, he took a few classes at the local community college.

When that didn't work out, Stanko turned to a life of crime.

By the early 1990s, Stephen Stanko was on probation for multiple charges of grand theft auto.

LIZ

Jane Elizabeth "Liz" McLendon thought she could spot a bad boy when she saw one. She'd written papers on juvenile delinquents, what they called in school "hoods," and considered herself a bit of an expert. Ambitious by nature, she hoped to turn it into a career one day.

She was a beautiful girl, elected homecoming queen. However, if you asked her what she wanted to be when she grew up, she gave a surprising answer.

"A criminologist," she would say. Specifically, she wanted to be an FBI profiler, who used details of murder scenes to predict what the killer was like.

As almost always happened to youthful dreams, real life got in the way. Liz married young, had a son, and was divorced when the boy was five. To her credit, even with the surprises, the wheels didn't completely come off her game plan. She completed college and earned a marketing degree.

Several years later, in 1992, the single mom was working as a sales rep for a telecommunications company.

Working for the same company, although in a different building a few miles away, was Stephen Stanko.

Liz's first impression of Stanko was one of suspicion. She even went so far as to tell her assistant manager that she thought the guy was "shifty."

The female assistant manager exclaimed with a twinkle: "Oh, but he's so cute!"

Liz furrowed her brow. "I don't know—there's just something about him."

After that, Liz couldn't get rid of him. He'd taken one look at her and his heart started pounding. Steve found every excuse to visit Liz's building.

"He was very persistent, and showing up in my office a lot," Liz recalled. He wore her down.

Stanko told Liz he'd grown up in Goose Creek, which was true, and had just gotten back from Savannah, Georgia, where he was attending art school, which turned out not to be true. He told her that he'd met an evil woman in Savannah and she'd taken every dime he had. He'd been stupid and had fallen for the woman's con artist scheme.

He was very polite, with such a nice personality—the world's most charming guy. And Liz wasn't embarrassed to admit that—forgetting all about Stephen's shiftiness—she was charmed.

He preferred calling her Elizabeth, rather than Liz, or sometimes "Rizarif," a version of her name in baby talk.

Stephen liked his beer, now and again, but he wasn't really a drinker. She never saw him show the effects of alcohol. "Not even a little bit," Liz recalled. No drug problems, either. That was a very good sign, Liz thought early on. That was one whole category of relationship dysfunction that she didn't have to worry about. He was just a "nice ol' Southern boy."

At first, dating Stephen was tremendous fun. Their nascent romance danced with a nearly gravity-defying bliss. They sang and looked into each other's eyes.

Although he couldn't play a musical instrument, he loved music. "He was a good dancer," Liz recalled. "Shagging (the dance) was one of his preferences, and he was good at that."

He enjoyed beach music and oldies. When they were together, they listened to a lot of Frank Sinatra and Neil Diamond. "Strangers in the night, dooby-dooby-do." Early on, he made her a cassette tape of music for her to play in the car, all stuff she liked: Van Morrison, Huey Lewis, Randy Travis, and the Righteous Brothers. That tape was her constant companion for a time, and those songs remind her even today of the good times with Stephen.

He wrote her love letters. He told her that he'd never felt as strong and close to anyone as he did to her. Love more than yesterday but less than tomorrow.

Liz's fondest memories were of going to college football games at the Citadel, where Stephen was a big fan. The Citadel's football team rocked in 1992, eleven wins, two losses, on their way toward capturing the Southern Conference championship. Stephen took Liz to the game at the old Johnson Hagood Stadium against Marshall in October, which set the all-time attendance record for the Citadel, more than 23,000 souls surrounding Sansom Field. The stadium and playing field had different names, which is what happened when you tried to dedicate the new without dissing the old.

Stephen told Liz that he wanted to be a writer—write about sales and achieving success. She said she thought he'd be good at that. She could see how he would be a very good motivator. He knew how to make people want to do well.

He said that his hero in the motivational area was Zig Ziglar, and he hoped to one day metamorphose, as Ziglar had, from champion seller to master motivator.

Stanko wanted to author best sellers, like Ziglar had penned, and be in constant demand for speaking engagements. The man could sell a pitch. He made it all seem so feasible.

Once, Stephen took Liz to an exclusive neighborhood and showed her a beautiful mansion. He told her that used to be his home, but he sold it to go to Savannah.

When that went over well, he took her to a boat marina, took her on a boat, and told her it was his—but he'd had to sell it, just like his beautiful home.

In one unusually candid moment, he told her he'd had a few disappointments, that he'd really wanted to go to the Air Force Academy, but it wasn't meant to be.

"I couldn't pass the eye exam!" he told Liz. It was a sensitivity to pressure or something in one eye. Nothing serious—just enough to keep him from flying fighter jets.

Stephen saw competition everywhere. Anything and everything was a competition he had to win. Liz remembered one time they had to go to a family function, her family, and Stephen felt anxiety that someone at that get-together might look better than they did. He insisted that he and Liz dress to the nines so that they would be the best dressed.

True, she sensed a chilliness on Stanko's surface—he countered her ardent embraces with boasts and swagger—but she chalked it up to his rigid upbringing, and—at first, anyway—didn't look deeper.

* * *

Liz noticed that Stephen's father was the key to his ego. If he needed to dress better, make more money, accomplish more things, or whatever it was, it was because he had been taught to be that way by his father. He had to be the best, or else he would disappoint his dad, which remained a horrible thought to him. His old man, who had gotten into his head and had never left. Every aspect of his life took on a grandeur that was almost entirely imaginary—his wishful imagination, the happier world in which his dad was proud.

The disconnect between Stephen's father and himself came over matters of discipline. Dad wanted Stephen to be the best at things because he worked the hardest and applied himself with the most tenacity. But that wasn't at all how Stephen went about life. Stephen was constantly searching for the shortcut, for the cheat, for the convincing illusion. He wanted everything to be easy—*expected* it to be easy.

Liz's son, a preteen by the time Stephen entered their lives, did not have many pleasant memories of the man his mother dated for almost four years. She came to believe that he was jealous of her relationship with her son. He was not only hard on the kid, but he sought to build a wall between mother and child.

Stephen was her son's baseball coach in Little League for a brief time, and it was most unpleasant. Stephen would come up with harsh punishments for kids who made an error, until it got to the point where it was no fun at all. Liz could really see Stephen's father coming out in his personality as he tried to teach the kids baseball. Like his father would have, Liz believed, Steve expected each kid to be perfect in every way, and became angry when they were less than that. It was very difficult for Liz's kid to deal with Stephen, to deal with a ruler, a dictator in his life. The kid's dad wasn't like that at all; his father was easygoing, not hypercritical like Stephen.

He didn't spend money on himself, but when Liz offered to take him out and buy him clothes, he always agreed, and directed her toward the finer labels. When he was home and being casual, he still wore Tommy Hilfiger jeans and Tommy cologne.

Stephen was seldom tenacious about anything, with the exception of cleaning. He was very clean and very neat—and he wanted his surroundings to be that way as well. Very anal, as a shrink might say.

He loved scrubbing and polishing and vacuuming and the rest of housework that most people found to be a drudge. When he had a sales job, he did best when selling cleaning chemicals to companies and hospitals—and part of the reason for his success was the enthusiasm and joy he showed while demonstrating the product.

When his surroundings were not neat and clean, he was quick to anger. He needed order. Chaos upset him. Liz figured this was probably typical of children of master chiefs. In households like that, she believed, you didn't experience or learn anything but *orderly.*

Over time, Liz saw Stephen's charm in a different light. In the vernacular of their song playlist, they went from "marvelous night for a moondance" to "you've lost that lovin' feeling."

His charm was fulsome—even excessive. She saw in him a stubborn unwillingness to rankle. He *needed* to be smooth with people, the better to sway them.

His inability to tell the precise truth, his unwillingness to be banal or pedestrian, was so pervasive as to be a detriment (certainly a complication) to his existence.

Life was so much harder for him than it needed to be. Seeing things as they were was not an option. He needed the kaleidoscope of his imagination to cope. He was constantly molding reality and trying to conjure spells. Hyperbole was his paintbrush. He even exaggerated minor happenings. If an ant crawled across his shoe, Stanko would claim it was a ladybug.

It wasn't just Liz. Everyone had a sense that Stanko enjoyed spinning a yarn or two. Everyone, including Liz, also felt his brags had some basis in fact. She didn't catch on to the fact that he was a pathological liar until after she fell for him, and by then, it was too late to quit him.

He was a rubber ball that always came bouncing back to her. Only years later would she realize that he had manipulated her most of all.

Stephen sensed Liz needed security and gave her that. He dominated the relationship, not because he was so large and in charge, but rather because his dependence on her was so absolute.

"He depended on me for praise, financial assistance, ego boosting, and helping him out of his many tight spots—and there were an exhausting number of tight spots," she said.

Liz felt like he was the sun, some huge gravitational mass, and she had gotten too close and fallen into orbit around him, then abruptly was "sucked right in." Get too close and you became a permanent part of his life.

She had known from early on, maybe six months after she met him, that there were a lot of things going on, plenty of trouble. But she was hooked. He kept her on her toes. She never knew what to expect the next time he walked through the door. To listen to him, he had the world's most eventful life.

For a guy who really couldn't hold down a job, he was always busy. He got up every morning, dressed in a suit and tie, ready for the day, and went out there to do whatever it was he did. And he would return ten hours later still looking kempt!

There was never enough solid evidence to tell for sure what Stephen was doing with his time, but he sometimes made jokes about his constantly plotting nature. What did he do all day? He kept all thousand irons in the fire, that's what.

There were so many imaginary jobs, and imaginary firings, that she had no idea which of them, if any, were real. She believed that he sometimes told little lies poorly so she'd be less likely to suspect his big lies.

There were always schemes. Stephen was like that showbiz act where the frantic man kept many plates spinning atop broomsticks. With Stanko, however, plates fell—quite often, in fact—and that was when his shoveling of the bull shifted into overdrive.

When Liz learned that Stanko was a habitual liar, she tried to determine reality, using outside factors. He concocted stories, left and right. He couldn't seem to help it.

Looking back on it now, Liz understood that Stephen Stanko was the classic psychopath, the man with no conscience, no capacity for empathy. Back then, she didn't know any of that. She just knew that Stanko lived in his own world, and she wasn't sure if the rest of humanity was there with him.

He was a chameleon, all right, but not everyone fell under his spell. Not everyone was sucked in. Those that weren't—women mostly, Liz found—withdrew when Stephen was around.

Liz sometimes thought women were more astute when it came to these things. There were several women she remembered who didn't want their boyfriends or husbands to be associated with Stanko.

"After three and a half years with Stephen, there were times when I questioned my own sanity," Liz said, likening that time to a "runaway roller-coaster ride."

Liz explained: "He was very good at what he did. He practiced it until he perfected it, and he used it on everyone. He made a career out of it."

There was a time period when Liz knew something was wrong with Stephen, even before he did—how he tried to hide his criminal activity from her—and she sensed the deception, even if she didn't know at first what was being hidden.

She tried to talk to him about it, but he denied anything and everything, and these discussions usually deteriorated into arguments. Some couples, Stanko would later note, could argue their way through their problems, but that was not the case with them.

He had a bad temper and "lost it" when he got mad.

Stephen and Liz went to a counselor for a time. But the counselor was too weak. Stephen was able to turn things around so that Liz felt she was the one being counseled. He tried to make her seem jealous. She'd admit to being suspicious of him, with good reason, but jealous? No way. That was another of his lies.

Any woman would have been suspicious. Stephen took telephone calls all day and all night. Sometimes he would go into the bathroom, close the door, and speak on the phone in a low voice. That was suspicious—with a capital *S*. She didn't confront him, though. He'd trained her that it was always wise to keep the relationship on an even keel. If there was a fight, she would lose.

"I felt like I walked on eggshells in my own home," she recalled. "I felt like, if I made the wrong move, I was going to be in trouble." She cried every business trip, because he found a way to make her miserable.

At one point, Stephen called Liz's boss and complained that her job was interfering with their relationship. She had worked hard to get where she was at that job, getting ahead in what was still a man's world, and she couldn't have been more mortified—humiliated!—by Stephen's phone call.

In 1995, Stephen was arrested for white-collar crimes, creating false paperwork at his job in order to collect commissions he wasn't owed. He told Liz he was innocent.

She got him a lawyer, but he ended up serving more than a month in jail. That was how Liz discovered Stanko was more than just a businessman with shaky ethics. He was a downright thief.

Stephen also made a big deal out of Liz's earnings and stated that he should bring home the money. Despite that, he stole blank checks from her purse.

"When he needed money, he couldn't resist pawning paintings and jewelry from around my home," she complained. One day, she confronted him about his criminal activities.

As usual, he abruptly became nasty; this time, his attack leapt beyond verbal, and became physical. He assaulted her in her home at one point, putting his hands on her throat.

Stanko got control of himself before doing Liz any harm—with the exception of scaring her. For the short term, she ran to her friend Mary Lou Culpepper.

Stephen and Liz broke up after that. For the long term, Stanko stayed with a couple of friends of his for a time, not far from Goose Creek. From there, to get even farther from Liz, he headed for the big city—Atlanta, Georgia.

"Once he was in Atlanta," Liz recalled, "he began his same old tricks, just with different people." He was pulling paperwork swindles at different jobs, and manipulating a new girlfriend. "What are the odds? He began to see a young woman I knew," Liz remembered. "Her name was Cynthia, and she had a young daughter. That's who he preyed on. He was always on the lookout for single mothers."

Stephen saw single mothers as age-appropriate damsels in distress, usually struggling in life a bit, in need of a man. It was a situation that he found easy to overwhelm. It was easy for him to interject himself into those incomplete families and make himself the hero.

"It would always seem at first that he was the answer to all of their problems, but in the long run, he just brought fresh problems into their lives," Liz said.

Stephen told Cynthia Wilson that Liz was calling him constantly; when, in actuality, the reverse was true. Liz was the one being pestered by unwanted phone calls.

He wanted to come back. She said no. He called again. Again, no. He was relentless and again she wore down. Despite all of Liz's resistance, there came a day when he was back.

He needed a place to stay and she supplied that—but their romantic relationship was finished. They were no longer boyfriend and girlfriend after Atlanta.

While Stephen was in Georgia, Liz moved into a new home in Goose Creek, where her next-door neighbors were Delray "Ray" and Natalie Crenshaw.

When Stephen returned to Goose Creek, he got a job

at a used-car lot, but that, as usual, wasn't enough. He wanted to start his own car dealership.

Although Liz certainly did not mind socializing with the Crenshaws, she begged Stephen not to bother them with his "business deals." Stephen said that was silly talk. Soon Stephen and Ray were more than friends, they were partners. Ray Crenshaw was in the orbit of the huge gravitational sphere that was Stephen Stanko, and had been sucked in.

Liz's conscience is still troubled over this part of the story. She knew Stephen was a con man, she knew that the Crenshaws were just the sort of people he would rip off, and yet she sat by and smiled and allowed it to happen.

The biggest question of all was: why did she let him back?

"I'll question that forever," Liz said.

So, by 1996, Liz no longer thought of Stephen at all the way she had when their relationship was still dewy and new, wreathed in romance. They weren't even buddies. He'd become a bully and a burden. She had long since figured out that his charm was always self-serving. She'd heard plenty of examples of him being misogynistic, verbally abusive to women. And she'd felt his hands around her neck. It was a simple case of cause and effect. Whenever she confronted him about anything, he "went mad." It was like he had a switch, and when you triggered it, there was no stopping him.

"The difference was like night and day," Liz recalled.

Why? Why? Why had she let him back? Naïveté, that's what it was. She thought he had changed. She still believed the things he said. No, amend that. It wasn't just naïveté. It was insecurity as well. Stephen had her convinced that she was powerless to change the way things were. Stephen was a social guy, and a popular guy, and he knew plenty of cops—both Berkeley County and Goose Creek. She remembered the first time he grabbed her throat. She called the cops, and when they arrived, Stephen went into his bs rap and blamed everything on Liz. The cop told Liz that he thought it would be for the best if she left and slept someplace else that night.

Leave? It was her house, but he was the one who got to stay; he was the one who had been attacking her. Liz realized Stephen had the cops in his hip pocket.

The reason for the police officer's suggestion was practical. Liz said she had a place to go, and Stephen said he did not. After that, Stephen told Liz that she should never call the police again or he would have them lock her up.

"I believed it was true," Liz said. He really did know those policemen and they were going to protect their own. He'd grown up in Goose Creek, went to school with those guys. She was a transplant from another part of the state—Johns Island.

And that's the way it was: Stephen was in charge and she had no say.

According to Stephen Stanko, it was he who eventually decided it was best all around if he left Liz McLendon. For one thing, he didn't want to harm her physically, and for another, he was afraid that she would be charged as a conspirator if he was ever caught in the possession of stolen items. So, in the "he said" version of the story, he started to pack a bag—to *protect* her.

The "she said" version differs, of course—and is, no doubt, far closer to reality. She said it was Sunday evening, February 18, 1996, when she confronted him with the fact that he'd been fired and hadn't told her. Of course, he scrambled, offered excuses. When she refused to buy it, the argument became nasty.

The following evening, Monday, February 19, she arrived home from work to find Stephen and Ray Crenshaw sitting in the backseat of an unmarked police car in Crenshaw's driveway, answering questions about stolen cars.

Liz's final argument with Stephen erupted early on the morning of February 20. He was too close, leaning. She pushed him; he pushed her back. They wrestled around.

"Get out!" she screamed.

"I will," he replied. He started packing. Liz went to bed and fell asleep. When she woke up in the morning, there was a strong scent of bleach in the air.

Typical, she thought silently. Stephen was cleaning again—well, good, maybe that would give his anger an outlet, if he set about the task of disinfecting something.

She opened her eyes and realized that disinfecting was not what Stephen had on his mind. He was standing over her, with the look of a predator on his face. In his hand was a wet cloth.

He leapt upon her.

When the attack was over and Stanko was gone, it took a while, but Liz finally managed to call 911, and emergency help arrived. First on the scene on Durham Drive were Detective D. Kokinda and Deputy T. K. Stern, and close behind was Detective Darrell Lewis, who was already familiar with Stanko because of the stolen-car investigation.

The call went out to all law enforcement in the area to be on the lookout for Stephen Christopher Stanko, who was six-three, 190 pounds, brown hair, brown eyes, probably wearing wire-rimmed glasses.

While Kokinda and Stern processed the scene for evidence, Lewis tried to obtain a written statement from Liz. But this was impossible, as the victim was still too upset.

Liz had given a brief and somewhat rambling account of events to Stern, who relayed them to Lewis, so he'd be up to speed. The victim had seen Stanko talking outside with his business partner and a cop, so she knew something was wrong—but when she questioned him about it, he became *extremely* hostile.

She said the next morning, *this* morning, he tried to asphyxiate her with chemicals. He said he was doing it to keep her from calling the police. Lewis thought this warranted an "intent to kill" charge. The victim certainly thought as it occurred that he was trying to kill her. When he couldn't asphyxiate her, he tied her up and kept an eye on her as he prepared to leave, showering and then packing his stuff into luggage.

With no more information immediately forthcoming from the primary victim, Lewis talked to Liz's next-door neighbors, the Crenshaws. Ray Crenshaw, a guy with longish chestnut hair combed back over his ears and a neatly trimmed gray beard, said that before the violence, Stanko had confessed to him that he was stealing the cars that they were supposed to sell at a used-car lot that they intended to operate together. Through Ray Crenshaw's help, Lewis was able to recover the stolen vehicles. Lewis made arrangements for both Liz and Ray to give thorough statements on February 22. Ray would come down to the sheriff's station to give his. Lewis would return to Liz's home for hers.

Lewis reviewed the files and found a report from a Virgil Cordray, an employee at McElveen Pontiac, of two vehicles that had disappeared from the lot. The report was filed on February 2, almost three weeks earlier. Lewis could see that Stanko's grip on civilized behavior had loosened abruptly during February 1996. He learned another piece of the puzzle after talking to people, at McElveen Pontiac, who told him that Stephen Stanko had been fired on February 17, just a few days before the attack on Liz. The cause for dismissal? He'd "unlawfully loaned" a woman named Teddy Monette a raspberry-colored Blazer from the McElveen lot. When they confronted Stanko about it, the car was returned, but he was fired, anyway.

Stephen Stanko fled Liz McLendon's house in a stolen GMC Jimmy, drove two hundred miles northwest, from the southern shore to South Carolina's northwest corner, headed toward the Blue Ridge Mountains, through Columbia to Greenville, where he took a hotel room.

Stanko claimed that he spent his brief time in the motel doing some soul searching. He pondered for the first time "the reality" of his crimes.

Regarding the violence to McLendon, he didn't know where *that* demon came from. Stanko, by his own recollection, spent a sleepless night in the motel, suicidal thoughts swirling in his mind. He lost the urge to flee, and he tried to summon up the strength to turn himself in.

As it turned out, surrender was unnecessary. He called McLendon to see if she was okay, and police already were prepared to trace the call. He called three times, each time from a different phone—but all three numbers were traced to the Days Inn on Congaree Road in Greenville, South Carolina.

According to Stanko, he was packing his bags to "go home," when the motel's parking lot filled with cop cars.

Stanko was booked for kidnapping, assault and battery of a high and aggravated nature, grand larceny, and breach of trust.

FEBRUARY 22, 1996

At 8:45 A.M. on February 22, 1996, Liz sat down in her home before Detective Darrell Lewis and answered questions for the purpose of formulating a formal written complaint. Since she had been telling him her complaint, his questions were pointed, and they quickly got down to brass tacks.

At Detective Lewis's prompting, McLendon verified that she lived in a home on Durham Drive, and her complaint concerned the man she lived with, her former boyfriend Stephen Christopher Stanko. Her complaint was that he'd kidnapped, assaulted, and battered her with the intent to kill.

"You said you confronted him about lying about his activities?"

"Yes, I've been suspicious of the activities of Stephen Stanko for a while now."

"How long?"

"Several weeks."

The suspicious thing was that he left for work each day very early and returned very late. She knew he had days off, but he always said he was going to work, anyway. She knew there had to be activities to which she wasn't privy.

"Did you ever ask him about those activities?"

"Yes, I would regularly question him about why he was at work so much, and he told me he had 'deals to finalize.'"

She said he worked at a car dealership, and according to him, he told her that he was meeting businesspeople who'd come in from out of town or was waiting for some guy who was supposed to deliver cars.

Her suspicions escalated in mid-January 1996, a month earlier, when she received a phone call from a man named Chuck Thornwald (pseudonym), who asked for Stephen Stanko. She said he wasn't home, and Thornwald asked if Stanko was at "his dealership" or was it McElveen.

Liz was flustered. No, she was downright *alarmed* by the question. What? "His dealership"? As far as she knew, Stanko owned diddly-squat. She suddenly realized there was a need for her to answer the question.

"Uh, McElveen," she said.

When Stanko got home, Liz grilled him about what Thornwald had said, and Stanko begrudgingly admitted that he did indeed own a car dealership. It wasn't open yet, though. She wanted to know who was putting up the money, and Stanko said it was Ray Crenshaw. Liz knew something was out of whack—all of this car dealership stuff was way too secret not to be trouble. She asked him why he hadn't told her any of this, and he said he "wanted it to be a surprise." The alarm bell in her head would not stop ringing.

He went into bs mode again. She could sense it. She'd get him talking about himself, and he wouldn't stop. He said he fully intended to tell her about the used-car lot when it was ready to open. He said that he wasn't stopping there. He had a second business in preparation as well, and this one was just for her, a real moneymaker, so she wouldn't have to work.

From that point on, Stanko and Liz fought frequently. She was in his face about the secrets. In dribs and drabs, she learned more details of Stanko's business, although it was, as usual, difficult to distinguish reality from daydreams.

He told her that Ray Crenshaw was investing in the initial car purchases, and they were getting their cars cheap, wholesale, from the supplier, who was Doug McElveen. She asked Stanko where McElveen was getting the cars.

"He buys them at auctions and sells them to Ray and me," Stanko explained.

Liz asked: "How much money have you and Ray invested?"

Stanko didn't give her a number, but he said it didn't matter. He'd already made all of his investment back and he was $12,000 in the black.

Liz thought at the time that was impossible. The damned lot hadn't opened yet!

"There," Stanko had said to her. "Now you know everything."

She could only shake her head.

"I *soooo* didn't know everything," Liz told the cop.

"Did you ever see any verification of any of this?" Detective Lewis asked.

"No, never."

"Any of it?"

"None of it."

"What happened next?"

She told Lewis that her domestic woes intensified dramatically on February 9, 1996, twelve days before he attacked her. Stanko called her on the phone and told her he was having a "bad day." He sounded terribly upset, so she had the florist send him a balloon at work to cheer him up. It didn't work. He was cheerless. *Oh-oh,* she remembered thinking. From that point on, he appeared to her to be on the verge of being out of control, teetering on the brink. She knew because she'd seen that "same temperament within him before." Now there was no talking to him. Complete silence was recommended, because there was no way to predict what would trigger an argument. Sometimes she thought it didn't matter what the topic was. His temperament was such that he could argue, and little else. Mention the weather and he'd pick a fight.

"How long have you known Stephen Stanko?" Detective Lewis asked Liz.

"Uhhhh . . ." The calendar in her head wouldn't work. She was still very shaken. Who could guess that one day she'd be having a regular life, and the next answering questions because her boyfriend tried to kill her? Finally she answered, "Several years."

"Ever in trouble before?"

"He's been in *a lot* of trouble," she said, her tongue clicking out the sound, and her eyes growing wide for a moment to emphasize her point.

As far as she could tell, Stanko was the kind of guy who made his living by making promises he couldn't keep. He was always raising money for something; then, when it came for him to supply whatever product was involved, the deal would fall through.

He'd scramble to avoid the wrath of investors, and then the process would start over again. Round and round, he went. There had been several companies that he couldn't have been more optimistic about, until the last moment when it turned out they didn't exist. Liz had a sneaking suspicion that this was true of the used-car lot he was starting up with Ray Crenshaw's money.

Then there were times when he got a job someplace, as an employee, and still he couldn't keep his nose clean. More than once, he'd gotten the pink slip because supervisors "falsely accused" him of something. Once, it was "falsifying orders," apparently to collect commissions he hadn't earned. Another time, it was "forging customer documents." There was a third time, too, but she couldn't recall the specifics. Maybe it would come to her later.

Stanko suffered legal difficulties at least once because of his misdeeds on the job. Stanko had dealings with a man she only knew of as Mr. Orr (pseudonym). Mr. Orr and his son, both of Goose Creek, got in trouble with Stanko over something. Because of that difficulty with the law, Stanko had to report periodically to Romeo Radoran, an officer of Berkeley County Probation.

"Did you and Stanko live at this same address back then?" Detective Lewis asked.

"No, previous," she said, and she gave Stanko's address in Ashton Drive in Goose Creek. "That was before I bought this house," she said, referring to the one on Durham Drive. She said she'd lived with her parents on Johns Island at that time and didn't purchase her house until July 2005.

"Now, this car lot deal, was that the first major business plan he'd kept secret from you?"

"Oh no," Liz said, shaking her head. "During the late spring of 1995—May, June—I discovered that he'd been pawning his personal items. He'd lost his job with Southern Chemical. He didn't want me to know."

The blowup that time had occurred on June 23, 1995.

She confronted him on several issues involving work, pawn slips, and a smattering of unexplained phone calls. The confrontation led to an explosive argument.

"At that time, he threatened my life and put his hands around my neck," Liz said. He didn't choke her, but she was terrified because she assumed he was about to.

Luckily, she got away from him. She ran to get her car and escaped to a friend's house.

"Which friend?"

"Mary Lou Culpepper."

"Where does she live?"

"North Charleston."

Detective Lewis established that the victim had filed a report with the sheriff's department after that attack—but she, in the long run, had decided not to press charges.

After that, she and Stanko only talked occasionally on the telephone. He was living at the time with Randy and Charles Bishop, in the Devon Forest neighborhood, along the northern edge of Goose Creek.

On July 1, or thereabouts—she wasn't sure of the exact date—he left the Bishops home and moved to Atlanta, where he met Cynthia Wilson, employed by Turner Broadcasting.

Liz didn't see Stanko during this time. She wasn't sure of the details, but she knew that Wilson was "taken" by Stanko for more than $4,000.

"There was a long-term statute filed, and, to my knowledge, a judgment was filed against him for that amount," she explained.

Continuing with her chronology, Liz said it was September 26, 2005, when Steve Stanko returned to Charleston. He showed up at her door and she let him in. The following day, he was taken by his mother and sister to the Berkeley County Probation Office, where he was arrested, and eventually he served thirty-five days in the Berkeley County Detention Center.

Liz went out and retained an attorney for Stanko's defense, a guy named Rick Buchanan. In addition to providing him with representation, she further bailed Stanko out of trouble by paying off some of his debts, many of which appeared to have been incurred between May and July of 1995.

Thinking ahead, Liz requested that a psychiatrist be called in to evaluate her boyfriend, and provide ongoing treatment following his release.

When he did return—he was released on October 30—not much had changed. He was supposed to make restitution for the money he'd scammed, serve his probation in a clean manner, and do community service hours. But it was the same ol' Stephen. Another deal was in the works, and Liz was to be the beneficiary. The deal was with Ray and Natalie Crenshaw, for a brand-new Yukon. And, as usual, Stanko always had a story as to why the deal was never finalized.

A psychiatrist did have sessions with Stanko, and Liz was allowed to sit in, almost like marriage counseling. She was concerned enough about the Yukon that never arrived to mention it in front of the shrink. This irritated Stephen to no end. She continued to cross-examine him about the used-car lot, and the obvious fact that he wasn't taking as close care of his legal responsibilities as he should. He wasn't visiting his probation officer, he wasn't making restitution, and he wasn't serving the community. She probably did sound like a broken record, reminding him that he was in dire straits here, and he wasn't adapting.

Straight and narrow? Stanko couldn't even *find* the

straight and narrow. In response to her nags, she told Detective Lewis, he became verbally abusive.

The next blowup came on January 26, 1996, when Stephen Stanko was supposed to deposit a check in Liz's account, to pay her back for the legal assistance she'd acquired when he was arrested. No surprise, the money never showed up.

Then, on Valentine's Day, 1996, a week before the attack, he told her that he had deposited the check in her account, just as he said he would. It was the bank. They must have put it into the wrong account or something. Later that day, he told her he'd been to the bank; the error had been discovered; he'd been issued a bank check, and had deposited it in her account. That turned out to be another lie.

Liz was starting to get the idea. Stanko saw other people as marks, and she was the biggest mark of all, defending him and spending money on him *long after* she should have learned her lesson.

Here was a guy who genuinely couldn't help himself. When everything told him that keeping his word and doing the right thing was the best way to insure a happy future, he nonetheless told only lies and did the wrong thing every single time.

After Valentine's Day she questioned him about all of it. She took his word for nothing and asked for verification. That made Stanko jittery and more than a little hostile.

"On Sunday morning," she said, referring to February 18, "I opened the trunk of my car, a '95 Honda Accord, to find Stanko had stashed some items from work in there." He'd been asked to clean out his desk. She confronted him immediately, asking him if there was anything he wanted to tell her, any news about his job that he wanted to share. He said the items were just some stuff that he couldn't keep at the office—which he referred to as "the tower," to make his new position seem more important.

By Sunday evening, Stanko was extremely agitated, telling Liz that he'd just gotten paged by Doug McElveen. The cars McElveen had purchased at auction were ready, and Stanko and Ray Crenshaw were going to pick them up for their used-car lot.

Trouble was, he hadn't been out of Liz's sight, and she knew there had been no page. His lies grew sloppier when he was agitated. At nine-thirty or ten o'clock that evening, Stanko left; he and Ray were going to go to McElveen's car lot. He was gone for about two hours, during which time Liz was "terribly concerned and upset." When he returned, she asked him if they'd been able to pick up the cars from McElveen, and Stanko said they had.

The next morning, Monday morning, Stanko didn't get up and go to work. Liz figured he'd lost his job, but Stanko said no, he was working a late shift, noon to nine at night. That afternoon, after he left, Liz called his job, and the receptionist said she hadn't seen him. Liz asked if Stanko was still employed there, and the receptionist said she didn't know. Liz called Natalie Crenshaw, who said she didn't know either if Stanko still had a job, but she did hear that there had been some kind of argument at work on Saturday. Liz sensed the old pattern coming to a head.

"I was aware of the signs," she explained. "He became defensive and argumentative in a violent and verbally offensive manner."

Late that Monday evening, Stanko went to Crenshaw's house. Liz drove around to keep tabs on Stanko's whereabouts. She saw him outside Crenshaw's house, sitting in what appeared to her to be an unmarked cop car. He was in there for a long time, maybe as long as ninety minutes.

Part of the reason she was so tenacious about keeping tabs on Stephen Stanko, of course, was that she cared for him. But there was another factor as well. She feared that she was somehow—albeit innocently—involved. Stanko had borrowed Liz's car and said he was having the passenger-side front-door panel repaired. In the meantime, he had her driving a GMC Jimmy, which he said came from McElveen. It had taken her a long time to get her car back, too long, and this just caused her to dwell harder on all of the unanswered questions she had.

She returned home and removed the pillows from Stanko's side of the master bed. She placed the pillows, along with a blanket, on the couch, so he'd know when he got home that he wasn't welcome in her bed. She then went to sleep with the lights out.

"When I woke up, he was in the bedroom, with a small flashlight. I asked him what he was doing, and he said, 'Where are my pillows?' I told him he was sleeping on the sofa. He said he was sleeping in the bed, and that I was a bitch."

He yelled the same things, over and over again, screaming that he hadn't done anything wrong and that he deserved better. He called her a "stupid idiot" and an "old hag."

At the end of a verbal tirade, Stanko rolled up a robe in his hand and threw it at her, striking her in the head "fairly hard." She told him she wasn't going to put up with this anymore.

He picked up a box of facial tissues and threw it at

her. She grabbed the box and returned fire. She told him to leave. He went to the garage and returned with his luggage.

He started packing in a somewhat haphazard fashion, the verbal abuse flying the whole time. In between insults, he screamed what were either more lies, or perhaps delusions.

"I'm doing well," he screamed. "I'm sleeping at night. I'm making money! I'm not lying! You are the problem! You are my problem!"

He grabbed her and threw her down so that she landed hard on the floor.

"If you touch me again, I'll call the police," she said.

He slapped her across the head.

"Go ahead and call the police," he said. "I've already talked to the police today. I've talked plenty."

She tried to dial 911, at least twice, but each time Stanko hung up the phone so she couldn't get through. One time he was too slow, and the call went through.

Using the system's caller ID, the emergency operator called Liz back. Stanko screamed that he was leaving and again began to throw items in his luggage.

Liz answered the phone and said her boyfriend was leaving, but if he came back, she would call again, and if that happened, they should send someone quickly.

Stanko didn't leave, however, but he did sleep on the sofa. The next morning, Tuesday, February 20, at about seven-thirty, the phone rang and Stanko answered it. He entered the bedroom and told Liz that her brother was on the phone. She spoke to her brother briefly, no more than five minutes.

When she hung up, Stanko reentered the bedroom and said, "I'm leaving today, and I won't be coming back."

"I think that is for the best," Liz replied.

His movements, she noticed, were becoming manic

again. While letting out a steady stream of rambling words, he was walking quickly in and out of the bedroom and going through the house, ostensibly making sure that he had left nothing of his behind.

He came back into the bedroom and plopped down in a blue chair by the window. He told Liz once again that he'd done nothing wrong. She was the one who'd been wrong by being so suspicious about everything and asking too many questions.

What did he expect? He'd recently been in jail! Liz thought. And he was only free because he promised to do certain things—and didn't even have it together to do them. He'd done no community service, and the times when she did manage to drag him to see the shrink, he steadfastly refused to take responsibility for any of his actions, always turning the sessions around so that the focus was on her and how distrustful she was.

She could see, and feel, his growing ire. He left the room and she could hear him rummaging through a laundry closet. "I thought he was just pulling out the dirty clothes that he wanted to take with him," Liz told Detective Lewis.

She heard the sounds of things being moved around in the closet, but she didn't give it much thought. She stayed in bed, hopeful that Stanko would leave before they had an opportunity to fight again.

He came back into the bedroom and she could see the wildness in his eyes. Now he stood at the foot of her bed, glaring at her. She could smell the strong odor of chemicals. Smelled like Clorox and ammonia.

Her first thought was to ask him what he was cleaning; but before she had the chance, he said, "We can't have you calling the police, can we? I have to shut you up." He jumped onto the bed next to her and pressed a chemical-soaked cloth over her face.

She fought as hard as she could. When he pulled the cloth from her face, she managed to tell him that she wouldn't call the police if he just let her go. "He said he didn't believe me, that I would call the police."

She told him that whatever he had done, that adding murder or doing this was only going to make it worse for him. No reaction. She knew then that she was in deep trouble. He wasn't going to let her call the police.

Liz grabbed quickly for the phone, but he was quicker, and he was on top of her before she could grab the receiver. His strong arms were too much. He held her wrists together with one hand and, with his other arm, flipped her onto her stomach on the bed.

Liz thought, *Oh, my Lord, he is going to kill me.*

Even as Stephen sat on her, she managed to wriggle her left hand free and again reached for the phone, the landline. She only needed to press four buttons— speaker 911—but she couldn't do it. He grabbed the phone cord and jerked it away.

"You're not calling anyone. I'm going to have to tie you up," Stanko said. He tried to get the cord, to pull out of the phone, but couldn't do it. So he reverted his attention to her, again holding her wrists together with one hand, while using the other to press the soaked rag over her face.

While still applying pressure on her face, Stanko said, "This always works in the movies. Why isn't it working now?"

Even then, in her panic, she picked up on the premeditated nature of the violence, the way he had watched a movie once and made a mental note to try that if he ever tried to kill somebody.

Stanko eventually took the cloth away from Liz's face. She gasped for fresh air, her face slick and shiny with tears. Liz got the impression he was trying to think of another way to kill her. The second he lightened up on the pressure, Liz managed to bite his left hand.

"Whereabouts on his hand?" Detective Lewis asked.

"Somewhere in the thumb area," the victim replied.

He held her wrists together behind her back and bound them together with a necktie. At first, she just lay there on the bed, too scared to move.

He told her to sit up on the edge of the bed. She was exhausted from the struggle and was running out of strength. He found rope and used it to bind Liz's wrists and ankles together. The scariest part of this for her was his manner. After he stopped trying to asphyxiate her with the smelly cloth, he reverted right back to his normal personality. As he bound her, he was talking to her in a calm voice, as if nothing had happened. She still thought she was going to die, but, in reality, the next attempt on her life never came.

"Please just leave," she begged. "Or let me get in my car and go." She realized that he'd put her dog outside, and had closed the bedroom blinds.

Stanko told her not to scream, not to make another sound. He would hurt her if she even tried to speak. He put her on the floor.

"I don't want to gag you, so please don't make a sound," Stanko instructed.

"Please don't gag me," she begged. "I'll be quiet."

Stanko went into the kitchen and she could hear him making several phone calls, but she couldn't tell what he was saying. While he was out of the room, she tried to wriggle her feet free so that she'd be able to make a run for it—but there was no way. The bondage was too tight.

"I just need to take a shower and get dressed—and then I'll leave," Stanko promised. "If you listen to me, I won't hurt you."

He made her sit on the floor while he shaved, and then he forced her to sit on the toilet while he showered.

"I wanted him to leave as quickly as possible, so I didn't make a sound," Liz explained. "When he got out of the shower, he told me that he had done some bad things. He said he couldn't help it. He always wanted to make himself out to be something he wasn't."

He told her he was sorry, how he never intended to hurt her. She risked speaking at that point and urged that he phone someone for help—whether it be his shrink, his probation officer, or his lawyer.

Stanko said he thought not. He was either going to kill himself or run. He hadn't decided.

"I said, just go, and let me go, so this will not be something else to cause you trouble," Liz explained. She noticed that Stanko appeared to be calming down somewhat.

He sat on the edge of the bed and said, "Don't move and I'll untie you." He did release her bondage and then said, "The bad guy is back. He is in control—and I don't know what to do." He told her he loved her, and repeated that he never intended to hurt her.

"He stopped the clock on the wall, sat on the floor next to me, and said he was leaving," Liz said. He kissed her on the head, said good-bye, and left.

Alone at last, Liz's mind was filled with multiple voices, all of them screaming. One dominant voice wondered what Stanko had done to make him go crazy like that. What had the "bad guy" done now that he was "in control"?

Another voice screamed that she was a mess and needed help, so she called her brother and instructed him to get someone over to her house. Ray Crenshaw called and instructed her to call 911, which she did.

Soon thereafter, the police, Natalie Crenshaw, and

members of Liz's family arrived—all, more or less, at the same time.

"Stephen tried to contact me several times that day," she told Detective Lewis. He told whoever answered her phone that he intended to turn himself in.

Darrell Lewis thanked Liz for her time and courage, and the interview ended.

On February 23, 1996, at 7:00 P.M., Frank Boedeker, of the Berkeley County Sheriff's Office (BCSO), drove to the Greenville Detention Center in Greenville, South Carolina, and served a warrant for Stephen Stanko's arrest on kidnapping charges. Boedeker then transported Stanko to the Berkeley County Detention Center, where he was booked at 11:30 P.M. and incarcerated. Filling out one booking form, under identifying marks, Boedeker wrote, *Scar on chin.*

While being booked, Stanko gave his address in Goose Creek, said he had been born in Guantánamo, Cuba, and gave as his next of kin "Elizabeth Stanko." This was not the last time he'd claim he and Liz were married, a false assertion that never failed to get under her skin.

STANKO'S GOOD INTENTIONS

By the midnight after his arrest, Stephen Stanko was wearing an orange jumpsuit, sprawled on the world's thinnest "mattress" in the county detention center. Seriously? Half an inch? It wasn't just uncomfortable, it was insulting.

Stanko was kept in isolation with no access to a phone. All civilized comforts were denied him. They wouldn't even let him have toilet paper, he later complained.

After stewing in his own juices for a few days, a deputy sheriff came and got him and took him to an interrogation room at the Berkeley County Sheriff's Office in Moncks Corner.

Darrell Lewis seemed like a nice guy.

"I need to know what happened, and I will do everything that I can to help," Detective Lewis said.

Stanko bought it. It was 6:40 P.M., February 24, two and a half days after Stanko attacked Liz. He was given a cup of coffee and he said he was ready to tell his story.

Lewis advised Stanko of his Miranda rights, one by one, and Stanko acknowledged that he understood his rights. He wasn't evil, he explained, but he did have a temper and he did "lose it."

Stanko told the investigator that he was twenty-eight years old, and had completed three years of college. His story started the previous Halloween, when he was released from the Berkeley County Detention Center after serving a little over a month.

Detective Lewis could tell right away what the theme of Stanko's statement was going to be. The theme: *Police had it all wrong. Once you looked at all the facts, you could see that Stephen Stanko was the real victim.*

So he got out of jail, and returned home to Elizabeth, his girlfriend, and wanted to impress on everyone his sincere feelings when he came back to the house on Durham Drive. His intentions were good. Pure. Immaculate, man.

"I had intended to start my life over again and make the wrongs I had committed once again right," Stanko told Lewis. That feeling of serenity, as it turned out, only lasted for nine days.

That serenity was violated during a job interview at 84 Lumber in Goose Creek. Just the night before the interview, Elizabeth had upset him deeply by telling him that he didn't care for her, and he was unappreciative of the many things she had done for him.

How could she be so thoughtless, to upset him, just before a job interview?

Their argument about whether he cared or was appreciative, he claimed, raged well into the night, and left him haggard when he should have been rested. Instead of a spring in his step, he was dragging. She hid the car keys so he had to walk to the interview. And then, unbelievable, she still wasn't done—she locked him out of the house!

As a result, the interview at the lumber company didn't go well, and he didn't get the job. Naturally. That went without saying. He didn't get back inside the house until much later in the day, when he was "finally allowed calm conversation" so he could convince Elizabeth of how unreasonable she was being.

Stanko told Lewis that for the first eight weeks after his Halloween release from jail, he did not break the law. Everything was straight business, until December 1995, when he first took money from Ray Crenshaw.

During that time, however, his domestic life was woeful. He and Elizabeth had multiple fights. Her beef was always the same: he wasn't *loyal* to her.

"These fights became more and more aggressive," Stanko complained.

Like any longtime girlfriend, he supposed, Elizabeth McLendon knew his weak spots. Figuratively speaking, she knew just where to kick him where it hurt. She knew just how to extract maximum fury from him.

"She would taunt me with my actions of the past, the way my family left me, and how I had lied before. But I wasn't. I wasn't lying to her," Stanko said. And there was no infidelity. She thought there was, but there wasn't.

He was true to her. He loved her. All he wanted was love and respect in return. "That was all I ever wanted from anybody," he said, getting downright sappy. He knew he was going away, and he had a right to be sappy, damn it.

Detective Lewis let him go, gave him a lot of slack rope, pleased that the suspect was so chatty. But Lewis eventually steered Stanko away from his tortured emotions and toward giving a chronology of facts.

* * *

Life, Stanko said, got better on November 14, 1995, when he got a job at McElveen Pontiac Buick GMC, at the intersection of Interstate 26 and Highway 17A in Summerville, South Carolina. Stephen Stanko was hired as a salesman, selling cars.

"I had a good couple of weeks to end November and brought home a good paycheck," Stanko boasted. He was bragging; yet there was a sad subtext. His "good" stretches were *so brief*—mere interruptions in his bad stretches.

Stanko cherished that strong feeling of pride that came with bringing home the bacon. He had always felt bad about not helping out as much as he felt he should at Elizabeth McLendon's house. The new job allowed him to help out with her bills and groceries.

Well, truth be told, he still couldn't help out as much as he'd hoped. He wasn't trying to get into the black, just out of the red. There was a $2,000 legal bill from the attorney Rick Buchanan, who handled his case.

He was trying to get out of debt; he was working hard. And when he went home, his girlfriend was giving him nothing but aggravation, nothing but a nightly battle, tonight's segment of a never-ending argument from hell!

There was a stretch there where his emotional roller coaster was rocketing out of control. He was actually doing well at work, and had entered a trial period that might lead to a promotion to assistant finance manager.

He felt higher than high about how the professional portion of his life was going. Even Elizabeth was impressed with his progress at the car dealership. She told him so. She said she was "proud and happy" for him.

He *responded* to that kindness—if only she had given him more positive feedback. He worked long, grueling hours so that he might be able to pay off his legal debt and help around the house as well. But, like all good things, this was short-lived.

Elizabeth's kindness was ephemeral. He'd heard of "cruel to be kind," but Elizabeth was the opposite—"kind to be cruel." And eventually, because of the fights at home and the belittling he endured, he "felt like nothing." He had a metaphor for Detective Lewis: "My self-esteem became a pit."

It was during this time, Stanko said, that he met and be-friended a thirty-four-year-old man named Delray Cren-shaw. They had a couple of brief conversations, had a catch with a baseball and mitts on the front lawn a couple of times—sunshine, pop the glove, really zipping them—and *boom,* Stanko and Crenshaw were good buddies.

They had a lot in common, Stanko claimed. Crenshaw was successful and Stanko wanted to be successful—make that, *deserved* to be successful. Crenshaw owned businesses so, Stanko said, "I had hoped that we could somehow combine these two lives and make more." More money, he meant.

The big problem, the way Stanko looked at it, was that he and Elizabeth had nothing to offer Crenshaw, nothing to attract Crenshaw into a business partnership. But that "problem" worked itself out the day Crenshaw said, without prompting, "Hey, let's do something together!" It was kismet.

Crenshaw didn't have anything specific in mind, and neither did Stanko at first. But once he started ponder-ing, a scheme practically sat down in his lap.

Stanko called Crenshaw and explained that he worked for a guy named Ricky Davis. Davis was the used-car manager at McElveen, and Stanko had an opportu-nity to, on his own, purchase a number of "late-model cars for a low price." Stanko said he needed $8,900 to buy the cars. He already had most of it. He needed only

Like heaven on earth, Sunset Beach, South Carolina.
(Photo by Tracy Minarik)

Stephen C. Stanko in 1986 as a senior at Goose Creek High School.

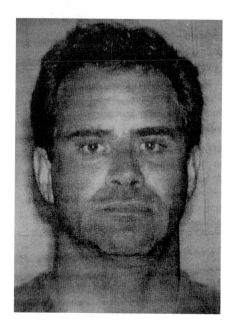

Stephen Stanko's Berkeley County Detention Center photo from 1995. *(Photo courtesy South Carolina Department of Corrections)*

Stanko as he appeared in 2006. *(Photo courtesy South Carolina Department of Corrections)*

Stanko on the eve of his second death-penalty trial in 2009. *(Photo courtesy South Carolina Department of Corrections)*

After Stanko's 2004 release from prison, he searched for a library that was suitable for his research, preferably one with a pretty librarian. The Socastee library, where Laura Ling worked, fit the bill nicely. *(Photo by Tracy Minarik)*

After knowing Laura Ling for only a matter of weeks Stanko moved in with Laura and her daughter in their home in Murrells Inlet, where water fun was only a few hundred yards away. *(Photo by Tracy Minarik)*

The house on Murrells Inlet Road where Stanko murdered Laura Ling and raped her teenaged daughter. *(Photo by Tracy Minarik)*

Dr. Kim A. Collins of the Wake Forest University School of Medicine Department of Pathology was the forensic pathologist called in on the case. *(Photo courtesy Horry County Police)*

Paramedic Chuck Petrella treated Penny Ling following her attack. He subsequently visited the teenager in the hospital and brought her a teddy bear. Penny would later clutch that bear tightly as she testified in court against the man who'd raped her and killed her mother. Solicitor Greg Hembree called Penny the bravest girl he'd ever known. *(Author photo)*

Stanko's second murder victim was Henry Lee Turner, a seventy-four-year-old man who lived alone. Stanko once referred to Turner as a "quasi-father figure." *(Courtesy Horry County Police)*

The clue that led to the discovery of Henry Lee Turner's body was Laura Ling's stolen red Mustang, which was found in front of Turner's house.
(Courtesy Horry County Police)

Stanko had remembered to throw his writings—including his book proposal regarding serial killers and the written version of his stand-up comedy act—into the back of Laura Ling's Mustang, but left them behind after stealing Turner's truck. *(Courtesy Horry County Police)*

Turner's home was on a cul-de-sac within Coastal Village Mobile Home Park in Conway, South Carolina. *(Courtesy Horry County Police)*

Turner's home was only a few feet away from neighbors, but no one heard the shots. *(Courtesy Horry County Police)*

Behind Turner's home, only a few feet from his body, was a Starcraft pop-up camper. *(Courtesy Horry County Police)*

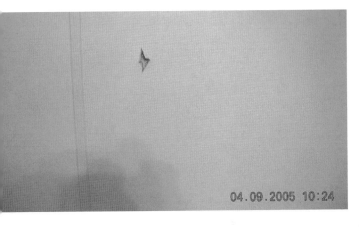

04.09.2005 10:24

One of the first discoveries police made after entering the home was a hole in a wall separating a bedroom from a bath. There was no blood or body nearby, however. Police later theorized that this was a test shot, fired by the killer to gauge if he'd adequately muffled the sound of the gun. *(Courtesy Horry County Police)*

One of Turner's last sights was of this sink. He was shaving and apparently using the sink as an ashtray when he was shot. *(Courtesy Horry County Police)*

A six-pack of Yuengling Lager with two bottles missing was found on the counter next to Turner's kitchen sink. *(Courtesy Horry County Police)*

A copy of *Playboy* rested on the tank of the guest toilet, on the opposite end of the home from where Turner's corpse was found.
(Courtesy Horry County Police)

Turner's bachelor pad, with pool table, cable, easy chairs and a kitchen area. When the first responding officer passed through the doorway at the rear and looked left, he saw Turner's body sprawled on the floor. *(Courtesy Horry County Police)*

Henry Lee Turner's body was found face down on the floor of the bedroom, with his feet just inside the bathroom. He was wearing blue jeans and a purple shirt, and had been shot twice, once in the chest and once in the back. *(Courtesy Horry County Police)*

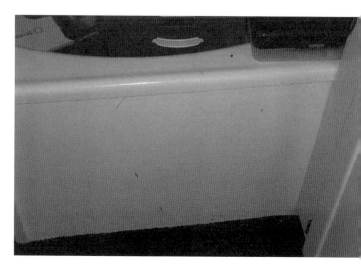

Blood later verified as Turner's was found splattered on the side of the tub. *(Courtesy Horry County Police)*

Police got a better understanding of what happened after discovering this pillow with bullet holes in it. That explained why neighbors heard nothing. The pillow had been used as a silencer. *(Courtesy Horry County Police)*

The police photographer at the Turner murder scene was Sergeant Jeff Gause of the Horry County Police Department.
(Courtesy Horry County Police)

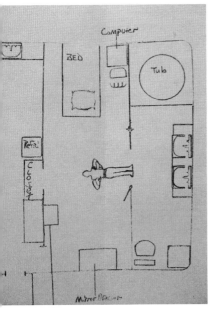

After photographing Turner's home in detail Sergeant Gause drew a schematic of the layout, including the position of the body, to help investigators put the photos in context.
(Courtesy Horry County Police)

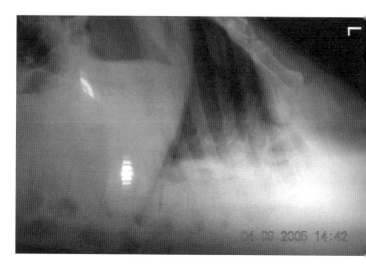

X-rays of Turner's upper body taken during his remains' post-mortem procedure vividly confirmed that there were still two slugs in him. *(Courtesy Horry County Police)*

Dust patterns on the carpet indicated that one of Turner's longarms was missing. *(Courtesy Horry County Police)*

Stanko had such a baby face. One of the reasons he was a successful
con man was that strangers couldn't imagine him doing anything bad.
(Photo by Elizabeth McLendon Buckner)

Elizabeth McLendon
Buckner as she
appears today.
(Courtesy Rick Buckner)

Stanko, here looking contemplative over Thanksgiving dinner, had a neatly trimmed beard for a while during his time with Liz McLendon. *(Photo by Elizabeth McLendon Buckner)*

The first victim of Stephen Stanko's violence was his longtime girlfriend and fellow Goose Creek resident, the beautiful Elizabeth McLendon. *(Courtesy Sharon McAlister)*

$2,200 more—but the thing was, he needed it in the next couple of hours.

That $2,200 figure, Detective Lewis noticed, would pay off Stanko's legal debt, plus give him some carrying-around money for a few days.

"Within hours, Ray had the cash in my hand," Stanko said. "Instantly I was important, and a *part of something*."

Stanko instructed Crenshaw to keep their business deal a secret from Elizabeth. Stanko wanted the new business to be a surprise. "It was a dream I truly had for us," Stanko told the investigator, his face a mask of sincerity. "Anyway, the twenty-two hundred went to paying the bills, and things like that."

For the first ten days, he had no trouble "holding off" Crenshaw. He made up stories about "problems here and problems there." There was "trouble transporting the cars."

He told Crenshaw that he had a GMC Yukon and a Sierra pickup truck that he was going to trade for the cars from Ricky Davis. Crenshaw didn't suspect, Stanko could tell. His mark had taken the bait, 110 percent.

"He thought I was the next best thing to sliced bread," Stanko bragged to the investigator. Unfortunately for Stanko, the key ending to any con is to get the hell away from the mark—to make off with the gold, so to speak.

But that was hard when you were tied down in a domestic situation, and the mark was your best friend. Crenshaw was pretty good-natured, and slow to suspect impropriety, but he did become impatient when day after day went by, and there were no late-model used cars arriving.

Stanko continued to lie to his friend, to invent new lies, but he could tell his credibility was eroding, and his lies became crazier. Despite this, Stanko felt safe taking a second bite from the apple. He told Crenshaw that he could get some pickup trucks at an unbelievable price, and, like before, the deal had to be made in the next couple of hours or the opportunity would be blown. Crenshaw, the saint that he was, forked over another $1,800 in cash.

Stanko emphasized to Lewis that the two cash payments from Crenshaw were his only payoff during the scheme. Ray and Natalie Crenshaw opened up a "used-car lot" bank account, with Stanko's name on it, but he never took any money from that account.

Plus, as further evidence that he was basically an honest guy, Stanko pointed out for the investigator that he had multiple opportunities to snatch cash at his job, but "never took a dime."

Now Stanko was on another "I'm innocent" jag. He actually said, "I did not do any of this for money." He wanted love, admiration, and respect. He understood now that he had gone about it the wrong way. He understood he had a psychological problem. He wasn't just an everyday, run-of-the-mill thief!

Lewis urged Stanko to get on with his tale.

Stanko told him that the time eventually came when he was going to have to "come up with some results" for Crenshaw. He had yet another idea. He went to the used-car lot where he worked. He knew there was a desk drawer where there were many duplicate sets of keys for cars on the lot. Stanko took keys that matched up with makes of cars that he'd promised Crenshaw. One by one, during business hours, Stanko drove the cars off the McElveen lot and to another location—in essence, delivering the cars, one by one, to Crenshaw. Stanko convinced Crenshaw that he had to keep the cars a secret from the people he worked with because he didn't want anyone on the job to know he was competing with them on the side.

Stanko took another car—and then another. He

enlisted Crenshaw's help. After hours, when the lot was unattended, Stanko would take a car, drive it to Crenshaw, and then Crenshaw would give him a ride back to McElveen's so Stanko could take another car.

Stanko stopped there and said that even though Elizabeth and the Crenshaws—Ray and Natalie—sometimes helped him with his schemes, none of them ever had the slightest inkling that there was any wrongdoing involved. They were all unadulteratedly innocent.

"Do you remember the makes of the cars you stole?" Detective Lewis asked.

"Sure. There were two pickup trucks, three Century, a Grand Prix, a Buick Regal, and that's not counting the Jimmy I gave to Elizabeth. I told her it was my demo," Stanko replied.

"What happened next?"

"After that, I contacted customers I met at work, who couldn't find the deal they were looking for, and steered them to the Crenshaw cars." He sold cars that way. He faked contracts. He knew just how to make the transactions look legitimate.

"Who'd you sell the cars to?" Lewis asked.

"Two of my customers were borderline crooks themselves," Stanko pointed out. One was named Chuck Thornwald. He was going through a divorce and not paying his bills. The repo man was after Thornwald's trailer, and he'd been lying to his creditors and his family.

The other slightly crooked customer, Stanko explained, was R. C. Criswell (pseudonym), who was two months late on every bill he had.

"Criswell lied to me about almost everything I asked him," Stanko told Lewis. Crenshaw sold one of the cars to his parents. It was a cash deal, and the Crenshaws put that money into the bank account that had Stanko's name on it.

Regarding lies he'd told Crenshaw, Stanko cleared up a couple of things. There never was any money from Thornwald or Criswell. There was no chop shop.

One time, by mistake, Stanko drove off from the McElveen lot with a car that belonged to a woman named Teddy Monette. He wanted to make it clear that that was not a theft. That was simply a mistake.

One night, Crenshaw brought over to the house a guy named Aldo Bassi, and Stanko simply retold all of the lies he'd told Crenshaw. So any information the sheriff's department got from Bassi should be taken with that in consideration.

He was really sorry about all of the lies he told, but what could he do? He'd painted his way into a corner and had to scramble. Elizabeth found out about the lies and was really pissed off.

It was right after the meeting with Ray Crenshaw and Aldo Bassi that Stephen Stanko went home, and Elizabeth was at him, relentlessly arguing with him, following him from room to room so she could let loose with a steady stream of insults.

It was the same old thing out of her mouth. She said he didn't care for her. She said he had to leave. She spewed the "usual hateful comments and threatened to call the police. A couple of times, I had to physically move her to get her out of my face," Stanko told the cop.

He said he went into the sunroom, and she followed him in there. She punched him, then kicked him. She threw various objects at him. "Finally we both ignored each other and went to sleep," he explained.

When he woke he packed his belongings into a couple of suitcases. She wanted him gone, he was leaving. But despite his compliance, the bickering continued.

His brain was swirling. All he could think of was keeping her from fighting so he could finish packing and get the hell out of the house. He put a combination of Clorox and 409 on a hand towel. He thought this would knock her out, and get her out of his hair.

"Never believe the movies," he said to Lewis.

The chemicals didn't render her unconscious, so he told her he was going to tie her up to keep her from attacking him. He would release her before he left.

"I never wanted to hurt her in any way," Stanko said. "In the past ten years, she is the only person I have truly loved, and who has shown me love. I love her, and I just can't go on hurting her. Or anyone else."

While he was shaving, and she sat bound on the floor, he remembered he tried to comfort her. His attempt to soothe his bound girlfriend continued as she sat on the toilet during his shower and then as he was dressing.

He untied her about ten minutes before he left, just as he had promised he would. He was nothing if not a man of his word. She cried and waved good-bye to him as he drove off. Stanko drove up Route 176 to Columbia, then took I-26 to Spartanburg to Greenville, where he checked into a Days Inn. Twice he called Detective Lewis, and police came and picked him up at the hotel.

No, he had no sexual relations while at the Days Inn. No, he carried no weapon. No, he didn't rob anyone. He felt better, now that he'd gotten it all off his chest, and was certain it wouldn't happen again.

That concluded the interview. A written statement was prepared and Stanko signed every page. He was returned to his cell and never again heard anyone mention helping him.

With Stephen's arrest, William Stanko turned his back on his son for good. The two would never speak again.

THORNWALD AND CRENSHAW

Later, on February 22, 1996, after statements were taken from Liz McLendon and Stephen Stanko, the Berkeley County Sheriff's Office expanded their investigation, interviewing a couple of Stanko's secondary victims.

By 6:30 P.M., Chuck Thornwald, who'd been mentioned by both Stanko and McLendon during their interrogations, sat in the sheriff's station, ready to tell everything he knew about Stanko. His questioner was the BCSO's Beverly Johnson. Thornwald was just a kid. A female questioner seemed like a good fit.

Thornwald told Johnson that his full name was Charles K. Thornwald, and he was nineteen years old. He was a high-school graduate and lived in an apartment building on Dorchester Road in Archdale, South Carolina.

No one told Thornwald that Stanko had called him a "borderline criminal."

"You are here in regard to a stolen vehicle, is that correct?" Johnson asked.

"Yes," Thornwald replied.

He said he'd gone to a used-car joint called McElveen Pontiac at the beginning of December 2005. He wandered among the cars for a moment before, as anticipated, a salesperson approached him and asked if he was in need of assistance. It was Stanko.

He said he was looking for a Trans Sport, and everything went swimmingly, until the subject of money came up. He was too young to be financed, so Thornwald left, feeling irritated. The trip to McElveen appeared to be a complete waste of time.

Not so fast. About a month later, just after the new year, Stanko called him and said, in essence, "Psst, have I got a deal for you." He said he was opening up his own used-car dealership, and he had a business partner named Ray Crenshaw.

The dealership he worked for might not give teenagers financing, but he would. Thornwald was all ears.

"I've got an S10 pickup that I could let you have for only nine grand," Stanko said. Thornwald wasn't completely green, and asked where the car came from. "It was bought from a government auction," the salesman assured him.

Stanko invited him to come look at the truck. Thornwald did—and he liked it. Stanko said it would be ten grand altogether—after financing.

Thornwald paused, and Stanko quickly threw in that he would finish making the payments on the teenager's current car. Thornwald again paused, and Stanko said, "Wait." He produced all of the legal forms necessary to make the transaction legal.

That did it. Thornwald said it was a deal, they shook hands, and the teenager drove the truck home.

"When did you first suspect that everything was not on the up-and-up?" Johnson asked.

"When I tried to switch my insurance. The company said that the lien holder had no information on me."

"What did you do?"

"I called Steve," Thornwald replied. Stanko told him, in effect, that he'd had trouble getting financing for Thornwald, but—since he was nothing if not a man of his word—he was going to finance the teenager "in house."

Thornwald said that was fine. Stanko told him it meant some more paperwork, and the next Saturday, the pair re-signed a bill of sale that changed the lien holder.

"The following Tuesday, Detective Lewis informed me the truck was stolen, and I returned it," Thornwald said, and that concluded the interview.

At 8:30 P.M., Detective Darrell Lewis took an oral statement from Delray Crenshaw, who said he was thirty-four years old, had an associate's degree, and the crime he was reporting was "breach of trust."

The respondent knew Stephen Stanko because Steve and Elizabeth were his next-door neighbors. That was no exaggeration, either. Crenshaw and his wife shared a fence with them. He and Stanko hit it off and had talked for a while. They discussed going into business together, specifically about opening up their own used-car dealership.

It was the day after Christmas, 1995, when Stanko called him and asked if he was still interested in doing that *thing*. Crenshaw said sure, so Stanko told him to drive over to McElveen. There was something he needed to tell him in person.

This part of Ray Crenshaw's story synched up with Stanko's version pretty well, Detective Lewis thought.

Crenshaw's story jibed surprisingly well with Stanko's, although their money figures differed. Crenshaw said Stanko told him that McElveen's used-car manager, a guy named Ricky Davis, was going to an auction and for about $4,500 he could purchase some used cars for them to sell. Crenshaw asked how much he needed.

"Just eighteen hundred dollars, and I'll put in the rest," Stanko said. Crenshaw gave him the money, but Stanko later explained that they could get a better price per car if they bought more cars, and Crenshaw contributed again to the used-car kitty.

At first, Stanko said the cars would arrive at Ricky Davis's warehouse in a week or so. Then he explained there was a delay. That guy Davis wanted in on the deal. That was the delay.

Then came more delays, and more excuses. On January 25, 1996, Ray Crenshaw visited Stephen Stanko to find out what was up, and Stanko said that for $2,080 he could get Crenshaw a Yukon for Crenshaw to drive. Stanko said that the Yukon could be delivered directly to them, rather than to Davis, because he had gotten them their "wholesaler's license."

A few days after that, Stanko said the cars had arrived and were parked on McElveen's lot. They picked up a 1994 Sonoma. Around that time, Stanko told Crenshaw that they'd made their first sale, selling a 1994 Escort to a kid named Thornwald.

That car, Stanko said, "was still in the shop." A day or so later, Stanko told Crenshaw that Thornwald had his car, and a second car, a 1995 green-and-silver Sonoma pickup, had been sold to a fellow named R. C. Criswell.

Stanko said that he had picked up a number of checks in payment and gave Crenshaw some cash to keep him happy. Crenshaw suggested that those checks be deposited in the bank account he'd opened for the business, so that there could be money for repairs and other overhead.

Stanko said he couldn't do that. He'd already made arrangements for the checks. No, he hadn't taken them to the bank himself. Instead, he said, he'd given them to a coworker whose wife was the branch manager at a local bank.

Later, Stanko explained that those checks were slow to clear because that same wife was suspicious that one of the checks wasn't good. Stanko said that relations between him and the guy Davis were not good. Stanko asked Crenshaw to help him move cars from McElveen's lot to their own so that Davis wouldn't be able to put them in his warehouse, where Stanko feared they would never see them again. Together, they moved two 1995 Centuries. On his own, Stanko moved another Century and a 1993 Firebird.

Stanko sold a car to Crenshaw's cousin. Crenshaw, who was beginning to get suspicious, thought this was a safe purchase. He knew his cousin had the same insurance as his parents had, and the insurance company would check the car's VIN number, which would tell them if the car was stolen.

Crenshaw was no longer easily placated. He hadn't received his Yukon. The original cars from the Davis auction had never shown up. Crenshaw threatened to rat Stanko out at McElveen's, but Stanko begged him not to, saying he would lose his job.

As for those original cars that Crenshaw had helped purchase, Stanko said Davis had moved them from his warehouse to another lot called Blue & Gold. Crenshaw went to that lot and asked about the cars. Nobody there knew anything about them. To that, Stanko said that the cars weren't at Blue & Gold anymore and had been transported to an illegal chop shop on Old Back River Road in Goose Creek.

A couple of times, Crenshaw recalled, he and Stanko had driven together to the chop shop. On those occasions, an African-American gentleman came out and talked to Stanko, but Crenshaw could not hear the conversations. Stanko told Crenshaw that "these people were dangerous," but he still assured him that they would get their cars.

Crenshaw had had enough. He talked to a friend of his who was a policeman. The cop said there were two Berkeley County deputies who could help him. Then he mentioned the police involvement to Stanko, and Stanko called him off. He said he knew someone who knew the captain, and they'd get better results from a higher-up. Stanko's lies began to involve law enforcement. He told Crenshaw he couldn't have his cars because "the chief" had them.

When Crenshaw expressed anxiety over where his money ended up, Stanko maintained that his own stress level was sky-high over the whole mess also.

Stanko told Crenshaw the stress was getting to him. He passed out—*boom*, completely lost consciousness—on one occasion after talking with Ricky Davis.

On February 19, Crenshaw visited a friend, Special Agent Aldo Bassi, who visited Stanko and interrogated him at length. Afterward, Bassi told Crenshaw that he suspected Stanko himself was the crook, *not* the people he'd been dealing with.

There was another full day of running around, going from place to place where the cars were supposed to be, but weren't. For part of the time, Crenshaw's cousin and another guy were with them, and Stanko always moved the adventure to a new location with a fresh lie.

Crenshaw called Stanko at eight o'clock, Tuesday morning, and Stanko agreed to meet him at McElveen. Crenshaw went there, but Stanko did not. At half past nine, Stanko called Crenshaw *collect*. Crenshaw accepted the charges.

Stanko had given up on the scam. Crenshaw confronted Stanko directly, and Stanko admitted to him that there was no Ricky Davis involved, or the chop shop, or anybody else. It was just him, just Stanko. Crenshaw asked where the cars that had arrived had come from, and Stanko admitted that they were stolen. In fact, he had stolen them. Now he could only think about one thing—getting away. Running away.

"Where's the money?" Crenshaw asked.

"There is no money," Stanko replied, adding that he had no intention of going back to jail. He said he was leaving, and he instructed Crenshaw to "help Elizabeth," because she knew nothing of his scheme and was completely innocent.

Crenshaw first called Bassi, who was busy and said he'd call him back; then he called Elizabeth, who was "very upset and crying and saying that Steve attacked her.

"My wife, Natalie, called 911 and then went next door to be with Elizabeth to wait for the police," Crenshaw told Detective Lewis.

"CERTAIN IT WON'T HAPPEN AGAIN"

The day after giving his statement to Detective Darrell Lewis, Stephen Stanko was taken out of isolation and had his first taste of what it was like living among "murderers, rapists, and thieves."

At six-three, 200 pounds, Stanko had size going for him, but that lent him no security. He still felt like easy prey to the vultures he was in with.

He was terrified, and the other inmates lacked fear. He liked to think he was a civilized man, and they were ruthless. To put it in his own dramatic and romanticized terms, for the next six months, he spent part of his time fighting a judicial battle, and the remainder fighting a social one.

Stanko was assigned a court-appointed attorney. His meetings with her were weekly, fifteen minutes long, and always discouraging. No one with a public defender ever pleaded not guilty.

The first thing she ever said to him was "It doesn't

look good. You gave a complete statement. There's not much I can do."

The second meeting was no better. His lawyer told him he was facing eighty-five years, and that was after they dropped the assault charge from "intent to kill" to "high and aggravated."

According to Stanko, Liz McLendon was on his side and joined his campaign to have the charges against him lessened. Stanko told his lawyer that he had doubts if the fifteen-page statement he gave was legal. He'd been duped into giving it. But his lawyer ignored him. She was convinced that his fate was "cast in stone" and the only effective strategy would be to emphasize the "first-time violent" nature of his offenses in order to work out less jail time.

Looking back on it, Stanko realized that his lawyer's tunnel vision when it came to plea bargaining didn't mean she was a bad lawyer. That was simply the way the game was played. Public defenders were so overloaded with cases that fighting for a client was out of the question. They bargained for the best deal and moved on to the next case.

One thing his lawyer did do for him, however, was arrange for examinations at a local mental hospital by a pair of psychologists. Those exams yielded a "borderline narcissistic" diagnosis, but nothing that called in to question his competency to stand trial. His choice was simple: ten years or eighty-five years.

In April 1996, the Berkeley County grand jury indicted Stephen Stanko for kidnapping; assault and battery, with intent to kill; nine counts of breach of trust, with fraudulent intent for stealing cars; and two counts of obtaining property by false pretenses.

His court hearing was held on a Monday morning. The solicitor gave the judge the gruesome details of his crimes against Liz—chemicals, attempted asphyxiation, bondage, and terror—while Stanko's lawyer emphasized his education and work history.

Victims were given a chance to make a statement—Liz and two others. Stanko was given an opportunity to speak in his own defense, and he made a plea for mercy, noting that his "assault" and "kidnapping" had resulted in no blood and no broken bones, and no weapons were used. (This ignored the fact that a rag soaked in toxic chemicals pressed over a person's face could easily be construed as a weapon.) He apologized to Liz for the violence, and to the other two victims for the cars he stole. He still lied. He always lied. All of their property had been returned, he later claimed, so no harm done. "I spoke honestly and calmly as possible," he recalled. Except for the part when he lied. Ask Ray Crenshaw if there was "no harm done." He was still out thousands of dollars.

Stanko pleaded guilty, as per his lawyer's instructions, and received a ten-year sentence. That worked out to ten years for the kidnapping and assault, and three to five years running concurrent for the nonviolent crimes ("breach of trust," "obtaining property"). He had been expecting three to five years for the violent, and ten for the nonviolent, but they'd been reversed by the court. When Stanko agreed to the plea deal, he understood that he'd serve between three and five years, but due to a new "truth in sentencing" law, and the fact that kidnapping was a no-parole offense in South Carolina, he had to serve at least 85 percent of his sentence—eight and a half years—before he could be released. That time would be spent in the MacDougall Correctional Institution.

Stanko would have thought that his transfer from the

detention center to the penitentiary would have been immediate. Not the case. Some say the most effective part of any punishment is the dread that precedes it. If that's the case, then Stanko got four days' worth, stewing some more, wondering about the hell they called Mac-Dougall and the next decade of his loser life.

When the time to transfer did come he wasn't alone. He was shackled at the ankles and belly to the prisoner in front and behind him, two feet of chain between men, and led with an impatient push or two by guards into a caged van.

Stephen Stanko's first stop at MacDougall was the Reception and Evaluation Center, where he was stripped naked, thrown into a shower, shaved bald, and deloused.

There was a comprehensive and invasive medical examination. Bystanders—the audience!—were allowed to suggest what parts should next be examined.

Forms were filled out.

Stanko understood immediately that he was going to have to reevaluate his sense of privacy in order to survive in his new environment. There was no dignity—only humiliation that set in right away, and threatened never to let up.

And, obviously, any resemblance to autonomy flew out the barred windows. All decisions—from here on out—were to be made by others. All he had to do was listen to the commands of the Man, and do as he was told. Anything else resulted in *discipline*.

When thoroughly received and evaluated, Stanko was assigned a number, and from then on, he answered only to that six-figure sequence. He waited in a holding area with the other rookies until he was assigned a six-by-nine cell with two roomies.

From then on, things became familiar, a routine: on weekdays a daily hour of recreation. No exercise on weekends. A shower every three-to-five days.

The only surprise interruptions came when he had to take one of many tests designed to pigeonhole the prisoner by intelligence and aptitude. These, along with the prisoner's criminal record, informed officials where to best place him in the system.

For all of the sophisticated thinking he demonstrated during his psychological exams, Stanko would later suspect that he was destined to be grouped with the hard cores. He was guilty of kidnapping, a violent offense considered pretty hard-core. Violent offenders were caged exclusively in *maximum-security* prisons, which were hell by design!

Stephen Stanko spent four years in maximum security, and then, because he'd been employed and kept disciplinary free, he was transferred out. Under the new arrangement, Stanko's jobs were more to his liking. According to Bob Ward, who was at the time the acting director of operations for the South Carolina Department of Corrections (SCDC), Stanko's prison jobs included being a library helper, a teacher assistant, and a chief clerk in the prison education building.

During his time in the prison library, Stanko not only read but wrote as well. He kept sort of a diary about his experiences. He researched the incarceration system, how it functioned and why it operated the way it did.

He learned the "why" behind some of the things that had happened to him. He wrote in a tiny and precise printing, both sides of the paper margin to margin, no negative space, no air on the page at all.

Stanko not only economized on paper with his writing

style, he was prolific. Of course, he had plenty of time, but
he managed to fill more than 2,000 pages, 1,000 pieces
of college-ruled loose-leaf paper, with his observations.

By 1999, Stanko was ready to tell somebody about
what he believed to be his literary accomplishment. He
chronicled every minutia of life at MacDougall and then
Turbeville Correctional Institution. He entitled the manuscript *After the Gavel Drops,* which was what it was about,
what happens to the man *after* he's taken from the courtroom in handcuffs.

As finally edited down for presentation, *After the Gavel
Drops* consisted of fifty short chapters. Stanko, of course,
would let any prospective publisher know that there was
a lot more where that came from. Prison was his muse,
and the pearls of wisdom flowed like "Ol' Man River."

Every word impacted poorly on the South Carolina
corrections system.

In Stanko's life, his manuscript was unique. It was, in
no shape or form, a confidence game. There wasn't anything flimflam about it. He created it and he was going
to sell it. *Who'd've thunk?* Maybe this *was* the new Stanko.

The appeal, Stanko realized, was that he wasn't writing a book about an average prisoner, he was chronicling
the experiences of an inmate in a Southern prison who
was white and highly educated. Readers were far more
likely to buy a book written by him than by some drop-
out street thug.

He wrote a solid proposal and sent it out. He was prepared to collect rejection slips, but, as it turned out, he
didn't need patience. Greenwood Press in Westport,
Connecticut, nibbled.

On June 18, 1999, acquisitions editor Emily Michie
Birch, with Greenwood's School and Public Library
Reference department, sent Stanko a letter thanking
him for his proposal. Birch wrote that Greenwood was

publishing a series of books for high school and public libraries about living in alternative environments—and his book might fit into that category nicely. Birch envisioned a book "suitable for high school students" (and she used that phrase), but still real. She also wanted a section for friends and family members with loved ones in prison, explaining how to relate to them. She envisioned the prisoner paired up with a university-affiliated scholar so that it would have the equal academic weight of the other books in the series. Birch told him a college-connected psychologist or a sociologist would be best—although if he had a working relationship with a psychologist, that would be fine, too, regardless if he or she were a college professor.

She didn't say anything about supplying him with an egghead coauthor, so he had to find his own. By August, Stanko had gotten nowhere. If Stanko couldn't find someone, she might suggest a name. She thought it might be a welcome addition to the manuscript to get some feedback from politicians and corrections officers.

Thus, during the autumn of 1999, Stanko sent the table of contents for his manuscript to the criminal justice department at the University of South Carolina, the largest CJ program in the state.

Stanko's package ended up on the desk of Dr. Reid H. Montgomery Jr., a professor there. Montgomery opened the package—a book proposal from a prisoner, you didn't see that every day—and began to read.

Although the grapevine was secret, Liz McLendon had a contact who knew something about Stephen Stanko's behavior in prison. Liz learned that Stephen was telling people that he was a lawyer and that he was inside on bum charges, some bogus white-collar crap, exacerbated by his nagging wife's accusations.

Wife? Liz thought, her hands balling into fists. Her role in the drama, the murder victim who refused to die, had been reduced in Stephen's telling to that of a nagging wife who was way too quick to get bent out of shape.

Even years later, she would anger at the memory. She managed to get past a lot of the things he'd done to her, but tell the world they were married, that *irked* her.

In addition to that anxiety, Liz had to deal with her fears that, despite Stephen's incarceration, he would find a way to harm her. As if to reinforce her terror, Stanko gave out Liz's phone number to other inmates and the family of other inmates. She remembered this as a scary time.

Reading the book proposal, Dr. Reid Montgomery found that the first paragraph on page one was a two-word glossary of "unfamiliar terms." The first word was "heart," which in prison meant the ability to stand up to others, not to squeal, and to take punishment stoically. The second word was "suitcase," which referred to the inside of an inmate's rectum, in which drugs were smuggled.

The TOC gave a one-paragraph summary of each of the fifty chapters, beginning with "Reception and Evaluation" and ending with "The Convict Enigma," in which Stanko talked about the fact that many ex-cons suffer from post-traumatic stress, making it difficult to reclaim a "life once held."

The document concluded with a two-paragraph "About the Author," in which Stephen Stanko described himself as a former honor student, former chemical representative and salesman who had spent forty-three months (1,309 days) inside, "journaling every event." He had 2,600 pages written.

Dr. Montgomery was intrigued by what he read—but too busy to coauthor the book himself. He recommended Stanko try Dr. Michael C. "Mickey" Braswell, professor emeritus in the Department of Justice and Criminology at East Tennessee State University (ETSU), who'd been Montgomery's collaborator on a book called *Prison Violence in America*, published in 1994. Dr. Braswell was also a book editor and knew how to doctor a manuscript from pedestrian to exceptional.

On November 1, 1999, Stanko wrote Dr. Braswell a letter from Turbeville prison to the professor's post office box at ETSU. Stanko apologized for the handwriting, explaining that his typewriter had been "lost" during a recent institutional transfer. He referenced Dr. Montgomery and explained that the book was "tentatively accepted" by Greenwood Press. He gave Braswell the name of the acquisitions editor at Greenwood with whom he'd been dealing. She said they would want a book between 90,000 and 110,000 words in length, and he was busy whittling it down to that size. *This is my invitation to you to co-author the completed manuscript,* Stanko wrote.

He enclosed a copy of his manuscript's table of contents with the letter, plus a blank "Request for Visitation" form. If Braswell was unable to accept, Stanko asked that he forward the message to any *university affiliated scholars who may find interest.*

Braswell turned out to be too busy, too (although he did end up writing the foreword to the book's final version). The timing was bad. He was already working on a couple of books.

He did, however, talk to Stanko on the phone several times and found him "obviously bright, energetic—and somewhat grandiose and manipulative."

During one phone conversation, Stanko expressed loneliness, feelings of being adrift without an anchor, of being disenfranchised. His family, he said, had disowned him. Braswell listened to Stanko from a psychology POV and did some on-the-spot analysis.

"I noticed that there was anger in his voice when he talked about his father, or anything to do with his father. There was a resentment," Braswell said. "My advice to him was that he was going to have to work through that. Anger wasn't going to get him anywhere."

Even during those few phone conversations, Braswell had pegged Stanko as a man suffering from an antisocial disorder. And Braswell knew what he was talking about. He had observed more than his share of antisocial personalities in his day, having for several years been a prison psychologist for Georgia Corrections. He worked at the Georgia Diagnostic and Classification Center (GDCC). All adult males entering the corrections system passed through the GDCC and had their mental health poked, prodded, and evaluated. The GDCC had a permanent prisoner population of a couple hundred as well, head cases who checked in for their psychological exam and never checked out. Braswell *knew* antisocial.

"Antisocials often don't have the capacity for intimacy but they are really good at pretending to be whatever you want them to be. Antisocials—psychopaths, sociopaths—are consummate actors. They are both charming and cruel," Braswell said.

Charming to get what they want. Cruel for fun. As long as they felt they might get their way, they would do any dance you wanted them to do. They were big into flattery. They would tell you that you weren't like the others, you understood them better.

"They are chameleon-like. It probably has something to do with how they were raised." Braswell felt that in many cases, antisocials have had something happen to them in childhood, an inconsistency, perhaps, that caused their psyche to be stunted in this way.

"People like to say it's brain chemistry and anomalies, and it can be," Braswell said. "But I have a feeling that at least as often as not that chemistry is a reaction to environmental factors."

Antisocials excelled when their lives were thoroughly structured, such as would occur in an institution. Braswell's experiences as a prison psychologist were that antisocials needed an inflexible list of things they could and couldn't do.

During his phone conversations with Stanko, the psychologist tried a couple of linguistic tricks to gauge his reactions. Interpersonally, Braswell found Stanko to be shrewd.

"Unfortunately, antisocials tend to be above average in intelligence," Dr. Braswell said. If you tried to disagree with Stanko, he would change his opinion, always reenforcing, never conflicting. He was never simply enjoying interaction with another person; he was always manipulating.

"And traditionally antisocials are not dangerous," Braswell concluded, "unless you put them in a corner. If you put them in a position where they aren't in control, can't talk their way out, in which they have no room to maneuver, then there might be unexpected violence."

The psychologist had never looked at Stanko's medical records and he had never given him a thorough examination, things that would be necessary to make an official diagnosis. So Braswell didn't know if being antisocial was all that Stanko was, but it almost certainly was a part of what he was.

Braswell recalled that Stanko wasn't happy with the sluggish pace and seemed very anxious to get the literary show on the road. Stanko, Braswell thought, had a grandiose perception of his connection with the editor at Greenwood. Braswell doubted that she was focusing on Stanko and his problems quite as much as he thought she was. Everything he said was tinged with a strain of grandiosity, but it was most noticeable when Stanko talked about himself as a literary "playa." He easily leapt ahead of himself, already thinking about a tour of speaking engagements after the book was published.

As Dr. Braswell remembered it, Stanko underplayed the violence of his kidnapping charge. Braswell assumed, however, that the violence was there. Stanko wouldn't have been given such a lengthy sentence if there hadn't been more violence than Stanko was fessing up to.

Dr. Michael Braswell called Dr. Gordon Crews, an associate professor in Washburn University's CJ department—and Dr. Crews said sure, he'd love to do a prison book with a literate prisoner.

"Apparently, I was the only one who had time," Crews recalled more than a decade later. He added with a chuckle: "Everybody else was too lazy."

Braswell told Crews that the idea had already crossed Reid Montgomery's desk, and Montgomery had given it an enthusiastic thumbs-up. Crews knew Montgomery well. He'd been Crews's teacher and mentor in college.

"I had a couple of books out at that time," he said. One was called *The Evolution of School Disturbance in America: Colonial Times to Modern Day.* "I was looking for something to write," Crews added. Crews sent Stanko one of his books, so Stanko would have an example of his work.

Not only wasn't Crews too busy, the Stanko project nicely filled a niche in his schedule.

* * *

Gordon Crews and Stephen Stanko talked about the crimes that had landed him in prison. Stanko freely admitted to flimflamming, and begrudgingly admitted that he had to get a little rough with his woman at one point because he was trying to pack and leave—and she was all *in his face.*

The professor made an effort to verify Stanko's criminal history. Crews used to work at the South Carolina Department of Corrections; so when he and Stanko first got hooked up, Crews contacted "all the buddies" inside the system looking for off-the-record info on Stanko. The list of convictions matched the list Stanko had given. The kidnapping charge was alarming, but Stanko had explained that. No one got hurt.

"I learned he was a model prisoner, who never caused any problems," Crews recalled. Stanko had no disciplinary record, which was why he was later released a year and a half early.

When Crews didn't immediately find evidence that Stanko was lying to him, he stopped his informal investigation. Like so many others who encountered the killer chameleon who was Stephen Stanko, Crews took him at face value.

"It's human nature," Crews said. "Good-looking guy, big ol' guy. Very smart." People don't think the worst of others. No one meets a charming person and asks themselves, *Gee, I wonder if this guy is a sociopath.*

Looking back, Crews could see how adept Stanko was at social manipulation, how his every word geared toward supporting his mark's preconceived notions. No mention of Clorox or asphyxiation, that was for sure. He said Elizabeth was trying to block him. He feared he would be arrested if he didn't split quick. He "overreacted." For a brief time, he tied her to a chair, but he untied her before he left! He only detained her until he could get his clothes packed and get out.

Crews had been naïve. Maybe Crews trusted him because Stanko was from the South. Maybe it was because Stanko was good at what he did. Crews, highly impressed with Stanko's ability to deceive, referred to it as an "art."

Stanko did his homework. "He talked to Braswell a little bit about me. He talked to Montgomery about me." By the time Stanko talked to Crews, he knew just where to place the compliments.

Crews said, "The way he approached me, 'Hey, Gordon, I'm like you, a young writer. The only difference between us is I'm on the other side of the tracks. If it wasn't for a couple of bad breaks, I'd be right with you. I would have gone on to college and become a writer. But, instead, because of the unfairness of the prison system I'm being victimized in prison.'"

This was playing right into Crews's sympathies. The scholar was, and had been for years, an advocate for inmates. Crews had seen in person how horribly inmates were treated.

"Even just over the phone, he could peg me," Crews recalled. He knew that his story would wrench sympathy from Crews. His story of being a white-collar criminal seemed designed for Crews—how he was forced to share a cell with hard-core, violent criminals; to use the toilet in front of three violent criminals, who stood there looking at him. That would be intimidating for anyone. Well, it just went to show how messed up the corrections system was. "Imagine the world from my POV," Stanko said. "I'm an educated, upwardly mobile guy who is now serving a long prison sentence in Lowcountry, South Carolina, because my stupid girlfriend got in my way. Look what I'm going through."

Crews found Stanko fascinating. The image of Stanko

on the toilet as the three black men, hard-core criminals, as Stanko described them, gave Crews the chills. It was the sort of thing people didn't normally think about.

Not all of Stanko's complaints impressed Crews. Crews had worked with the corrections system and knew that a lot of things that Stanko took personal offense to were standard operating procedure.

Everything out of Stanko's mouth was about Stanko. There was no subject that wasn't first painted with a thick coat of the sociopath's narcissism.

Gordon Crews remembered the first version of the manuscript that Stephen Stanko sent him: "His chapters were kind of like Stephen King chapters—three pages or so." Still, he was struck by the coherence of Stanko's argument against the current penal system. It was Stanko's contention that prison created more violent criminals than it reformed. He noted that nonviolent criminals were given long stretches behind bars, where they had no choice but to learn how to be violent, thus making them more likely to hurt someone once they got out.

Crews applied for visitation rights with the prisoner and was turned down—although he was granted telephone rights. It was during this time that Crews realized that South Carolina Corrections was not going to be helpful when it came to Stanko's book.

Just because Stanko was not a disciplinary problem in prison didn't mean he wasn't a pain in the ass. The system *hated* an intelligent and articulate prisoner.

Stanko saw himself as better than the corrections system. He observed his surroundings with thick condescension. And when dealing with prison employees—the very people who had power over him—he couldn't help but allow his condescension to show, to push at the boundaries whenever he could.

I am special was what Stanko was saying, and he felt he deserved to be treated special as well. And why not? The smallest schoolchild could see he didn't belong there.

Intelligent prisoners noticed what was being done to them. Many prisoners lived hellish existences on the outside, and came to feel they were treated better inside than outside. *Go ahead and beat me,* they say, *it's better than what I was going through as a free man.*

The educated ones, on the other hand, say, *This ain't cool. They can't do this to us.*

Plus, educated and articulate prisoners knew how to make complaints in such a way that they commanded a response. Stephen Stanko, a bit of a jailhouse lawyer, researched his rights and called out the system whenever one of those rights was denied.

"He filed many injunctions and complaints and lawsuits against them over the years," Dr. Crews remembered. "Grievance after grievance after grievance was filed with the South Carolina Department of Corrections—so naturally, they labeled him a troublemaker."

In 2000, records show, he sued the South Carolina Department of Corrections and won. The suit involved work time lost, and he was awarded by the court the grand sum of $5.69.

In 2001, he sued the SCDC again, claiming that instead of being in minimum custody, he deserved to be in minimum out restricted (MOR) custody. This time, he lost. The case lingered in the courts for a while, but on March 31, 2003, administrative law judge Ralph King Anderson III ruled that MOR custody was not appropriate because Stephen Stanko was a kidnapper.

Prison officials had had it up to here with Stanko. He

was aggravating to the nth degree. Then came the final straw: they found out he was writing a book.

Stanko made the mistake of mentioning his literary efforts during one of his prison interviews. Stanko said he was writing a book about *them* and what a shitty prison system they ran, about all the evils they'd done to inmates.

Oh, you think so? was their response. The prison fought back.

"They cut him off at the ankles every chance they could," Crews recalled. "They shut him down at that point."

First they took away Stanko's computer privileges. He had to smuggle his writing out, passing his mother pages when she came to visit. She would later send the stuff to Dr. Crews. Then they took away his paper and pencil.

By that time, Dr. Crews had all the manuscript he needed to fashion a winner. He never was granted visitation rights.

At one time, Stanko had been granted phone visitation rights from a list of thirteen people. These were mother Joan, all three surviving siblings—brother Jeff, sisters Peggy and Cynthia—friends Bob McMurray, Bill Kupter, and Pattie Perkins, literary collaborators Braswell and Crews, and his editor at Greenwood Press, Emily Birch. Also on the list were three lawyers, Harry L. Devoe, Wesley Locklear, and John Shupper.

Devoe was a Clarendon County lawyer who represented Stanko during a postconviction relief hearing. It was through Devoe's efforts that Stanko's name was not placed on the state's sex offender registry, an addition that was normally routine for those convicted of kidnapping.

By the time Stanko was released from prison, the phone rights of everyone but the three lawyers had been revoked. Even Stanko's mother was no longer allowed to call him.

Crews negotiated a contract for himself and Stanko

with the Greenwood publishers. He began to edit Stanko's manuscript and write his own portion of the book.

Along with the theme that corrections were being handled all wrong, Crews noted that there was a "never again" motif to Stanko's writing. He vowed that he would never go back to prison. That could mean one of two things: he intended to go straight, or he would take his own life before returning to prison.

From 2000 to 2002, Stephen Stanko and Gordon Crews worked on the book together, communicating only by phone. They finished their masterwork and submitted it to Greenwood.

It was quickly rejected. It *bounced* back.

"Not appropriate for high-school students," the publisher said.

Crews almost blew a gasket. Today, he has smoothed out, but acknowledged that Stanko had the misfortune of attracting an editor at Greenwood who was determined to make a square peg fit a round hole, no matter what damage she had to do to the peg. She had written in her very first letter to Stanko that she wanted the book to be part of a series she was putting together for high-school students. That caveat to the contract, however, was soon forgotten.

"I didn't pay any attention to that for five years, you know?" Crews said.

Now the manuscript was being rejected because it was too adult. Crews thought that was the point. This was a Scared Straight scenario. Telling the truth to high-school students about life inside prison could only be a good thing, right? The word "appropriate" wasn't appropriate.

Crews burned a bridge or two, and was removed by the publisher from the project. Greenwood replaced

Crews with Dr. Wayne Gillespie, an assistant professor of criminology at East Tennessee State University.

Gillespie cut out about 90 percent of what Crews had written, cut back Stanko's section to about one hundred pages—and he wrote the rest of the book himself.

It was finally published, a slender hardcover, in 2004, with the title *Living in Prison: A History of the Correctional System with an Insider's View.* The book had three authors listed on the cover: Stanko, Gillespie, and Crews. They had to give Crews credit because they were still using a couple of chapters he'd written. The book came out two months before Stanko's release.

Crews talked to Stanko about the book. Crews said that he didn't like it. Stanko said he didn't like it, either—but he couldn't help but be excited about being *published.*

In his book, Stanko wrote he had two concerns regarding his return to society: one, that he would carry an ex-con stigma wherever he went, and two, that he would bring some of the hell of prison with him when he returned to the outside.

Dr. Gillespie would later say that Stanko's coauthors were unaware of the details of the crimes that had Stanko living in prison. They had asked him what he had done, and had taken his word when he told them.

"He was very selective in the information he revealed to me," Gillespie recalled. "He presented it as a domestic situation—nothing hard-core. He kind of said they were having problems because of problems at work. He was general in his description, and that is why I was led to believe his main crimes were fraud and breach of trust."

"I never knew—none of his collaborators knew—the details of his past. How could we be so stupid?" Crews wondered.

* * *

To write the book's foreword, the publisher brought back Dr. Michael Braswell, who'd originally turned down an offer to coauthor.

Braswell taught courses emphasizing peacemaking, social justice, and restorative justice. He believed in giving criminals and their victims opportunities to interact: criminals could accept responsibility for the damage they'd done, and victims could regain emotional wholeness. Braswell's courses included: Ethics and Social Justice, Themes of Justice (a film course), Human Relations and Criminal Justice, and Peacemaking Practicum. He was a former prison psychologist, a licensed marriage and family therapist, and a college teacher for fifteen years. It was Braswell's goal to improve the relationship between personal and institutional transformation in ways that would tend to create a more compassionate community and criminal justice process. He was strongly opposed to the death penalty— a problem solver based on fear, greed, cynicism, and an overreliance on the notion of punishment. The college professor taught humility, compassion, and service— what he called a "commitment to the possibility of forgiveness and restoration."

Pragmatists thought Braswell viewed the world through rose-colored lenses, and his daydreams, though interesting to contemplate, lacked relevance in the real world.

Braswell's foreword to Stanko's book contained spooky harbingers, right from the first paragraph, invoking as it did the name of Jack Henry Abbott, another inmate/author who proved there is no relationship between writing ability and criminal rehabilitation. At least, sometimes—even sociopaths can write.

Abbott was a career criminal who, after learning that

Norman Mailer was writing a book about the life and death of murderer Gary Gilmore, became pen pals with the author. Mailer slobbered over Abbott's letters—they were "intense, direct, unadorned, detached, and unforgettable"—that he had them forged into a book called *In the Belly of the Beast*. Mailer didn't stop there. Calling Abbott "intellectual, radical, and a potential leader," the author campaigned for the prisoner's parole. Asked if it wasn't risky to put a guy like him back on the streets, Mailer would say that "culture is worth a little risk." Abbott's freedom lasted only six weeks, ending when he stabbed a restaurant employee to death for denying him access to an employees-only men's room. In retrospect, Abbott's book should have been called *In the Belly of Anyone Who Annoys Me*.

"I think Abbott ended up scaring Mailer before it was over," Braswell opined. He said that Abbott's behavior after release, as well as Stanko's, illustrated one of his corrections-reform power points. The brainwashing prisoners received in the system served them counter-productively when they tried to reenter society. Simple as that.

While Stephen Stanko was still in prison, Liz heard he had a book in the works that was to be published. She felt her blood pressure skyrocket. And that was before she read it. Reading the damn book, months later, infuriated her.

In the book, Stanko referred to Liz as his "spouse." It made the steam come out of her ears. True, he didn't use her name, but to try to make people think his attack on her was just a marital squabble was unconscionable.

Stanko was released to community supervision in July 2004, a two-year program, squinting into the sun and relying on the kindness of Hummer, the mother of his fellow inmate whom he'd befriended. Only days later, Liz was notified by a victim's advocate group, whose job it was to keep potential future victims aware and up to date, that Stephen was a free man. After that, though, Liz was in the dark. She later said she had no knowledge of where Stephen was staying or what he was doing following his release from prison.

"And I didn't want to know," she said. Although she did suppose he might be staying with his parents; in which case, they were on opposite sides of Goose Creek and not likely to run into one another.

During those early days of new freedom, Stephen Stanko made no attempt to contact Liz McLendon. He *did* receive periodic phone calls from his original coauthor, Gordon Crews, who was urging him to rewrite his original prison manuscript—the one that was inappropriate for high-school kids—and send him the stuff.

Stanko said he was planning on writing again, and he would send Crews the pages when he was done, but he didn't want to write about prison anymore. By that time, Crews had relocated to Rhode Island. He and Stanko never did meet in person.

"I was up the Coast, and I never found time. I never pushed myself to go see him," Crews admitted.

They talked on the phone. During one phone call, Stanko told Crews that he was working on something. He was doing a lot of research in a library he frequented. He said he was being helped by a pretty librarian and a friendly old man he'd met.

Crews encouraged Stanko to keep it up, to continue going to the local library. Knowing what he knew now, remembering that encouragement made him feel, as he put it, "sick to my bones."

But Stanko's creativity was never the main thrust of the conversation. Mostly, he whined about how hard it was for ex-cons to assimilate into free society.

Stanko had a list of complaints. Couldn't keep a job, couldn't *whatever*. Folks discovered he was a convicted felon and he got the stink eye everywhere.

The tone of the conversation was perfectly in keeping with their relationship over the years. Stanko complained and Crews listened. Stanko still knew how to push Crews's buttons. Crews had dedicated years of work into researching the problems inmates had reentering society, so the ex-con had his coauthor hanging on every word.

Crews responded to Stanko's complaints with a "good-ol'-criminal-justice-faculty-type" condolence: "It sucks," Crews told him. "Do the best you can."

Crews recalled Stanko's "perfection." No one would have figured him out. "You can tell by his writing how articulate and smart he is."

During this same period, as Stanko struggled with reentry, he also called his foreword-writer, Dr. Michael Braswell. Stanko, Braswell recalled, was in some sort of financial straits, his demeanor different from when he was in prison. Now living a life without institutional structure, Stanko's grandiosity got the best of him. He couldn't tell the truth, when it felt better to brag. Braswell picked up on the hustling-and-hectoring nature of Stanko's phone pitch. He no longer sounded like a new kind of journalist. More like a fast-talking salesman. "He sounded like the kind of guy who could sell anything," Braswell remembered.

* * *

In the days after the Laura Ling and Henry Lee Turner murders, there were calls on the radio and TV for those who had encountered Stephen Stanko to come forward and tell the county solicitor what they knew.

Among those who called was Kelly Crolley, whose family's Owl-O-Rest Factory Outlet furniture store had been scammed out of $125 by Stanko posing as a charity fund-raiser.

Crolley came in for an interview and was questioned by Fifteenth Judicial Circuit deputy solicitor Fran Humphries, who could tell that Crolley was going to make a great witness, communicating for the court just how despicable Stephen Stanko could be even when he wasn't on a spree of violence.

On that Masters weekend—while Stephen Stanko was still running free, simultaneously fleeing from the law and enjoying happy hour—the U.S. Marshals were trying to predict what his next move might be. After all, Stanko was on a spree. As the killer haunted taverns and saloons in search of fresh marks, fresh victims, law enforcement was elsewhere providing protection and setting up surveillance around people they considered likely future targets. One of those possible targets was Gordon Crews, who worked at Roger Williams University in Rhode Island at that time. The first Crews heard of Stanko's new violence was when a local reporter chased him down and asked him for a comment. U.S. Marshals showed up at his house and took Crews and his family into protective custody. The university closed for two days, such was the fear that Stanko was heading toward their campus to kill Crews. Two of Crews's colleagues, with whom he'd had squabbles, complained to the university that Crews might have hired Stanko to kill them. "I love academics," Crews later said with a laugh.

It *was* funny in a way, looking back: As the Crews family was being locked up in Rhode Island, Stanko was in Georgia knocking back shots of tequila with great ceremony and laughter. Crews recalled the total craziness. *America's Most Wanted* came to his house!

All that publicity was having a positive effect on book sales. There was a rush to buy *Living in Prison*. There were copies on eBay selling for $250. Crews's personal copy was seized by a U.S. Marshal. In the weeks that followed, libraries in South Carolina reported that copies of the book were being checked out but not returned.

Crews said he was available to do TV, as long as he had an opportunity to plug the book. He was on *Good Morning America,* and appeared with Nancy Grace, Anderson Cooper, and Greta Van Susteren on their shows.

One of the people police most wanted to talk to was Liz McLendon. Police feared that Stephen Stanko might consider his attack on Liz as an incomplete murder, something unfinished in his life. Police tried to extract from Liz info that would help them catch the guy. She said that she'd learned that Stanko was a wanted man, again, when her next-door neighbor, Natalie Crenshaw, who knew Stanko well, had called her and said it was on the news.

All of that time trying to push Stanko out of her brain and in one instant he was *baaa-aack.* Liz's fear and anxiety were back as well. *Damn him,* she thought. Liz had spent years, nine years or something, trying to forget Stanko, and she'd done a pretty good job of it. Now that it was all relevant again, she found memories were not returning as coherently as police would have liked.

They asked questions for which she didn't have good answers. Why had she helped him even after he was arrested? She tried to explain that she was more fiercely loyal than she was suspicious—until the nightmare struck like a two-by-four in the forehead. It was so painful that she tried to forget.

They would ask her how she could not know, and she had no explanation. Liz came out of the interrogation with increased sympathies for all victims, for everyone who had ever fallen into a sociopath's web of seduction and deceit.

She told the cops that she believed him because he believed himself. He had himself convinced that his lies were true, and that was how convincing he was.

"Unless you have lived it, you can't fully understand how it happens," she explained. If you confronted Stephen about his "truths," he would become adamant. His reality was complicated enough, and others were not to poke at it.

On April 12, 2006, the first anniversary of Stanko's arrest in the Augusta Exchange parking lot, Stanko was still sitting in his Georgetown County Detention Center jail cell, awaiting trial, which was scheduled to begin that summer.

To commemorate the anniversary, one newspaper ran a feature article regarding the case. A reporter asked Gregory Hembree if he planned to seek the death penalty. Hembree said he was, but when asked why, he zipped his lips.

"It's too serious a case for me to be playing fast and loose," Hembree said.

Richmond County sheriff Ronnie Strength said that

while it was true that his men had made the arrest in the Augusta Exchange parking lot, it was really Dana Putnam who was the hero.

"Without her, we may not have taken him into custody here," the sheriff said.

HUMMER

Not everyone was grinding their teeth at Stephen Stanko, eager to see him die. He didn't have many friends, but they did exist. And one was Kate Bradley (pseudonym), who went by the nickname of Hummer. She met Stanko when he was doing his kidnapping time.

Hummer's son was in Stanko's cell block on trumped-up "sex with a minor" charges. "My son went to prison for a crime he truly did not commit," she said. Every lawyer she spoke to looked at the evidence and wondered aloud, "What is this kid doing in jail?"

Stanko knew the system and helped Brian (pseudonym), her son, with the necessary paperwork that came when a prisoner attempted any legal maneuver. She and her son met Stanko while filling out legal forms. Stanko befriended the woman, and added Hummer to his phone visitation list.

Because of her son's experience, and the experiences of other ex-cons like Stanko, Hummer Bradley had become an advocate, and wanted everyone to know how screwed up the South Carolina justice system was.

She began one interview with: "I'll tell you, like I told

the detective, Stephen Stanko never did anything wrong to me." She still thought about Steve in such a positive way. "He never did anything bad *to* me or *around* me. What I'm *aware* of is the difficult time Steve had after he got out of prison, the things he went through. It was just horrendous."

South Carolina gave no help whatsoever to prisoners released back into the free world, no programs to help them adjust, nothing to prepare them to become part of the legitimate workforce—making their return to crime an inevitability.

There was a time when released inmates received a new suit of clothes. But no more. Today, prisoners walked out of prison wearing the same outfit they were arrested in years before.

If they didn't have any family or a place to go, they might have to steal for their *first* meal, Hummer said. Even if they were lucky enough to get a job, and jobs were like miracles to ex-cons, they often didn't have a vehicle to get to and from the job.

Talking about Stanko, she said: "Due to the fact that he was just out of jail, no one would hire him. He tried every store within miles. Best Buy. Home Depot. Wal-mart. You name it."

The human resources departments at those stores weren't evil or mean. There were a lot of bosses in a position to hire inmates who didn't do it, not for philosophical reasons, but because their insurance companies balked.

"There you go again with the insurance companies. They seem to rule the world," Hummer opined. "When somebody finally did hire Steve, they didn't give him a chance. I don't know anybody who can get a new job in a new field and produce out of the gate. It takes months."

People talked about Stanko being a con man. That

burned Hummer up. No one talked about the job applications, the steady stream of applications that Stanko wrote. He was always honest about his past, and everyone took a pass.

The prison was at fault. It was just a cage. It ruined men. Unless you were trying to pass your high-school equivalency test, there was no teaching. And they were released with no money. "Zero!" Hummer exclaimed. "Bus money, that's it. In the name of heaven!" She urged everyone to picture themselves in that situation— released into a new world, broke. It was not fair. These men almost immediately became desperate and did desperate things.

As Hummer put it, "They resort to whatever."

She didn't think they wanted to go back to prison; it wasn't a matter of being institutionalized and ill-prepared to deal with freedom of choice. They liked their freedom, the same as everyone else. They resorted to crime because they were penniless.

"What are they supposed to do, look for change on the street?" she asked.

Hummer was lucky enough to help some ex-inmates. She had a small business and hired ex-cons to work for her. She wished she could give more of them an opportunity, but her business wasn't that big.

She said she might be in the market for a ghost writer to help her produce the book she envisioned, ripping the lid off the screwed-up South Carolina justice system.

She said the system worked on a simple premise: "If you don't have money, you're going to jail. Innocent or guilty, you are in jail. If you have money, you could get out. Am I bitter about it? You bet."

Her son was accused of stopping off on his way home from taking a test at college and having sex with a minor.

It was ridiculous. There was not a shred of evidence against him—but it didn't matter.

She had an investigator tell her that to get from his school to the scene of the crime to fit the prosecution's timeline, he would have needed a helicopter. But the price tag was $250,000. Come up with the money and Brian walks; don't and he's going away. Truth meant nothing. And when they get out, they might do okay for a brief period; then a lot of them started doing drugs and drinking. She really wished she could have done what she had to do, come up with the quarter million, and kept her son free. If she had known what her son was going to have to go through, she would have raised the money. It wasn't like she didn't spend money on the case. She emptied the kitty, again and again, for lawyers, none of whom did her son any good, and one who retired from his practice because he was fed up with the corruption.

"You're dealing with the South here," Hummer explained. "It's like a Third World War."

Getting back to Steve, if he couldn't get a job after eight and a half years behind bars, who could?

"He was an extremely educated person. He's a genius, I can tell you that much," Hummer said. She remembered him having some official title that allowed him, at first, to have visitation rights with other prisoners and their families, to help them fill out forms.

In light of the most recent allegations, Hummer said she was still shocked. She never considered Stanko capable of doing anything violent. It was a double shock because she'd gotten to know Laura Ling and her beautiful daughter through Steve, and they were very nice people.

"He had such a mellow disposition," she explained. "Very laid-back. When he got out of prison, I had him laughing a lot. He definitely did not have the makeup of a murderer."

There was only one explanation: "He just snapped." He was like a pressure cooker. Laura wanted him to get a job. She was tired of supporting him. "But she was asking him to do the impossible," Hummer explained.

She said too many people—and by that, she meant writers—were portraying Stephen Stanko in a bad way, which only went to show they didn't really know him.

It was part of the Stanko legend at this point, for example, that his flimflam behavior included pretending he was a lawyer. Not so, Hummer said. He was as smart as a lawyer; and he knew how to do some of the things that lawyers do, because he was so smart. He assisted people in the law, but she never heard him claim he was a lawyer. She did hear him say that he *had* a lawyer who could help push the paperwork through, and though she couldn't recall his name, she believed the lawyer to be real. "I heard him on the telephone a few times with that attorney," Hummer recalled.

Like just about everyone who knew Stanko, Hummer didn't know much about Stanko's family. She knew his father would have nothing to do with him. His mother was still receptive to him, and he was in touch with one sister, Peggy, in California, but that was it.

Hummer remembered one time she drove Steve back home to Goose Creek and she met Stanko's mom. Stanko was there to pick up some stuff they'd kept in storage for him while he was away. Stanko's mom gave him some pastries.

Seemed like a long time ago now. Would she be attending the trial?

"No, I couldn't handle it," Hummer Bradley said, with a shake of her head.

THE PHILOSOPHICAL DEBATE

During the run-up to Stephen Stanko's trial for the murder of Laura Ling, there was much discussion about Stanko's punishment, if found guilty. One such debate during the late summer of 2006 appeared in the Myrtle Beach *Sun News* as part of an ongoing series on criminal justice, responsibility, and the death penalty.

It was a conversation between journalists Tom W. Clark, of the Center for Naturalism in Somerville, Massachusetts, and journalist Isaac Bailey, from South Carolina. The exchange was highly philosophical. Did evil exist? Did all humans have the capacity for self-control? Was there a third factor beyond heredity and environment? Something organic, perhaps. And what effect would the answers to those questions have on the judicial system?

If a scientific explanation existed, and Clark obviously believed it did, all retributive punishment should be abolished. Obviously, that included the death penalty.

Tom Clark said taxpayers' money was better spent on

reducing crime, healing communities and victims' relatives, and *lastly* rehabilitating imprisoned criminals.

Stanko lacked the capacity for self-control, Clark said. He didn't deserve the death penalty because he was a product of his "environmental and genetic makeup." Stanko could not be held accountable for the genetic factors he was born with, nor had he any control over his upbringing. It wasn't his fault.

Despite the fact that he felt Stanko bore no responsibility for his seemingly evil behavior, Clark did not think the prisoner was completely insane, either—not in the legal sense. Stanko knew what he did was wrong. Obviously, if a police officer had been in the room, he wouldn't have committed those horrible crimes against the Lings, and he wouldn't have shot Henry Lee Turner.

His self-control existed, but it was compromised severely by both nature and nurture factors. His lack of self-control could be exacerbated. When combined with his other antisocial characteristics, bad things happened.

Isaac Bailey responded that maybe it was harder for Stanko to control himself than it was for other people, but he could still do it. *He can choose to resist,* Bailey wrote, adding that he believed genetics and environment influenced behavior. He did not believe that genetics *caused* bad behavior.

Clark said Bailey's theory brought up an interesting circle of questions. If certain genetics and environment did not cause bad behavior, then *what did*? What made Stanko choose to act as he had acted? If there is evil, what caused it? Was it caused by genetics, environment, or something else?

Summing up the South Carolina POV, Bailey said that because he believed Stanko could have prevented himself from raping and murdering, he chose not to.

Because of that, he was a "self-made monster" and deserved the death penalty.

Yes, Clark countered, but we can't know that Stanko could have resisted his urge to rape and kill. And if—*if*—he had no choice, then it was immoral to execute him.

Bailey asked what recommendations Clark had for the justice system given his opinion about killers like Stanko, probable sociopaths with neither conscience nor impulse control.

Clark laid out a series of bullet points. One, keep Stanko the hell away from society. Two, in order to deter any possible future killers and rapists, Stanko should maintain his isolation from the general public for at least twenty years. Three, his time away should include classes to teach him social and job skills. Four, he should receive treatment for all physical and mental problems. Five, Stanko should be taught relentlessly of how much he hurt his victims' families, and should be made to apologize and somehow make restitution. Six, after he had completed victim restitution and community restoration, and had fulfilled the terms of his sentence, he still should not be released back into society until it had been determined that he no longer presented a threat.

Clark said the goal was to reduce crime. Public safety was the first concern. Public safety, in reality, he said, often became secondary to punitive concerns.

The public liked harsh sentences. Many even liked the death penalty. And why? Because it felt good to get back at the bastards who did those horrible things.

What sort of society do we want to be? Clark asked.

In response to the *Sun News* article, Nils Rauhut, chairman of the Department of Religion and Philosophy at Coastal Carolina University, said that there could never be a clear-cut winner in the debate between Bailey and Clark. They were discussing things that were mysteries. How could we ever know how much differently we could act from the way we actually act? There is no test for that, and any attempt would spawn bad data warped by self-consciousness. We could never know how free we actually are, nor could we ever, with any accuracy, determine what degree of our activity was determined by past occurrences. Because of this, Rauhut concluded, we could never eliminate a system based on punishment.

DEFENSE LAWYERS

Because he had no money, Stephen Stanko was originally to be represented by public defender Reuben Goude, a former marine who earned his law degree at the University of South Carolina in 1979, and was admitted to the state's bar that same year.

Public defender in Georgetown County was a part-time position. In addition to his work for the South Carolina Commission on Indigent Defense, Goude also had a private practice, so he was a busy fellow.

"At that time, I was appointed to all of the public defenders' murder cases," Goude later recalled. But not exclusively murder cases. A wide variety of criminals came his way as a public defender; while in his private practice, his specialties were real estate closings and title searches, personal injury, car wrecks, divorce, bankruptcy, adoption, and workers' comp.

But Goude remained Stanko's lawyer for less than a year. The beginning of the end for their legal relationship came when the solicitor decided to go for the death penalty.

In South Carolina, defendants in jeopardy of the

death penalty were entitled to two lawyers to represent him, one of which, by law, had to be appointed from outside the public defenders' pool.

"Death penalty cases are extremely time-consuming for the lawyers," Goude said. "If I had hung onto the case, I would have had very little time to do the two hundred other cases I had been assigned." Plus, he would have gotten paid the same money for a lot more work.

Goude noted that the whole process was made more efficient when death penalty specialists handled death penalty cases: "They are familiar with the procedures and the forms, and they have the routine down pat."

Two other lawyers volunteered to take on the case, and Goude volunteered to get off. Stanko was consulted and agreed to release Goude. And a judge made the switch official.

So, during the autumn of 2005, Goude was released from the case and replaced by two private lawyers: the bespectacled and mustachioed William "Bill" Isaac Diggs, whose long gray hair was usually tied into a ponytail down his back, and Gerald Kelly, both of whom had death penalty experience.

Bill Diggs was born June 8, 1950. He'd earned his B.A. in poli-sci at the University of North Carolina at Charlotte in 1977, and his J.D. at the University of South Carolina School of Law at Columbia. He'd been a lawyer since 1980.

From 1984 through 1989, he was the chief attorney of the South Carolina Office of Appellate Defense. During that stretch, he defended a thousand clients at postconviction and appellate hearings. Over the years, he'd served on several committees, helping draft South Carolina's current rules of appellate procedure. He had been approved by the U.S. District Court to be the appointed defense counsel in South Carolina's capital murder cases.

Diggs knew the answer to why Stephen Stanko had done what he did was locked up inside his client's head. He decided to use whatever means he could find to "look inside" Stanko's brain in search of an explanation for what had happened. He searched the country and came up with a team of experts that could show a jury, with evidence they could see, why Stanko did the things he did, and why it would be wrong to punish him for those actions.

On May 18, 2006, at Diggs's request, Stanko was transported to the University of South Carolina Medical Center where, at about noon and under heavy guard, state-of-the-art 3-D color photos were taken of the inside of his brain.

In addition, Diggs had shrinks poke at Stanko's psyche. Not everything that came out pleased his defense as a mitigating factor. Some of Stanko's statements merely underlined his despicable nature. At one point, Stanko told a psychiatrist that he hadn't raped Penny. The sex had been consensual. In fact, it was Penny's threat to tell her mother about their affair that started the trouble that night.

For most of the twentieth century, South Carolina law was simple. A prisoner could be executed for murder, rape, and kidnapping—but only in cases where there was no legitimate argument for mercy.

The determination of punishment was in the hands of the judge and the jury. No one else had any say-so. That was the way it was until 1972, when the U.S. Supreme Court declared those rules, in effect, unconstitutional.

In 1976, South Carolina law was changed to make the

death penalty mandatory in some cases. This law didn't fly, as judges repeatedly ruled that there had to be a process of mitigation and aggravation before a prisoner was condemned to die.

In 1985, the death sentence was back, now with a separate trial to follow the defendant's conviction, using the same jury after a brief cooling-off period.

The toxicology report on Laura Ling was not released by SLED until more than a year after Laura Ling's murder. According to tests performed by forensic toxicologist Tim W. Grambow, there was no alcohol, barbiturates, or opiate painkillers in Laura Ling's system. She did, however, test positive for a "potentially toxic" level of amphetamines. Prone to weight fluctuation, Laura was frequently dieting, and perhaps she was using stimulants to "burn fat."

Two months later, Grambow released the findings for Penny Ling that revealed she had no intoxicating substances in her at the time of Stephen Stanko's attack.

STANKO SPEAKS

Sitting in jail, waiting for his trial to begin, Stephen Stanko was interviewed by Troy Roberts, of CBS News. He affected remorse, his voice wavering as he pitched the notion that he never wanted to hurt anybody. He had a split personality. There were two of him: good and evil. Jekyll-Hyde on a wonder ride. It wasn't fair to punish the good half for what the bad half did. He couldn't hurt anyone on purpose. It wasn't in his makeup, in his moral code. The last thing he remembered he'd been arguing with Laura Ling and she *slapped* at him, knocking his cigarette out of his hand and in between his glasses and his face, burning him. He felt a swelling anger and then . . . nothing. He couldn't remember anything after that. The next thing he knew he was in the shower and he had blood on him. He put a towel on and went into the big bedroom, where he felt for a pulse on both women, and didn't find one on either. So he packed and left and contemplated suicide.

Although he claimed to have no memory of being violent, he did recall conning people on a regular basis, ever since he was a teenager and found himself in community college rather than the Air Force Academy. He felt like he was in a race, racing to become successful. Since he wasn't the fastest, he had to cheat to have any chance of winning. Once he started cheating, he couldn't stop. He wanted everybody to know that, no matter how his trial turned out, he had to believe that the gray matter inside his head was of value. Scientists could study him, do test after test on him, and maybe learn something about this thing that was going on inside him, this switch in him that sometimes was flicked and turned him into someone else. Maybe they'd find something that would help other guys down the road who might be suffering with the same malady. Maybe even help find a *cure*.

Of course, science could make use of his brain whether he was dead or alive, and he wanted to live. At first, not so much, but now yes. He'd been of two minds—no pun intended—when he heard he had a brain defect. It was good news, because it explained so many things about his past behavior and why he'd done bad things. On the other hand, it wasn't curable. He was always going to be a guy with a brain defect. It was a downer if you looked at it that way. But now, he knew; he *knew* why he destroyed the things he loved: Laura, with whom he shared an unconditional love, a woman he *still* thought about every day, and Henry, who had been a friend and, yes, even a "quasi father figure" to him. Man, Henry was "good people." Stanko thought and thought and tried to figure out the *trigger*. It was conflict, that much he was sure of. The only time it had ever happened was when he was confronted with violence. Someone would throw a set of keys at him or slap his face, burn him with a cigarette, and *boom*, something in his brain, the chemistry in his brain, just changed.

Stanko thought back to his years with Elizabeth

McLendon. Same thing. He kept screwing up, running sloppy con games, big on ambition, short on endgame. He wanted to be forthright about his flimflam past. He did a lot of stuff without a license. He recalled the lies he used to keep his marks off his butt: He was a paralegal. He was a corporate attorney. Check's in the mail. FedEx lost it. Lies on top of lies. No check ever arrived. He remembered that stuff clearly. But not the violence. He wished he could remember the violent things that had happened, but he couldn't. He'd asked himself, there was so much conflict and violence in prison. How come he hadn't killed anybody when he was behind bars? He eventually came to the conclusion that it was because of witnesses. Every time he got into a fight—and by his count there had been thirty-nine of them—there had been too many people around.

That Mr. Hyde part of his brain was reluctant to emerge under such circumstances.

Informed of Stanko's statements, Solicitor Greg Hembree was concise in his assessment: "Stephen Stanko is a remarkable liar," Hembree opined.

Hembree went on to describe Stanko as a man incapable of remorse, a "cold-blooded killer."

A review of Stanko's disciplinary records from his first stint in prison indicated that he hadn't gotten into thirty-nine fights during those eight and a half years. He hadn't gotten into *any* prison fights. *Zero.* Some might say this was because he was never confronted by women, little girls, or old men—that he was frightened of getting into a violent altercation with a strong young man. A fellow could get hurt that way. Hembree couldn't help but conclude that Dr. Jekyll was a tad reluctant as well.

PART III

FIRST TRIAL

The bailiff said: "Call the case of *The State of South Carolina* versus *Stephen C. Stanko*. All rise. Circuit Court Judge, the Honorable Deadra L. Jefferson presiding. The court is now in session."

The judge entered and sat, the courtroom sitting with her. She was a forty-one-year-old African-American female, and a local product through and through. Known in her youth as "Dee Dee" Jefferson, she grew up on Simons Street, attended Charleston public schools, and earned her B.A. in political science and English in 1985 from Converse College in Spartanburg, South Carolina. She earned her J.D. at the South Carolina School of Law in Columbia. After a stint as a clerk for a judge, and some time in private practice, she was elected by the South Carolina General Assembly to the position of resident family court judge in 1996. She became a circuit judge in 2001 and had served in that position since. She prided herself in her impartiality, and believed in following the law—balanced with common sense. She personally saw herself as a judge who relied on "a great level of discernment in seeing that there is something more to a case than my eye can see. People are not just throwaways. You can't send everyone to prison. There is just not enough room." Despite her self-opinion, she was seen by her colleagues as a "tough judge" when it came to sentencing. Of the 112 jurists in South Carolina who sat on the state's circuit, appeals, and supreme courts, Jefferson was one of the youngest.

The defendant was brought in last for security reasons. He'd been transported from the detention center to the courthouse in a police prisoner transport vehicle, which was basically a cage on wheels. His hands were cuffed in front of him and he wore a thick leather belt with an electrical device that could instantly drop him with a lightning-bolt shock if he tried anything funny.

As a spectator entered the courtroom from the back, the defense was on the left and the prosecution on the right, closest to the jury, which would sit in a box along the right-hand wall. One thing that made this courtroom a little different was that the stenographer—a female, with long red hair—sat in her own box directly in front of the witness stand, where she could hear the testimony good and loud.

The bailiff read the charges: one, murder; two, assault; three, criminal sexual conduct; four, kidnapping; five, battery with intent to kill; and six, armed robbery.

During the first days of the trial, Stephen Stanko was without a jacket or tie. He wore a crisp white dress shirt, buttoned all the way to the top, brown suit pants, and freshly polished brown dress shoes. Later, he would be allowed to wear a jacket and tie.

During preliminary hearings, Judge Jefferson determined that Stanko was mentally competent to stand trial, but that an insanity defense would be allowed.

Now, at the start of August 2006, she called for voir dire. Four hundred prospective jurors had been summoned, a far greater number than normal because of the case's notoriety.

During voir dire, William Diggs attempted to question a potential juror as to her views on the insanity defense. Greg Hembree immediately objected. Judge Jefferson sustained the objection and ruled that Stanko's defense team could ask potential jurors whether they could consider affirmative defenses "and list them all," but they would not be allowed to ask if they would consider the specific affirmative defense of insanity. After a lengthy sidebar, Diggs informed the court that he was "abandoning" asking potential jurors questions specifically regarding the insanity defense.

Following several days of voir dire, twelve jurors and two alternates were in place.

Because of the numerous media outlets covering the trial, including *48 Hours,* the jury was sequestered during the trial—isolated from other people, newspapers, and television news.

The trial's setting looked straight out of a movie, a beautiful small-town Southern courthouse—the one with the fresh white paint, thick pillars, balustrade, and six-foot-thick walls. The courtroom had unadorned walls, also painted white.

With the exception of Stephen Stanko himself, the principals were typecast for their roles. As was often the case, the solicitor, Greg Hembree, was a good-looking guy, neatly kempt and impeccably dressed. Sitting next to him during the trial would be his equally well-groomed assistant solicitors Fran Humphries and Bo Bryan. In the meantime, across the aisle on the right side of the courtroom, defense attorney William Diggs had a long gray ponytail and a thick mustache. His second chair was filled by Gerald Kelly, who would have to power through the trial on crutches, with a cast on one leg.

Stanko's wrists were handcuffed as he entered and left the courtroom, but they were free when he sat at the defense table with his lawyers. Of course, there would be no time when he wasn't under the watchful eye of Georgetown County deputies.

The defendant wasn't the only one closely observed. Security was tight across the board. Prosecution witnesses who had yet to testify were kept in a room together, and were not allowed to watch the proceedings, not even on a TV monitor. That was because no one wanted witnesses to be influenced by previous testimony.

Kelly Crolley, who wasn't scheduled to testify until the penalty phase, befriended Laura Ling's daughter, whose horrors were unimaginable.

Penny was impressive, unbelievably solid, Crolley observed. She seemed like a good kid, who really had it together—in spite of everything that had happened to her. As the young victim waited for her turn to testify, she worked on origami.

Also waiting was Henry Lee Turner's girlfriend, Cecilia, and Charles "Chuck" Petrella, the young paramedic from the Murrells Inlet Rescue Squad who treated Penny at the crime scene and gave her a teddy bear the next day. Now, in the courthouse, the paramedic and the teenager hugged, the first time they'd been together since the day after the attack. Penny had the teddy bear with her—she showed him brightly—and she promised she would have it with her when she took the witness stand.

All of the witnesses were nervous, but there was a lot of laughter. The room had a small-town feel. Two witnesses, present for unrelated testimony, had once been married to each other.

Also Dana Putnam was there, the woman who'd loaned her couch to the killer before calling the cops.

Liz McLendon was there, now remarried and known as Liz Buckner. She was married in 2001 to a man who, understandably enough, did not care for his wife dwelling on the distant past and that really bad boyfriend she'd had. "I'm a victim of your circumstance," Liz's husband liked to say, which always made her laugh. Liz thought being a witness in a murder case was "just awful." Listening to the details of what happened to Laura Ling and her daughter was especially difficult to Liz because, as Liz later remembered, "how closely it was related to what happened to me." When she listened to everyone's story, she put herself in Laura Ling's place, which was a very stressful thing to do. She lost control of her emotions a couple of times. She met Penny Ling and they had long talks. Liz felt empathetic toward the teen victim, felt herself climbing aboard an emotional roller coaster, nonstop undulation until the trial was over.

"I kept putting myself and my son in that situation, and I couldn't help but think, 'Oh my, that could have been us,'" said Liz. Liz knew she shouldn't *but couldn't* help it: She felt guilt. Could she have taken steps to prevent Stephen Stanko from being released early on his kidnapping conviction? She wondered how things might have been different if Stanko had been forced to serve his entire ten-year stretch instead of being released a year and a half early. Would Laura Ling still be alive? Would her daughter be free of the emotional and physical scars Stanko left? "I felt I was carrying the guilt for everyone," Liz recalled.

* * *

When the jury—twelve, plus two alternates—was in place, Judge Jefferson sat at the bench and addressed the jury. She explained that this was the case of *The People of South Carolina* v. *Stephen Stanko*. She ran down the charges against the defendant, defining each charge as she went. She explained that their job was a very important one because of the seriousness of the charges against the defendant.

"A person who is convicted of or pleads guilty to murder must be punished by death, or by imprisonment for life," she said. It was the first death penalty case in Georgetown County in almost ten years.

She gave the jury a brief course in how trials worked. Her job was to determine how the law was to be applied, and that everyone understood those applications. It was the jury's job to determine what the facts were and to apply the law to those facts. They were a team. Their responsibilities were perfectly complementary. They were to base their decisions solely on the evidence—which consisted of the witnesses' answers, not the lawyers' questions—as well as any physical items that might be introduced by either side. They were not to come to any conclusion regarding the defendant's guilt and innocence until they had heard all of the evidence. They were not to discuss the case with anyone, even fellow jurors, until the trial was over and it was time for them to deliberate. The defendant had a right not to testify on his own behalf—and should that happen, the jury was not to hold the decision against him. Sometimes they would be asked to leave the courtroom, and proceedings would continue without them. Despite this, they would miss *no allowable evidence.* First they would hear opening statements, then the prosecution's case, the defense case, and closing arguments. Because this was a case with a defense of mental illness, there were four possible outcomes they could choose from: guilty, guilty but mentally ill, not guilty by reason of insanity, and not guilty. She thanked the jury for their service, and warned them that the trial might take a couple of weeks, so they should do their best to concentrate on the evidence just as hard on the last day of the trial as the first.

"Okay, opening statements. Mr. Solicitor, you may proceed."

"Thank you, Your Honor," Gregory Hembree said, buttoning his jacket as he rose to his feet. He promised to show the jury that Stephen Stanko's violent outburst during the spring of 2005 was not a onetime thing but part of a continuing pattern. They would learn that Stanko was a guy who did very bad things, but he didn't feel all that bad about it afterward. The defense was going to claim that he was mentally ill, but there was no evidence to suggest that. Just because he engaged in criminal behavior, that didn't make him crazy. Heck, if that was the case, you'd never be able to prosecute anyone for anything. He'd *seen* mentally ill and Stanko wasn't it. Stanko didn't do anything bizarre. He didn't kill because a voice from his washing machine was ordering him to do so. He was a grifter who became violent when he was cornered. Simple as that.

During his opening remarks, Stanko's defense attorney Bill Diggs explained that the reason Stanko did the things he did was insanity. He couldn't help it. He lacked the basic body part, part of his brain, that in other humans prevented people from doing unwise things. Once he had an idea he couldn't inhibit himself, and the results were tragic in this case. Tragic, yes. His fault, no.

"After you have heard all of the testimony, I want you to look at the facts of this case. Would a normal person do the things Stephen is accused of doing? A healthy person? Steve looks normal. He looks healthy. Why would a human being do this to someone they love and depend on? How does someone in their right mind do these things?" Diggs said. "I suggest to you *they don't*. Stephen Stanko has a brain defect that keeps him from knowing right from wrong. He is not an evil demon-possessed person. He operates as a person who borders on insanity all the time. My client was insane when he murdered Laura Ling."

Diggs explained that when he said insane, he didn't mean psychotic or schizophrenic, but rather psychopathic to the nth extreme. Stanko said that he became so outraged during his April 8 argument with Laura Ling that the last thing he remembered was being burned by the cigarette. After that, nothing. Total amnesia. He must have been in some sort of fugue state.

Diggs shrugged. Sure, you could take that with a grain of salt. Defendants will say anything to lighten their punishment. But the jury didn't have to listen to anything Steve Stanko had to say. Diggs was going to present experts who had photographed Stanko's brain. They were going to see hard evidence based on cutting-edge technology.

"This will be as close as we can come to showing you *what insanity can look like*," Diggs said.

When opening statements were finished, Judge Jefferson instructed Solicitor Hembree to call his first witness. The prosecution called Lieutenant William Pierce, who testified regarding his initial observations of the crime scene. It was his unfortunate duty to introduce much of the case's physical evidence, photos of Laura and Penny Ling after the attack. He held up, for the jury to see, the bloodstained gray-and-black tie that had been used to bind Laura Ling's wrists behind her back.

Dr. Kim Collins, pathologist at the Medical University of South Carolina in Charleston, testified that she was a professor of pathology at that school, and that hospital's director of the autopsy section. She said she'd earned her medical degree at the Medical College of Georgia School of Medicine in Augusta, and completed her residencies in forensic pathology at the North Carolina Baptist Hospital and the Bowman Gray School of Medicine at Wake Forest. Another noteworthy item on her résumé was that she was coauthor of a book called *Forensic Medicine,* an illustrated text that has been called the "atlas of forensic medicine." She said that her clinical expertise was in general forensic pathology, sexual assault, child abuse, and elder care. She testified regarding the autopsy of Laura Ling.

Dr. Collins brought a large board upon which two diagrams of Laura Ling's body had been drawn, front and back. On those drawn figures, the pathologist had marked every injury the victim received during the attack.

Every bruise, each cut and gash and gouge. Even wounds inside the victim's mouth were marked and labeled. With a pointer in her right hand and her written report in her left, she itemized those wounds for the jury.

There were contusions on the back of the left thigh, on both buttocks, ligature marks on the wrists, bruises on the arms, abdomen, and uppermost thigh, severe face trauma, etc.

"See how the necktie is tightly wrapped around both wrists before the wrists were tied together," she said.

Lucky for Liz Buckner, she was one of the first to testify. "It will be good to get it over with," she remembered thinking. For the occasion, she wore a light blue collared blouse under a black-and-white–patterned jacket.

She testified that she met Stephen Stanko in 1992. They met at work, a telecommunications job. They became boyfriend and girlfriend, and for a long time things were good, and they cohabitated in Berkeley County, South Carolina. Then there were difficulties. Cause? Stanko was a con man, not the man he was claiming to be.

"I was becoming increasingly upset with Stephen," she testified, "because I felt I wasn't getting the whole truth. Some things were beginning to take place that I did not like."

Borrowing money. Starting phony businesses with a neighbor. Pocketing all the money. She discovered he'd been fired from his job and they had a row, started out as an argument but escalated into pushing and shoving. She told him to leave and he said he would. She saw him pull out a suitcase and start to throw stuff in it. She went to bed and cried herself to sleep.

"What, if anything, happened when you woke up?"

"When I woke up, he was standing at the foot of my bed—and he had a *horrible* look on his face. I asked him what he was doing and he said he was getting ready to leave. I asked him, 'What is that that I smell? What are you doing? Are you cleaning the house?' And, at that moment, he jumped over me with the cloth that was drenched in Clorox-409 mixture. He proceeded to try to suffocate me. He flipped me on my stomach and he put the pillow over my head."

During much of Liz's testimony, Stanko kept his eyes down, on the table in front of him. But during this part, he flashed her a quick glare, as if silently accusing her of lying. After a few seconds, he gave it up and lowered his eyes again.

"What were you thinking as he did this?" Hembree asked.

"I thought he was going to kill me. I thought I was going to die."

Liz told the jury how Stanko held the cloth tightly over her face. But, as was frequently true of first-time asphyxiators, he underestimated the required time and energy to kill someone in that manner.

"What happened next?"

"He actually did say, 'This isn't working. It worked in the movie.'"

"Did that statement have a meaning to you?"

"I took it to mean that he'd seen a movie in which someone was killed that way, but it didn't work in real life, so he was going to have to think of another way to kill me."

"What, if anything, did he do next?"

Liz's voice, urgent but unemotional up till this point, began to crack. She pulled out a tissue and prepared for the impending tears.

"The instant he stopped trying to kill me, he reverted back to his normal personality. He began to talk to me like nothing had happened. He took a couple of neckties and tied me up."

"Neckties?"

"Yes."

The jurors had just seen a photo of the neckties that bound Laura Ling's wrists, so they were familiar with what that looked like.

"What did you do?"

"I was screaming for him to get away from me, and I was praying that he would leave. I told him, if he just left, I would never say anything to anybody about this."

Dabbing at her eyes with the tissue, she described how he carried her, now bound and gagged, into the bathroom and sat her on the toilet while he took a steamy shower.

"I could hear him humming in the shower, humming

and murmuring, like he was happy and he didn't have a care in the world, like it was just another normal day."

When he got out of the shower, Liz testified, he left her tied up in the living room. He kissed her on the head and left. Later, she heard he had been arrested.

Liz Buckner was cross-examined by the defense's second chair, Gerald Kelly, who wasn't afraid to butt heads with the witness, despite her victim status—a very risky thing to do in front of a jury, because it was so easy to appear villainous.

She answered Kelly's questions—aimed toward making her seem to have exaggerated the violence of the attack, and an unwillingness to accept blame for the fact that there was a row in the first place. Hadn't she thrown a set of keys at Stephen Stanko, escalating hostilities?

She sensed that her interrogator knew she felt guilty and was trying to use that to make her look bad in front of the jury. She felt that she was being victimized all over again. He asked her if she had a dog at the time she dated the defendant. She said she did, and he asked if the dog was still alive. At that time, the dog was still alive, but Liz couldn't help but wonder why he asked. He seemed to be picking around, searching for sore spots. What did he hope to prove? Did he want to anger her so that the jury would get to see the hellcat who needed gagging and bondage for her own good?

Liz personalized her experience, painting upon the defense attorney motives he no doubt didn't have, projecting her emotional state onto him. She came to believe that he was sadistic, that the defense lawyer was enjoying the process. Liz could tell. Enjoying it just a little bit *too much,* she thought.

TESTIMONY OF PENNY LING

Penny Ling, with teddy bear, took the stand. She wore a black sweater over a white blouse and a black-and-white–patterned skirt. Those who knew the young woman's story noticed immediately that as she took the oath and had a seat, she was wearing a scarf that hid her neck from view. As her testimony began, it was instantly obvious that this was a strong woman of great courage.

On the ledge in front of her sat the Bible used for swearing in witnesses, a plastic cup filled with water, and a box of facial tissues.

Her testimony, no matter how difficult, was nice and loud and clear. She broke down a little bit during one portion, describing the death of her mother, but she was strong when she described her own pain and suffering. When she teared up, the jury and the spectators teared up with her.

It was a small courtroom, almost intimate, and not crowded. In a room like that, everyone was close to one another, and it was difficult for the spectators to be completely quiet. Even during the most dramatic testimony, there was usually a background noise of fidgeting, shuffling, and coughing. But not as Penny testified. The courtroom was silent—except for the sound of her voice.

She understood that many rape victims preferred to stay anonymous, to hide their faces, but she knew she had not done anything to be ashamed of and had allowed the press to print her name. The Associated Press had her photo. So what? It was *the man* who did these things to her who should be ashamed, not Penny.

She was determined to take the horrible thing that had happened to her and make it into something positive. There were people out there watching the news on TV and reading the newspapers who had had similar things happen to them, and she wanted all of those people to know that it could be *all right*. With the right mind-set, you could piece your life back together again. She used her mother's memory as a source of inspiration. Her mother had taught her to work hard and she could do anything she wanted to do—and those were the words she was going to live by.

She had not seen the attack coming. Looking back, she'd noticed that Stephen Stanko was a little bit more aggressive around the house than before, but she never thought he might be a rapist or a murderer. The attack, she felt at the time, was out of the blue. She didn't know what had triggered it.

Only two people knew what the final straw had been. One was gone—the other a pathological liar.

She remembered waking up and feeling like she was in the Twilight Zone, encased in a miasmic cloud. Stanko was in her room, telling her not to scream. If she screamed, she and her mother were both *dead*. Now, looking back, she understood that it didn't make any difference if she screamed or not. He intended on killing them both, anyway. At the time, she believed him. People were always believing him.

She recalled that the reality of the situation came with a blast of adrenaline. She threw off the covers and burst into action. She needed to get to her mom, and get to her quick. She needed to gather up her mother so they could both get out of there.

She ran into her mother's room and saw her mother on the floor. She was still alive. Penny could hear her moaning, and she thought her mother was trying to say something. But Laura Ling was too incoherent to form the words.

At that point, she testified, she must have been hit over the head or something, because she suddenly lost consciousness. When she woke up, she was on her back, on her mother's bed, and Stanko was raping her.

She told the jury that despite the blow to her head, she continued to struggle. She didn't want to make it easy for him. She kicked and fought as hard as she could, but she couldn't come close to matching her attacker's strength.

The rape was completed. Stanko flipped Penny over onto her stomach and placed one of his knees on her back. He held the teenager down as he returned his attention to Laura.

"And this entire time, my mom was still alive," she testified. "I mean, I could tell because she was moving."

She pressed her chin against the head of the teddy bear as she described the horror of watching the monster kill her mother. "He began choking her, and I immediately thought, 'Oh God, he is going to kill her,'" she said. She had fought, fought harder than ever when the defendant was murdering her mother. She said she told herself, "If you're going to die, die saving your mom."

Her mother's moaning turned into urgent choking

noises—noises that became weaker and quieter, until they stopped. Penny forced herself to look away, because she knew that Stanko was too strong to be stopped and he was killing her mother. She didn't want the murder to be her last image of her mom.

"The next thing I know, he was behind me. He held my head up and he slit my throat—twice," Penny testified.

She described how "lucky" she was. If the killer had sunk the knife into her neck just a little bit deeper, she would have been dead. But he didn't.

A number of things had to go right for her, or she wouldn't have made it. She described the manner in which she, despite her wounds, had managed to make an emergency telephone call and maintain a dialogue with the dispatcher for the sixteen minutes it took for first responders to arrive.

With that, the tape of her 911 call was played for the jury.

"I want my mommy," Penny was again heard to say.

She described the days after her injuries, when, as she lay in a hospital bed, she watched the progress of the manhunt for Stanko with great interest.

"I realized that the reason he was wasting all this time is because he thinks I'm dead," Penny said. "He was enjoying himself and taking his sweet time, because he thinks he doesn't have anything to worry about."

As Stephen Stanko listened to Penny testify, he put on a little show of his own for the jury, for he could feel their eyes upon him as the young girl described what he'd done. Stanko pulled out a handkerchief and began to dab at his eyes, but those close enough could see that there were no actual tears to wipe. The gesture with the handkerchief was as phony as everything else about the defendant.

When she finished telling the story, the solicitor asked

her to remove the scarf from around her neck. She untied a knot with nimble fingers, then allowed the scarf to fall away.

There was a gasp followed by a hush. The scars from the slitting of her throat were still clearly visible.

Penny's family, including her dad, sat right behind the prosecution, his sunglasses atop his head. Chris Ling was a big man, with a rock-hard jaw and a cleft chin. Those who saw it would never forget the expression on his face as he listened to his daughter testify about what Stephen Stanko had done to her. He was listening to her, but his eyes were on him. The old cliché "If looks could kill" was never more apropos.

"You couldn't have had a scene like that in a movie," one spectator commented. "I've never seen so much hate and anger in a man's face. I was wondering, 'How in hell is he staying in that seat?'"

Chris Ling was only twenty feet or so from the man who had raped his daughter and murdered his ex-wife. Every time Penny's dad shifted in his seat, the deputies in the courtroom shifted their weight toward him. If there was one thing to keep the deputies on the four walls of the courtroom relaxed, it was the knowledge that every spectator had passed through security screening. Penny's dad was unarmed.

When her testimony was through, the judge asked the defense table if there was cross-examination. William Diggs realized he had nothing to gain here. If he was too sympathetic to the witness, he reinforced her testimony in the minds of the jury. If he was even the slightest bit aggressive with her, he would come off as cruel.

"No questions," he said.

Gregory Hembree would later recall Penny Ling as

one of the most courageous individuals he had ever encountered in a court of law. To testify to the things she did, while the man who murdered her mother and raped her was in the room, only a few feet away, took nerves of steel, and Penny had them.

When it was over, Chris Ling still felt the hate and the anger, but it was obvious by his countenance that he felt something else swelling in his breast: *pride.* He couldn't stop telling anyone who would listen how proud he was of Penny. She was the strongest and most courageous young lady in the whole world.

Everyone agreed.

STANKO THE GRIFTER

To establish the defendant's confidence-game lifestyle, Gregory Hembree called Harriet Cunningham to the stand. She explained that she lived in Socastee, not far from the library where Laura Ling had worked. She frequented that library and knew both the defendant and his murder victim.

"How would you describe his demeanor?" Hembree asked.

"Highly professional," Cunningham replied. "I even invited him over for supper one night."

Stanko had been her lawyer, she explained, and had taken $1,300 from her in exchange for $200,000 in Veterans Administration benefits he claimed she was owed. She only later learned that she had been hoodwinked.

He had been so smart and polite. It never occurred to her that the nice young man was lying.

"Did Mr. Stanko give you any money at all?" the solicitor inquired.

"No. It was supposed to come by FedEx," the elderly witness replied. "I received no money from the VA."

After Cunningham, an auto mechanic named Robert Ollsen (pseudonym) took the stand and described how he had been conned by the defendant, giving him a $1,000 retainer for legal services, which never materialized.

Sitting in the courtroom that day, as well as every day of the trial, was Stephen Stanko's coauthor Dr. Gordon Crews and his wife. They were in the process of moving and had the summer off; so luckily, they had the freedom to attend the trial in its entirety.

"It was fascinating to sit through that. It was unbelievable," Dr. Crews said. This, despite the fact that Crews was not a witness, and the book wasn't mentioned once. The most memorable thing about the trial, by far, Crews thought, was listening to the testimony of the surviving victims, Penny Ling, in particular. "To hear that young victim describe what happened to her was something I'll never forget," Crews said.

Stanko didn't know Crews was coming. The coauthors made eye contact briefly, but Stanko quickly looked down. Crews could tell Stanko recognized him. The defendant had seen his former colleague's "About the Author" photo on the dust jacket of the Crews book he'd received while in prison. In addition, Stanko had had computer privileges when Crews first started working with him, and had probably seen a photo of Crews on the Internet somewhere.

But there was only that one brief flash of recognition, and that occurred at the start of the first day. For the most part, Stanko kept his head down and his eyes lowered the rest of the way.

Crews wondered what triggered the homicidal spree.

In a lot of ways, Stanko's collaborator suspected, it was similar to the buildup to his attack on Liz nine years earlier. Stanko knew the adage of weaving tangled webs through deceit. Well, Stanko's deceptions were chronic, complex, even layered. When the tangled web fell on him, it was always way too complex in its structure for even Stanko's considerable intellect to untangle. He'd tried a straight job, but it didn't work. He assumed it wouldn't *ever* work. His con jobs were falling apart. He was selling stuff that didn't exist. He owed everyone money. And his own inability to deal fairly with his fellow human beings had again painted him into a desperate corner, where, in Stanko's mind, the only solution was violence. "I'd like to know what broke bad that night," Crews later said. Deepening the mystery, there was a sexual component to the attack in the Ling case that, according to both parties, didn't exist with the McLendon crimes.

Crews was slightly nauseated by the way Stanko had fooled him years before into believing he was basically a white-collar criminal, but who was a monster, instead.

Now that the truth was out, Crews wanted the details. The author didn't just sit and watch. When court was adjourned, he was social and did some informal research.

"I got to meet his victims and victims' family," Crews recalled, "and realized how bad something like this hits them. It is stuff I teach every day in my class, but a reminder for me as well." Sometimes he sought them out and sometimes they approached him.

One afternoon during the trial, Liz Buckner approached Crews in the parking lot outside the courtroom. He remembered that she chewed him out once on live TV for profiting off a tragedy, and his first thought was that he was going to receive a second dressing-down. Instead, Liz impressed upon him the sickening details of Stanko's attack on her, and details of the buildup to the attack that were obviously similar to Stanko's buildup to murder.

"It was a direct parallel," Crews recalled. "He had trouble with anger every time he was confronted. This is classic sociopathic stuff. He builds this box, and I think he really believes half of the lies he tells. Like any con man, he is convincing because he has himself convinced. If he says he's an attorney, he believes it."

His murders were cons gone bad. He killed his marks. It wasn't that he killed the people he loved most, it was that he killed the people he *used* most. Crews thought how lucky Liz was to be alive. She survived because of the killer's blunder, not because of his mercy.

Crews never caught Stanko in a lie, and Stanko never made a promise to Crews that he didn't keep. Of course, Crews was conned by Stanko in that he didn't reveal or give any indication of his own capacity for violence. But, on the other hand, Crews's interaction was different from others in that the book was real. It wasn't like the used-car lot he claimed to own, the charities he claimed to collect for, or the legal services he claimed to provide. Stanko really did write a book, and it really had literary and scholarly merit. In that sense, who could expect Gordon Crews to see through to the real Stephen Stanko?

According to Dr. Michael Braswell, there was probably a solid reason why Stanko went from flimflam to legit when incarcerated, and back again when freed. One of the surefire ways to treat a person with an antisocial personality disorder was to give their lives a lot of structure, structure such as is offered by institutionalization. If provided with enough structure, antisocials were unable to manipulate the situation, which, in turn, allowed them to partake in nonmanipulative activities. Now looking back, Crews wished he had spent more time asking Stanko about topics other than his difficulties in prison, or assimilating into society following his release. Crews wished he'd spent time finding out what made Stanko tick. He'd worked with the man for years and knew nothing about his childhood. The only family member Stanko ever referred to was his mother. He mentioned no siblings. Crews had the definite impression that Stanko was an only child. He did allude to his dad once—who, he said, was dead—but it was a subject that for reasons unexplained angered him.

"His mother was his only supporter," Crews remembered. "She was top dog, behind him four hundred percent. I've got letters from her yelling at me because I wasn't moving fast enough." Stanko was impatient when it came to the collaboration. Crews's part of the writing, or editing—or whatever it was—was never happening fast enough for him, and he enlisted his mother's help to quicken the pace. When Crews and Stanko had problems with the editor at Greenwood Press, because they hadn't produced a manuscript that was suitable for high-school students, Stanko's tone became desperate. "Please, you've got to publish this. This is my life," Stanko would say.

"He didn't understand the system," Crews recalled, "didn't know that publishers will end up doing whatever they want to do, which was pretty much what happened."

As a rule, the hallways were cleared and secured before the defendant was led into or out of the courtroom. There was one time, however, Crews observed, when there was a mix-up.

"The timing was screwed up or something, and everyone ended up out in the hallway together," Crews said.

Stanko and Penny Ling's father for an awkward moment found themselves standing only a few feet apart.

The situation didn't last long. As soon as the guards saw their error, they got Stanko out of there, and didn't bring him back until the hallway was cleared.

With the exception of that one error, the courthouse had its act together. They had a system designed to keep parties from opposite sides of criminal trials from encountering one another. They were kept in separate rooms—defense here, prosecution there.

Which door a witness used to enter the courtroom depended on which side he or she was on. The victim's family, for example, was always escorted in through a side door, which assured that they would never be in close proximity to the defendant, his supporters, or his counsel.

During the trial, as all spectators do, Crews spent a lot of time observing the jury. It seemed to him that the panel felt no sympathy for the defendant—or defense counsel, for that matter.

They looked at the solicitor when he was speaking as they would a friend or trusted neighbor who was explaining something to them. But they looked at the defense counsel with suspicion. This man William Diggs wasn't from their part of the world. He used too many words.

The prosecution knew how to make the jury cry. The defense counsel could only, at best, confuse them. At worst, the jurors clenched their teeth and balled their fists. Sometimes they had no idea what the defense was talking about *and* they didn't like it.

If it wasn't a done deal, it was the next thing closest to it.

"I remember turning to my wife and saying, 'Look at

that jury,'" Gordon Crews recalled. They hated Stephen Stanko's guts.

Not relying solely on eyewitness testimony, the prosecution presented damning scientific evidence as well.

Testifying for the people was SLED agent Robin Taylor, the division's lieutenant supervisor of DNA casework.

"You are a forensic scientist?" asked Gregory Hembree.

"Yes," Taylor replied.

Taylor said that her lab had received a wide array of biological evidence from the Ling crime scene, via the Georgetown County investigators. Among that evidence were blood swabs taken from the Ling crime scene, from the blade and handle of the pocketknife taken from the defendant at the time of his arrest, and the gear shift and steering wheel of the red Mustang. The swabs from the car had proven to be, unfortunately for the prosecution, insufficient for reliable interpretation.

"I also processed Penny Ling's Sexual Assault Evidence Collection Kit, head and pubic hair—pulled to include the follicle—from both victims, pubic combined, and vaginal, oral, and rectal swabs, plus fingernail scrapings and miscellaneous body fluid." Taylor tested the droplets of blood found in the hallway and bathroom of the Ling home after Penny's rape and Laura's murder.

There was a concentration of blood on the medicine cabinet, perhaps indicating that the killer, bleeding from the hand, was rummaging around in search of first-aid materials.

"Did you identify the blood found on the knife blade pulled from the defendant at the time of his arrest?"

"Yes, I did. That blood's DNA profile was a match for the control blood sample from the victim Laura Ling."

"There is no doubt?"

"The chances of an unrelated individual having a DNA profile identical to Laura Ling's is one to twenty quadrillion," Taylor replied.

"Was semen among the evidence found at the crime scene?" Hembree asked.

"Yes."

"On which swabs was the semen found?"

"It was found on the vaginal and outer-anal swabs."

"Was DNA profiling able to identify that semen?"

"Yes, the semen belonged to Stephen Stanko," Taylor stated.

During cross-examination, William Diggs asked about the fingernail scrapings that had been taken from both Penny and Laura Ling.

"Were you able to positively identify Stephen Stanko's DNA in those scrapings?" Diggs asked.

"No," Taylor said.

On redirect, Hembree asked if the scrapings had yielded only the DNA of the victims.

"No, there was a second contributor to the DNA," Robin Taylor said.

"Could Stephen Stanko be ruled out as that contributor?"

"No, he could not."

Dr. Pamela Crawford, a forensic psychologist, testified that she had given the defendant a lengthy interview following his arrest. She'd examined his medical history and interviewed friends and family members regarding his behavior over time, and she had come to the conclusion that he had a "personality disorder with narcissistic and antisocial features." He had a "grandiose sense of self-importance," lacked empathy, and took advantage of others. "For his achievements and talents, he requires excessive admiration."

"Did you find in this defendant any mental disease?"

"No. He has a personality disorder," Dr. Crawford answered.

"Did you find any mental defect?"

"No."

A chilling look into Stephen Stanko's cunning came with the testimony of John Gaumer, Laura's boss at the library. He said he'd received a phone call at 9:30 A.M., only a few hours after the murder.

The call was from Stanko, who said he was calling on Laura Ling's behalf. She probably wouldn't be making it to work that day, Stanko calmly said, as she was still recovering from a bout of food poisoning.

The prosecution concluded its case by replaying a portion of Penny Ling's 911 tape. The last thing the jury would hear before the defense took their turn would be the horrible sound of the shattered little girl, her life horribly and irrevocably altered by the monster who sat before them.

DEFENSE CASE

One thing Stephen Stanko and his defense team agreed upon was the importance of science. "Science is the one thing on my side," the defendant said before his trial. He was mentally ill, and he could prove it. It sounded crazy, but he had the pictures *to prove it.*

To demonstrate Stanko's insanity for the jury, William Diggs would bring in a team of medical experts to explain to the jury that Stanko wasn't responsible for his bad acts.

First up was Dr. Bernard Albiniak, whose job it was to make understandable and credible the science—the latest technology—upon which the defense's theory precariously perched.

Dr. Albiniak explained that he earned his Ph.D. in 1976 from the University of South Carolina. He was a forensic psychologist, and a professor at Coastal Carolina University, teaching courses in substance abuse, statistics, research methods, and health psychology. During his career, he had been a forensic consultant in a variety of criminal proceedings.

His testimony concerned positron emission tomography (PET) scans of Stanko's brain taken at the Medical University of South Carolina. He explained what PET stood for, a reference to a nuclear medicine imaging technique that produced a three-dimensional image. The PET camera detected radiation from the emission of positrons. Point was, the resulting image not only showed the physiological makeup of the brain, but also revealed the level of activity in each portion of the brain.

How were PET scans taken? As was true of other internal examination methods, a preparatory radioactive "tracer" was introduced into the body, usually via direct inoculation into the bloodstream. The PET scan system indirectly emitted gamma rays in pairs that could be captured in an image. The tracer was allowed to remain in the body for a waiting period before the scan was taken. Flat images were captured at minutely varying depths within the target organ, and a computer subsequently assembled those slides into a 3-D image. The scan created a picture that didn't just illustrate the size and density of a human organ, but also made sort of a map of its functional processes.

Now that the jurors knew what PET scans were, they needed to be told what the scans of Stanko's brain meant.

On Thursday morning, Dr. Thomas Sachy took the stand. He was a young man, as far as experts go, with a thick head of brown hair, prematurely graying a bit at the front and top. He had a gentle voice. He explained, under William Diggs's questioning, that he was a forensic psychiatrist and founder of the Georgia Pain and Behavioral Medicine center, which specialized in the use of neuropsychiatric imaging techniques and other concepts of behavioral neurology. In other words, he looked at photographs of the brains of people with mental problems, and tried to determine if he could *see* illnesses, injuries, diseases, or other abnormalities. He moonlighted as a public speaker, giving talks to interested groups in pain management, forensics, or other aspects of neuropsychiatry.

Dr. Sachy offered the jury a summary of his education and professional career: certified by the American Board of Psychiatry and Neurology in both general and forensic psychiatry; two Bachelor of Science degrees, in electrical/computer engineering and general studies from the University of Calgary; master's at Georgia State; medical degree in 1995 at the Medical College of Georgia; licensed to practice two years later.

"Do you belong to any professional organizations?"

"Yes. American Academy of Psychiatry and the Law, American Neuropsychiatric Association, and American Psychiatric Association."

"What do you do now?"

"I am in private practice in Georgia," Dr. Sachy said. He treated patients of all ages, from children to geriatrics. As a pain specialist, he said, he relieved suffering and discomfort during a medical or surgical procedure, or because of a disease or condition.

"Dr. Sachy, how would you describe Stephen Stanko's brain function?"

"Stephen Stanko's brain function was highly unusual. There were parts of his brain that were not as active, compared to other parts of his brain."

For Dr. Sachy's testimony, a TV screen was set up so that the jury could see. On it were two colorful PET scans, one of a "normal" brain, one of Stanko's brain. Dr. Sachy said Stanko's mental difficulties could be seen.

This testimony set a precedent in South Carolina— the first time in the state that PET scan evidence had ever been used as part of the defense case in a criminal trial.

Areas of red indicated high levels of brain function. The normal brain had plenty of red in the frontal lobes. Stanko's had *none,* the witness emphasized.

"We can see particularly right here," Dr. Sachy said, pointing to the darkness and shadows that were Stanko's frontal lobes, "he's less functional as compared to a normal brain."

Those lobes were inactive, leaving him with diminished impulse control, he explained. There was also a matter of weight. If you removed Stanko's brain and weighed it, you'd find his brain weighed less.

"Why is that?"

"Because his brain has too much water in it."

"You say the defendant's brain weighs less than the normal brain—but what about its size?"

"It is smaller. He has a condition known as hypofrontality. He has a decreased function in the medial orbital frontal lobes of his brain."

"How small?"

"His left frontal lobe was in the smallest two to three percent of the population."

"Could you explain the significance of that in terms the jury could understand, Doctor?"

"Sure. It is this frontal area of the brain that makes us essentially human, prevents us from bad behavior, from being impulsive and aggressive. Because of brain damage, he cannot control his impulses when he becomes angry."

The doctor pointed at the center of his own forehead. "My brakes are right here."

People with damage to the frontal lobe of their brain, Dr. Sachy explained, were prone to fits of anger and violence. Due to brain damage, the "emergency brakes" between impulse and action are missing.

"Because of Mr. Stanko's frontal-lobe damage, he lacks the ability to appreciate the difference between right from wrong, predisposing him to psychopathic behavior."

"What, if any, are your conclusions regarding the functionality of Steve's brain?"

"I'm one hundred percent sure that his brain is just not working right."

"Your diagnosis?"

"He is a psychopath."

"Does he choose to be that way?"

"No. Neither Mr. Stanko nor the other psychopaths I've examined have ever made a conscious decision to be psychopathic. It is a malady that has been forced upon them by bad luck, or God, or genes, or what have you."

"He was insane?"

"He met the moral and legal definition of insanity. It's my opinion that Mr. Stanko had diminished capacity twenty-four/seven, but at the time of this act, he was beyond that. He was insane."

"Yet, he is an intelligent man?"

"Oh yes. His IQ is one forty-three."

"That classifies him as a genius?"

"Yes, but it is entirely possible for a person to be intellectually smart, yet still exhibit mental problems beyond human control."

"How long would you estimate Mr. Stanko has suffered from damaged frontal lobes?"

The doctor said that Stanko's medical history showed that he'd suffered from brain problems since birth, nearly killing him as an infant. At that time, doctors documented that the defendant had "possible cranial damage."

The defendant's medical records were "crystal clear." There was "no question" that he was born with "some form of neurological dysfunction." He'd had a temporary blockage in his windpipe at birth—caused, according to his medical records, by "early vomiting"—and suffered from jaundice. Either could have been the culprit.

"It is interesting that they documented this in 1968 and not 1998," Dr. Sachy said. He noted that while Stephen appeared to develop normally through childhood and into adulthood, the key part of his brain affected by the oxygen deprivation during infancy did not. "Later, that same problem caused him to exhibit antisocial behavior as an adult. Those same problems prevented him from distinguishing right from wrong."

Asked to speak briefly as to the legal and medical history of PET scan technology, Dr. Sachy said PET scans were used during a criminal trial in New York in 1994, and had been used to diagnose brain damage and other illnesses since the 1970s.

"No further questions," William Diggs said.

"Mr. Hembree?" Judge Jefferson said, turning toward the solicitor's table.

"Thank you, Your Honor," Gregory Hembree said, and began his cross-examination by establishing that Dr. Thomas Sachy lacked board certification in forensic neurology, and that he worked predominantly in Georgia, where the standards for mental competency differed from those in South Carolina. Hembree argued that Stephen Stanko knew the difference between right and wrong as well as the next fellow, he just didn't care. He felt no inner conflict when doing bad things.

"There's a difference between mental problems and behavioral problems?"

"Yes."

"Isn't antisocial behavior a behavior and not a mental disease? What's the difference between this psychopath and that psychopath?" Hembree asked.

"You're right," Dr. Sachy said. "It's difficult to make that distinction."

"Dr. Sachy, you interviewed the defendant about his actions, did you not?"

"I did." Stephen Stanko, in fact, had given him details of the immediate buildup to the murder and rape. Stanko said he'd been planning to end his relationship with Laura Ling that night. He'd planned on moving out. He said that Ling's daughter was the one who threatened him. She said that she was going to expose him as a child molester. Laura became furious after hearing her daughter's accusations and attacked Stanko, slapping him and burning him with a cigarette.

"And then?"

"That was the last thing he remembered," Dr. Sachy said. "There was a period of amnesia. The next thing he remembered, he was showering, washing blood off."

Hembree made the witness admit that, on the night of the violence, Stanko's behavior remained cunning. He checked the pulse of both of his victims, and stole a bracelet right off the wrist of Laura Ling's remains. He packed his electric guitar before leaving. He went to an ATM and cleaned out Ling's account. Cunning, not crazy, right?

"Dr. Sachy, would you characterize the defendant as a killing machine? Stephen Stanko, he's a killing machine, right? He's a great white shark, right?"

A chorus of objections came from the defense table.

"Legally, he knows the difference between right and

wrong, but mentally, he doesn't care. Dr. Sachy, is it your position that persons diagnosed as psychopaths are not responsible for criminal acts?"

"That's a philosophical question," the witness replied. "If imagery from brain scans proves abnormalities, then yes, I believe that."

Hembree drew Dr. Sachy's attention to Stephen Stanko's infant medical reports. He'd earlier testified they indicated brain damage. But the witness had been selective, hadn't testified as to the contents of those records in their entirety. So now, to be fair, Hembree asked Dr. Sachy to read some passages from the records that he'd previously ignored.

"What does that say, Dr. Sachy?"

"'Neurological OK.'"

"'Neurological OK'?"

"Yes."

"Isn't that good news?"

"That's great news."

"That's great news! And the baby was released from the hospital two days later, wasn't he?"

"Yes."

"And you, Dr. Sachy, are a professional witness, are you not?"

"I wouldn't characterize myself that—"

"You are getting paid by the defense for your appearance today, isn't that correct? You are getting paid right now?"

"Yes."

"And, if I may ask, at what rate are you being paid?"

"Four hundred dollars an hour," Dr. Sachy said.

"Is there a ceiling on your fee?"

"Yes, up to forty thousand dollars."

"If you put in one hundred hours on this case, the defense pays you forty thousand dollars?"

"Yes."

Hembree seemed to be having fun as he cross-examined Dr. Sachy. He got the defense witness to say that he had testified in about fifty trials, and in all fifty, he had been a paid employee of the defense. Plus, in those fifty cases, he had never—never once—found a patient to be sane.

"No further questions," Hembree concluded with disdain.

Dr. Evelyn Califf, a Myrtle Beach family counselor, had been employed by the defense to examine Stephen Stanko's life and come up with factors that might help to explain Stephen Stanko's behavior. The defendant didn't just have organic damage, the defense wanted it to be known, but his nurturing environment contributed to his mental disease as well.

Dr. Califf pointed out that much of Stanko's family had turned their backs on him a long time ago. She added that Stanko was estranged from much of his family and hadn't spoken to his father in ten years.

Stephen Stanko's defense called Dr. James Thrasher, an older Myrtle Beach psychiatrist who established his expertise by pointing out that he was a professional in a variety of ways: doctor, lawyer, engineer. He testified that he had studied the defendant's medical records dating back to his birth. In addition to studying the defendant's past, Dr. Thrasher said he'd examined Stanko not long after the murders.

Thrasher supported the theory of the previous doctors, that Stanko had a diminished ability to resist the urge to kill because of his severe personality disorder and damaged frontal lobes.

Dr. Thrasher was a Rennaissance man, no doubt about that. He had delivered babies, and he'd been in the navy. "Everything but an Indian chief," Gregory Hembree later said.

Name it, and he was an expert in it. But what Dr. Thrasher wasn't was good at standing up under cross-examination. Hembree attacked.

Though Dr. Thrasher had done some ob-gyn work early on in his career, as all medical doctors do, that was not his specialty, was it? No. Despite that, he was the guy the defense picked to interpret the records of Stanko's *birth*, correct? Yes.

Dr. Thrasher acknowledged that Stanko did not show signs of mental problems during his youth, as one might expect when a brain injury was congenital, and that Stanko was raised in a "normal home," had played sports in school, had regularly dated, and was of above-average intelligence.

Stephen Stanko claimed during the interview that he'd suffered memory loss. The first thing he remembered after Laura Ling's murder was taking a shower. First he was covered with blood, and then he was clean and toweling himself off.

"Dr. Thrasher, did Stanko tell you his actions after his memory kick-started in the shower?"

"Yes, he did."

"What did he say he did?"

"He said he was very concerned about the condition of his victims. He tried to find a pulse in both victims but couldn't."

"He thought they were both dead?"

"Yes."

Hembree also made Dr. Thrasher admit that—despite Stanko's claim that he was in la-la land during his violent spree, with a memory that blinked in and out—he was cool and cunning enough to steal a bracelet, $700 in cash, and a red Mustang.

"These appeared to be steps taken in a sequential fashion by somebody who knows they did something substantially bad," Hembree said. "Wouldn't you agree with that, Dr. Thrasher?"

"It appears that way," the witness replied.

Hembree made Dr. Thrasher refer to the defendant's medical history—again and again—looking for any mention of brain abnormalities. Hembree also cited specific points in the medical records in which doctors said baby Stanko's condition was improving.

"You don't have a record of brain abnormalities, do you?" Hembree asked.

"Only a suspicion," Dr. Thrasher replied.

"According to the records, the baby was getting better, isn't that right?"

"It appears that way," Dr. Thrasher said.

"How much is the defense paying you for your testimony?"

"One hundred fifty dollars an hour," Dr. Thrasher replied.

Hembree later characterized James Thrasher's appearance on the witness stand as disastrous for the defense. While being grilled by the solicitor, he needed to refer to notes. He couldn't get through a statement without misspeaking. That resulted in frustration that further diminished his impression on the jury. After a time, he appeared wound "tight as a tick" on the stand.

Gregory Hembree's favorite moment came when he approached the witness stand and was helping Dr. Thrasher find his spot in a document they were discussing. One page brushed up against Thrasher's arm and he almost jumped out of his seat.

"He looked like I'd just hit him with a Taser," Hembree

said. To make matters worse for himself, he complained to the judge that the solicitor had struck him with the paper, which made some in the courtroom laugh at the poor guy.

On that negative point, the defense rested.

The prosecution called a rebuttal witness, Dr. William Brannon Jr., who informed the jury that he had received his M.D. degree at the Medical University of South Carolina in 1961. He served residencies at the U.S. Naval Hospital in Bethesda, Maryland, in 1962, and the Georgetown University Medical Center in Washington, D.C., in 1965. He was a distinguished professor of neuropsychiatry and behavioral science, with special interests in clinical neurology, headache, stroke, movement disorders, and epilepsy. He had served on the faculty of the University of South Carolina School of Medicine since 1980. Dr. Brannon's job was to disagree with every scrap of Dr. Thomas Sachy's testimony. He said that Dr. Sachy was reading the PET scan wrong for one thing, that Stephen Stanko's PET scan showed *normal* brain activity.

"His data is faulty from the start," Dr. Brannon said. "He based his study on *forty-one* people." His intonations made it clear that he found this a ridiculously small sample. Dr. Brannon had looked at Stanko's PET scans and found them "perfectly normal."

BACK PAGES

On the morning of Friday, August 11, 2006, with the jury out of the courtroom, Judge Deadra Jefferson asked the defendant if he planned to directly address the jury during the closing arguments of the trial.

Stephen Stanko said he did not, but he added that he had a few questions he'd like to ask the court. "My questions concern the four possible outcomes you said the jury should pick from—guilty, guilty but mentally ill, not guilty by reason of insanity, and not guilty."

"Go ahead," Judge Jefferson said.

"We have never said I was guilty but mentally ill. There is no treatment in the system for a person who is convicted of that," Stanko said.

"I can't change the jury's options," Judge Jefferson explained. "State law says that it is mandatory that we offer that to the jury."

Stanko reiterated that at no time did he plan to speak in front of the jury.

"All right, let's bring them back in," Judge Jefferson said. The panel resumed its position along the wall, and closing arguments began, starting with Fran Humphries, the deputy solicitor, speaking on behalf of the people.

Fran Humphries led with a subject that had gone largely unspoken during the trial. The Lolita factor. Was Stephen Stanko a pedophile? Did he premeditate raping Penny?

"Where did it begin?" Humphries asked. "Did it begin when the defendant and the victim just met? Did it begin after he moved in? Did it begin night after night when he watched that young girl go to her bedroom? When did his thoughts turn to lust?"

The jury looked at photos of the teenager's battered face.

"Is there any doubt of the defendant's guilt of assault and battery with intent to kill? Is there any doubt that the girl succumbed to the assault while unlawfully confined? There is no question. None."

He asked the jury if any of them really believed that, as the defense maintained, the defendant had a mental disease or defect that prevented him from knowing right from wrong, and reminded them that they'd heard testimony from a forensic psychologist stating that Stanko did not have a mental defect, but rather a personality disorder—and bad, bad personality was simply *not* a legitimate criminal defense.

Did Stanko know right from wrong? Here was a man who robbed his victims blind and then partied hardy in Columbia and Augusta before his capture.

Was he legally insane? Here was a man who called his victim's boss and said she wouldn't be in that day because she'd eaten a bad clam the night before.

"The defendant was clearly trying to cover up for something *he knew was wrong,*" Humphries said.

Humphries referenced the defense witnesses who had testified that Stanko was insane. "How convenient a standard that is," he said. "If your conduct gets really bad, you are insane. When I am really, really bad, when I am evil, you can't hold that against me."

He knew the jury could see through the defense's medical smoke screen, see the truth: "Stephen Stanko is antisocial. He's mean. He's narcissistic. He wants what he wants *when he wants it*. He has the ability to conform his conduct, but what's to gain from that? He is not insane."

During his closing, Bill Diggs characterized his client as a man "forsaken by his family," a man who hadn't talked to his father for more than a decade, who would probably never talk to his father again.

"What is more telling than for Stephen to be rejected by his own family?" Diggs asked the jury. "He grew up with these people. He loves these people."

Diggs described his client as a man who was "a victim of brain abnormalities." Stephen Stanko's condition could be compared to a patient with Alzheimer's disease, in that he "couldn't control himself" when he murdered and raped.

"He was insane, and that is the only verdict that is justified by the evidence in this case."

Diggs stood beside a TV screen that showed the PET scan of Stanko's brain and his visibly inactive frontal lobes. In case the jury didn't quite get it, there was also a PET scan of a normal brain, frontal lobes *glowing* with conscience and inhibition.

Because of a frontal-lobe defect, Diggs said in his final argument, his client lacked the ability to control his limbic system, his "fight or flight" emotions. Maybe it was jaundice, maybe the early vomiting. Oxygen supply was diminished causing a variety of lifelong brain difficulties.

Diggs summed up, "The only explanation is insanity. You can see it in his birth records. The brain controls our conduct. It's that simple. It's not hard to understand. His brain made him do it. It's on its own. Just goes and does things. And while I'm over here, my brain's out running around, murdering and raping people."

Diggs again pointed to his own brow, reminding the jury that this insanity defense wasn't a last-ditch effort, wasn't just a load of psychobabble, but also had a measurable—indeed, photographable—physical component. "That's where the brain defect, the mental defect, is," Diggs said. "That's where the ability to distinguish between right and wrong is. He doesn't have the brain function to do that, to make that distinction."

TWO HOURS IN
JURY ROOM #1

Judge Deadra Jefferson addressed the jury, explaining that the time for deliberation had arrived, and that they were to choose one from four possible verdicts: guilty, guilty but mentally ill, not guilty by reason of insanity, and not guilty.

She instructed the jury that in order for Stephen Stanko to be found not guilty by reason of insanity, the defense had to demonstrate "by a preponderance of the evidence" that Stanko had a mental disease or defect that rendered him unable to distinguish right from wrong.

She dismissed the two alternate jurors, thanking them for their service and apologizing that, after all their hard work, they did not get to deliberate with the others.

The jury retreated to Jury Room #1 and took only two hours to reach its verdict. The only interruption came when they sent a note to Judge Jefferson asking her to define "guilty but mentally ill." Everyone assumed their normal positions in the courtroom, the judge last to enter. Law enforcement was present and alert. Verdicts were emotional moments.

Judge Jefferson called for the jury and the twelve jurors filed in. The foreperson, a diminutive African-American woman, wasted no time reading the decision.

"'*The State of South Carolina* versus *Stephen Christopher Stanko,* as to count one, we the jury by unanimous consent find the defendant guilty." Stanko stood motionless with his hands clasped in front of him as the verdict was read. There was emotion in the courtroom—a sign of relief, a relaxing of the shoulders, knowing it was over—but it was quiet and subdued.

The defense immediately moved for the routine bench ruling regarding Stanko's sanity. Judge Jefferson promptly upheld the jury's decision, saying, "There is sufficient evidence in the record that Stanko was sane."

William Diggs asked the judge for a new trial. The jury needed one of the charges *defined* during their brief deliberations. That was a solid indication that they were confused.

Judge Jefferson said it was no such thing. It was a sign they were careful, not confused, and denied Diggs's motion. She reminded the fulminating jurors that the penalty phase still lay ahead, and that they were to return following the mandatory cooling-off period. The judge pounded her gavel and court was adjourned.

Still holding her teddy bear, Penny Ling hugged her family members and then walked over to the prosecution table to give a hug to the solicitor and his assistants.

Outside the courthouse, Gregory Hembree was asked about the death sentence. He said, "We've already won. Stephen Stanko is never going to be a free man. He may victimize someone in the prison system, but he'll never victimize another free citizen."

Penny's dad, Chris Ling, told one reporter that Penny

was his hero. He called Stanko a coward and a bully. That was the reason he was a model prisoner during his previous incarceration. He lacked the *nads* to stand up to someone his own size.

Chris Ling applauded the jury for putting aside all of the psychological mumbo jumbo to get to the crux of the matter.

Another reporter asked Penny if she was bothered by the fact that Stanko never apologized to her for what he had done. She shook her head no, saying she was "beyond an apology." She couldn't say she'd ever be able to forgive what Stanko did to her mother, but she did forgive him for what he did to her. She refused to go through her life with hate in her heart, never able to move on.

TO LET DIE

On August 15, 2006, the parties met in court without the jury to set up the ground rules for the penalty phase of the trial. William Diggs moved that no testimony regarding the murder of Henry Lee Turner be allowed, that this case was about the Lings alone. Evidence regarding the shooting of the man in Conway would be prejudicial to the jury.

Argument ensued and Judge Deadra Jefferson said she was going to need time before announcing her decision. She said that previous South Carolina Supreme Court decisions had allowed such evidence because the burden of proof was less strict in the sentencing phase. "Case law seems to offer that the purpose is not to introduce guilt. The supreme court seems to indicate it is relevant to his character," Judge Jefferson said.

Among the scheduled prosecution witnesses were relatives of Henry Lee Turner, as well as Horry County police officers who had investigated the Turner murder. And, Gregory Hembree added, he wanted to show the jury photos taken at the Turner crime scene, including those showing the victim facedown on the mobile home's floor.

Hembree argued that the jury needed the complete picture: "Stanko knew exactly what he was doing and why he was doing it."

Arguing for the defense was Gerald Kelly, who pointed out that since Stephen Stanko had never been convicted of murdering Turner, he was, according to the law, presumed innocent of that crime. Kelly said that it had not even been proven that Turner *was* murdered, and that allowing the Turner evidence would "virtually guarantee" that his client would be sentenced to death. "If you want to hang him out to dry, then that's what will happen," Kelly continued. "No human force can stop it if this is allowed. What kind of foolishness is this? The solicitor is going to stampede the jury into believing Stanko killed Henry Lee Turner. You can't take the quack out of a duck."

Judge Jefferson eventually said she did not want to create a record that might have an effect on a subsequent murder trial in Horry County. The Turner stuff was out. She then called the jury into the courtroom and explained that they had to sit through what amounted to a second trial, with opening statements, testimony by witnesses on either side, and closing arguments. They were to determine if the defendant should be executed or receive life imprisonment without hope of parole. If they chose death, Judge Jefferson noted, "your decision must be a unanimous one."

In his opening statement before the jury, Hembree said, "Justice is the very last thing that the defendant wants—and justice in this case is to sentence Stephen Stanko to death."

* * *

Kathleen "Kelly" Crolley then testified that she worked in Surfside at her family's furniture store, and Stephen Stanko came into the store in 2004 and looked at desks for his wife. He said they were building a house on Pawleys Island. As he was browsing, he received several calls on his cell phone.

"Could you hear his side of the conversation?" asked Hembree.

"I could. I gathered from what I heard that he was collecting money for some sort of charity."

"Did you ask him about his charity work?"

"Yes. When he got off the phone, I asked him about it. He told me he had a young niece with cancer, and she was hospitalized at the Medical University of South Carolina."

Crolley told Stanko that she had a soft spot in her heart for that hospital. Her baby was born prematurely there, and everyone did a great job.

He told her that he'd taken a year off from his job as a lawyer to start the "Children's Cancer Research Foundation." He didn't buy any desks, but the store ended up giving him a hundred dollars and she gave him another twenty-five.

"What, if anything, did you subsequently learn about the Children's Cancer Research Foundation?"

"I learned that he made it up, that it never existed," Crolley testified.

Regarding her role at the trial, Crolley later remembered, "My little part seemed so insignificant." She was there to tell the jury what a snake Stanko was, capable of exploiting children's cancer.

For the penalty phase, the defense once again brought in its panel of legal experts, including the doctors

James Thrasher and Thomas Sachy, who repeated their theories.

The defense then offered numerous blasts from Stephen Stanko's past in their attempt to demonstrate that his life was worth saving. It was like an episode of *This Is Your Life*. Stanko appeared downright entertained as "blasts from his past" took turns testifying.

The nostalgia program began with three Goose Creek High School employees. On crutches, with a cast on his leg, Gerald Kelly did the questioning. First witness was John H. Fulmer, who had also been the defendant's assistant principal and football coach.

Fulmer described Stanko as a good high-school student who didn't have a behavior problem. To demonstrate how normal Stanko was, photos from his senior yearbook were shown to the jury.

There was Stanko with the homecoming queen. There he was with the Odyssey of the Mind, the school's science club.

William Diggs showed the jury a newspaper clipping about that club. They'd taken first place in a local competition. (Stanko smiled with nostalgia when viewing those photos.)

Academics? Stanko scored 1120 on the SAT, belonged to several academic clubs—*and* had no disciplinary history. Fulmer called the defendant "beneficial to the school" and "a model student."

Referring to the yearbook, which the defense attorney still held, the man said, "I can go through that yearbook and pick four or five people that I thought would have been trouble—but not him. He was a well-dressed, good-looking guy, even in high school. He was never in trouble. He was not a loner but a popular guy. There were no oddities. He didn't fit the profile of a student headed for trouble."

Stanko was a member of the Beta Club, which required its members to be honest, just, cooperative, responsible, industrious, humble, and charitable.

"Beta Club people don't usually go to jail," the principal added. "If Stephen had stayed the way he was in high school, he would have been a successful college student with a good career. He was in the top twenty-five in his class."

Stanko's old chemistry and physics teacher, Clarice Wenz, verified for the defense that she was a onetime Teacher of the Year winner, who'd also received a Sigma Xi award for teaching chemistry. Regarding Stanko, Wenz said, to the best of her recollection, she met him when he was a junior. Maybe he was a sophomore, but she was pretty sure he was a junior. She'd been his teacher, yes, but she really got to know Stephen better when she sponsored the Odyssey of the Mind team, the one that won the local contest and went to the state competition. He'd been over to her house. He was typical of your brighter-than-average and better-looking students. There was no indication that he would ever do anything negative.

Kelly handed Wenz a note and asked her if she recognized it. She did. It was a note written by Stephen and some of his friends back in the day, expressing appreciation for her efforts.

"Could you read the note aloud, please?"

"Certainly."

Gregory Hembree could have easily stopped this process, objecting to the fact that, through the note, the defendant was being given the opportunity to testify without the risk of cross-examination. But the solicitor held his tongue. He didn't think *This Is Your Life* was hurting his case. It didn't matter what Stanko *was*. It was what he'd *become*: a monster who needed to be put down.

After reading the note, Wenz continued praising Stanko. It wasn't just that he was smart. He was a hard worker as well. He hardly ever goofed off, had tremendous potential, and could have gone into any field he wished. She said Stanko was "a student who not only stood out for his achievements at school, but also in the way he interacted with me and his peers." He got along, too. He had many friends, and he worked well with others, both when it came to schoolwork and extracurriculars.

"Did you ever meet Stephen's parents?"

"No, I never did."

"Never?" Kelly sounded incredulous.

"No."

Hembree had one question in cross-examination: "Was there any indication that the defendant was mistreated at home?"

"Oh no," Wenz said. "He had good manners and was polite. He seemed well brought up."

The third Goose Creek High School witness was attendance clerk Wanda Brooks, who had lived right across the street from the Stankos on Kenilworth Road. Stephen visited her house as a kid so often that he felt like he was one of her own. She said he was very friendly and outgoing.

"How would you describe the house that Stephen grew up in?" Kelly asked.

"Very unfriendly. I talked to his mother sometimes outside."

"What was it like inside the house?"

"I didn't go inside the house very much," Brooks said.

In an apparent attempt to blame Georgetown County for the murder and mayhem at the Ling residence, Pam

Harrelson was called to the witness stand and described herself as a former employee of the South Carolina Department of Parole, Probation and Pardon Services. She testified that when the defendant was released from prison in 2004, he was supposed to report monthly to the agency's office in Conway. Stephen Stanko complied until December 2004, missed his January 2005 meeting, and did not report after that.

"Ms. Harrelson, did your office receive any complaints about Stanko's behavior following his 2004 release from prison?" Gerald Kelly asked.

"Yes. There were several calls."

"And what was done in response to those complaints?"

"I believe that, according to our policy, those complaints were referred to the police."

"Do you recall the name of the person making those complaints?"

"Yes, her name was Connie Price."

Connie Price took the stand and testified that she was from Socastee, South Carolina, and had been a frequenter of the Socastee library, where Laura Ling worked, in 2005.

As recently as two days before Laura Ling's murder, Price had been making phone calls complaining about Stephen Stanko's "bizarre behavior."

Although it was true that she never filed an actual incident report until *after* the murder, Price had spoken in person, two days before Laura Ling's death, to a Myrtle Beach police officer about scams she thought Stanko was running. She could tell the officer was not impressed by her story because he took very few notes. She told the cop that Stanko was posing as an attorney, and had conned her out of money by agreeing to, for a fee, help her with a medical malpractice suit. "Plus, he was acting erratically," Price concluded.

"What did you mean by 'erratically'?" Gerald Kelly inquired.

"He told me wild lies. Like he said that he was bringing in big guns to help me with my lawsuit. He said he was on his way to meet (former North Carolina senator and vice presidential candidate) John Edwards, and he was waiting on a package for me. He said (*60 Minutes* correspondent) Mike Wallace was going to help."

Price paid him close to $1,000 in legal fees before realizing he was "the biggest con artist in the world." She told the jury that "the straw that broke the camel's back" came when Stanko told her he needed to "get inside my house because he needed to check my wiring and make sure it was up to code."

"What did you think about that?" Kelly asked.

"I thought he was crazy."

She said that she called many agencies—Horry County police, Horry County Solicitor's Office, SLED, the Drug Enforcement Agency, the FBI, and the U.S. Marshals—complaining about Stanko, but none of them seemed able to focus on her.

"I was getting the runaround," she concluded.

"Did anyone ever get back to your complaint?"

"No, sir."

Price's testimony, William Diggs felt, helped his case in a couple of ways, not just that the authorities had multiple reasons to get Stephen Stanko off the streets before he began his violent spree, but also Stanko had demonstrated mental difficulties during the buildup to that spree.

* * *

Reinforcing Connie Price's charges that no one was focusing on the defendant's growing menace was the testimony of former assistant solicitor Karen Sauls. After a rundown of who she was—poli-sci degree from North Carolina State University in 1997, law degree from Saint Louis University in 1992, now assistant district solicitor—she testified that assistant solicitors were not intended to be investigators. If Connie Price had a complaint about Stephen Stanko, the police were the people she needed to contact.

U.S. Marshal Thedus Mayo testified that she had contacted Pam Harrelson at the parole board regarding complaints about Stanko. Harrelson told her that warrants were typically issued only when there were serious breaches of parole conditions, such as when parolees absconded. Stanko's failure to report, Harrelson told Mayo, was merely a "technical violation."

During the conference to determine the appropriate jury charges for the penalty phase, Judge Jefferson informed both sides that she intended to charge the jury on two statutory mitigating factors. William Diggs did not request a charge on any additional mitigating factors—in particular a consideration of "the age or mentality of the defendant at the time of the crime"—and told Judge Jefferson that he had no objection to the jury charges.

Diggs argued before the jury one last time, trying to save his client's life. He repeated his earlier statement that institutionalization often had a positive effect on psychopaths. The last time Stephen Stanko was in prison, he had written a book. He could be a leader in prison. "Stephen could be a good inmate. With his intelligence, he could help other inmates."

* * *

On Friday, August 18, 2006, after another two hours
of deliberation, the jury gave word that they were
through. Judge Deadra Jefferson called them into the
courtroom and they took their positions in the jury box.

"Has the jury reached a decision?" Judge Jefferson
asked.

"We have, Your Honor," the forewoman said.

"The defendant will, please, stand for the publication
of the jury's verdict," the judge instructed.

Stanko rose to his feet.

The forewoman said, *"The State of South Carolina,
Georgetown County,* versus *Stephen Christopher Stanko,* recommendation of sentence, death penalty."

Judge Jefferson took the jury's recommendation and
sentenced Stephen Stanko to death. The judge also
sentenced Stanko to 110 years in prison on the other
charges, including criminal sexual conduct, kidnapping,
and armed robbery.

Stanko was deadpan.

William Diggs asked the court to set aside the verdict
and allow Stanko to be tested further for his condition,
adding, "It's beyond a doubt that Mr. Stanko has this
particular brain defect. It would be fundamentally unfair
to go ahead with his execution."

Judge Jefferson explained that the prosecution in this
case, as well as the court, agreed from the start of proceedings that Stanko's mental state was a question of fact
for the jury. There had been plenty of time for tests,
tests, and more tests.

"It really came down to who the jury believed," the
judge added. "Did they believe the state's experts, or the
defense's experts? There is no need for any more testing
of Mr. Stanko." The defense case had demonstrated

that Stanko already had been examined by a slew of physicians and scientists. "I can't imagine anyone else who would test him," the judge concluded.

Stephen Stanko's execution was originally scheduled for October 17, 2007, but that date would be set aside because of Stanko's appeals process, and the fact that he still faced trial for the murder of Henry Lee Turner.

Gregory Hembree, glowing with his victory, fielded questions from reporters, saying he felt the death penalty was the appropriate sentence in this case. "I wouldn't have sought it if we didn't believe in it," the solicitor said.

Asked how long he felt Stanko had to live, he said it would be for quite a while. Appeals could take years. "Typically, it lasts between six and eight years," he added.

No, he didn't think the jury ever took Stanko's insanity defense seriously. "He knew what he was doing. He wasn't just some loony tune who didn't know what he was doing."

Also "doing press," although far more emotionally, was Chris Ling, cheeks wet with tears, telling reporters that he had learned three important lessons during the trial: "Number one, the process works. We'll be putting down a man who victimized old men and little girls. Number two, our probation system needs a total overhaul. It needs to be totally reviewed. And three, I've got the greatest daughter in the world, and I love her. Thank you," Ling said.

"What was the hardest part for you?" asked Michael Smith, of the *Horry Independent*.

"I think that came on the first day of the trial. To see

him uncuffed and wearing street clothes. It was hard for me to not get closer and closer to him," Ling replied.

About half of the jurors made themselves available for interview after the penalty phase. They were all not only at ease with their decision, but enthusiastic about it. The man was guilty and he deserved execution. None of them would lose sleep over it.

Did they buy into the defense's medical witnesses at all? No way. One male juror explained what it was like to hear the defense's scientific theories. He felt "dazzled with brilliance, and baffled with bs." A female juror said she felt it was possible for a man to do these heinous things and *not* be insane. Another male juror characterized Stanko as "worse than a monster," a guy who "had everyone conned." What about the testimony that he'd had brain damage from the time he was a baby? They didn't believe a word of it. "He was temporarily insane when he wanted to be temporarily insane" was how one put it.

The jurors agreed that the witness who most influenced them was Penny Ling. The teenager's words were something they never would be able to forget. She communicated how brutal, vile, and disgusting the attack had been. One male juror said that listening to the 911 tape was one of the hardest things he'd ever done. The little girl calling for her mommy. It brought tears to his eyes. A female juror noted that even though Laura Ling had not been around to testify, they felt like she was. Dr. Collins's testimony, and her drawn diagram of Laura Ling—with all of the wounds clearly marked—made it seem as if the victim was testifying from the grave, telling the jurors what a monster Stanko was.

* * *

Anyone who was used to watching murder trials on TV, such as trials involving celebrities in California, might have expected to see Stephen Stanko's trial go on for many weeks, if not months.

But that was not the way things were done in South Carolina.

"I've never seen a quicker slam-bang job in my entire life," recalled Dr. Gordon Crews, who was there for all of it. "One week, *boom*, guilty. One week, *boom*, death. Over. That's South Carolina justice, man. It was cold and quick."

Just the way the taxpayers like it.

Outside the courtroom, a reporter found Laura Ling's mother, Sue Hudson, who was in town from Garland, Texas, to see justice done. Asked what she thought of the sentencing, Hudson said she was "tickled to death" that Stephen Stanko was getting the death penalty.

APPEAL

Up until the late 1900s, South Carolina executions were carried out by the same staff that manned death row, forcing state executioners to kill men they had grown to know. In the modern system, separate staffs tended to the prisoners and executed them, and there were fewer debilitating cases of depression to worry about.

From 1912 to 1990, South Carolina's death row was at the Central Correctional Institution in Columbia. From 1990 to 1997, it was at the Broad River Correctional Institution, before moving to its current location.

Following his sentencing, Stephen Stanko was sent to live on death row in the Lieber Correctional Institution in Ridgeville.

Executions were carried out at the Broad River Capital Punishment Facility, the state's only death house. Since 1912, South Carolina had executed prisoners in the electric chair. A fourteen-year-old black male once took the long walk—but that was ancient history now.

Prisoners on death row for crimes committed before 1995 had a choice: the electric chair or lethal injection?

If they refused to pick, they got the chair. The last prisoner to go out crackling and smoking died in 2008.

Criminals whose crimes came after 1995 received the lethal injection, which was administered in the same area as the electric chair. Even those who got the shot saw "Ol' Sparky," looking like a terrifying Grand Guignol set piece, just before they died.

Three members of the media would be allowed to witness Stanko's death—one print, one electronic, one wire service. Three members of the victim's family could be there.

Also allowed to watch Stanko die would be a man or woman of the cloth, a lawyer representing the rights of the prisoner, and Gregory Hembree, the solicitor who earned Stanko's conviction.

Perhaps it was a good thing that an obligatory marathon of legal activity preceded an execution. DNA testing proved that sometimes the system got it wrong.

Executions now occurred in South Carolina between once and three times a year. So it was par for the course that Stanko didn't figure to die any day soon. Before South Carolina could make plans to off him, there was a plethora of legal business to tend to, most of it in Horry County where Stanko's responsibility for the Turner murder remained unresolved.

At the end of the summer of 2007, Stephen Stanko had his first appellate hearing in a Columbia, South Carolina, courtroom. His appellate attorneys were Kathrine Haggard Hudgins and Joseph L. Savitz III, both assistant appellate defenders for the South Carolina Commission on Indigent Defense.

Savitz—B.A. in English from Clemson, 1977, J.D. from the University of South Carolina School of Law—

had been one of the defenders since 1982, and he specialized in death penalty cases. Hudgins, who went to the
same law school, earned her B.A. at the College of
Charleston. Hudgins proved to be a woman who, when
given a choice, always chose both. She had a bundle of
experience working both sides, as both an assistant solicitor and as a public defender. She also had a private
practice that handled crime cases, both state and federal, and at both the trial and appellate level. Into jour-
nalism, too, she served on the criminal law committee,
and the editorial board for the renowned *South Carolina
Lawyer* magazine.

In March of 2008, Savitz and Hudgins argued that
Stephen Stanko didn't get a fair trial because, during
voir dire, the judge wouldn't allow potential jurors their
opinion on the insanity defense, and she had failed to in-
struct the jury on an additional and unrequested statutory mitigating circumstance during the penalty phase.
Regarding voir dire, the supreme court noted that when
Judge Deadra Jefferson refused to allow William Diggs
to question potential jurors regarding their feelings
specifically on the insanity defense, Diggs had stated for
the record that he was "abandoning" that line of questioning. Therefore, no issue was preserved for appellate review, since the objecting party accepted the court's
ruling and did not contemporaneously make an additional objection. In order for Judge Jefferson's ruling
during voir dire to constitute a reversible error, the lim-
itation she placed on questioning must have rendered
the trial fundamentally unfair, and that was not the case.
In fact, the court characterized the voir dire as impartial
and unbiased.

The supreme court voted four-to-one in favor of denying the new trial. Chief Justice Jean Hoefer Toal wrote
that the jury process was fair because *the qualified jurors*

were impartial, unbiased and capable of following the law.
There was no indication that the trial had been rendered fundamentally unfair by the court's limitations on
voir dire. The lone dissenting vote came from Justice
Costa Pleicones, who maintained that Stanko's attorneys
should have been able to "probe jurors' bias" with respect to the insanity defense.

Disappointed, Savitz said he would appeal to the U.S.
Supreme Court, adding, "People that don't think insanity is a defense aren't qualified to sit on the jury. We
don't know if we got twelve jurors who just don't think
insanity is a defense, thought he was insane but thought
that was all the more reason to give him the death
penalty."

Connie Price, the woman who tried to report Stephen
Stanko to the authorities just days before the murders,
was contacted not long after the trial by Los Angeles television producer and author Larry Garrison, president
of SilverCreek Entertainment.

Garrison told her he wanted to write a book and produce a feature film on how she "eluded" Stanko and
later testified against him.

When Kelly Marshall Fuller, of the Myrtle Beach *Sun
News,* contacted Garrison, he admitted that he had books
and feature films in the works on a number of subjects,
including Michael Jackson (who was alive then) and
the L.A. murder of Bonny Lee Bakley.

Stephen Stanko was noteworthy enough for CBS to
dedicate an entire episode (January 13, 2007) of its *48
Hours* program to him. Troy Roberts, a network investigator, spent days interviewing Stanko, trying to find out

what made him tick. Stanko made a very strong first impression on Roberts. He had manners, looks, and smarts. It didn't seem at first to Roberts that Stanko was capable of depraved deeds. And that was what made the story so compelling.

One of the key witnesses interviewed by CBS was Dr. Thomas Sachy, who explained that he "took on" the Stephen Stanko case because from all of the things he'd read in the literature—in the news articles regarding his capture and what he had done—Stanko was probably a psychopath. He described PET technology and how cool and shriveled Stanko's frontal lobes were.

In response, Gregory Hembree was concise. "Junk science," he said.

Not all of the trial's participants watched the *48 Hours* episode on Stanko, and some skipped it even during an encore appearance. "I have had three or four people tell me they saw me on the *48 Hours* episode, but I missed it both times," Kelly Crolley said.

On Friday, March 16, 2007, Stephen Stanko's mother, Joan, passed away at the age of seventy-two in Summerville Medical Center.

Two and a half months later, Penny Ling, now seventeen, graduated with honors from Dutch Fork High School, home of the Silver Foxes, in Irmo, South Carolina. The Associated Press covered the event, and Penny repeated for them that she didn't mind being identified in the media. She hoped her openness and her story would help other assault victims.

She said, "If there's anything I can do to show anyone who's ever been the victim of domestic violence, or who's been through something similar, that you can piece your life together, even at fifteen. You can make something out of this."

Asked her plans, Penny said she was attending a nearby university that autumn. She said that every day she lived, every success she enjoyed, every accomplishment she achieved, was not just a reminder of her strength, but also a reminder of Stephen Stanko's weakness.

She smiled as she told the reporter she was a living example that he "failed at one of the last things he'll ever do."

In the days and weeks following Stanko's death sentence, Penny said, she closed the door on that chapter of her life. The day she walked out of that courtroom, after testifying, was the day he died as far as she was concerned.

"It's done," she said. "Even though he took my mom away, I'm probably the best representation of who my mom was. So in a way, she's still here."

SECOND TRIAL

Time passed. By June 2009, Stephen Stanko was appealing his conviction by claiming his trial lawyer was inadequate. *Despite this,* Stanko had no intention of switching lawyers for his second trial. William Diggs was his man—inadequate or not. Stanko's second death penalty trial, for the killing of Henry Lee Turner, was scheduled to begin November 9, 2009, in the Horry County Courthouse.

It would be the first capital case to be tried in Horry County since February 2008, when Louis "Mick" Winkler was accused of shooting to death his estranged wife, Rebekah Grainger, in her condo complex while he was free on bail and wearing an ankle bracelet, awaiting trial on charges that he'd kidnapped and raped her. After the shooting, Winkler fled on foot. A golf course employee on the job spotted a man in the woods off the fairway, and called 911 on March 20, 2006. The suspicious man was wearing torn clothes and was covered with dirt. He was chased through the woods near River Hills by police with dogs for three hours before he was captured. Jury selection for that headline-maker began on January

2008, and a pool of two hundred was needed to build a panel of twelve. Gregory Hembree had been representing the people at that one, too. The judge was James Lockemy, and the jury brought the verdict in late on a Saturday night. During the penalty phase, Hembree focused on the reasons they were seeking the death penalty. Hembree was on the record as feeling that only the "worst of the worst" killers should be executed, and he felt Winkler qualified. Here was a guy who killed a woman that he, in theory, had once been in love with, and why? To save his own skin! Colder than cold. Such depravity gave you the shivers.

In South Carolina, the death penalty was saved for cases with aggravating circumstances—say if the victim was a child, or a cop, or involving rape. In this case, the aggravating circumstance was that Winkler killed a witness against him of a previous crime. South Carolina was not quick to kill prisoners. Horry County had five men on death row during the Winkler trial; one had been there since 1996. Hembree thought the time between sentencing and execution should be cut. "There is room for reform," he said. "There are ways you can speed up the process." Reformation, he warned, shouldn't be reckless. There were people who thought the execution process wasn't punishment enough. The killers had an opportunity to say good-bye to their friends and loved ones, but the victims of their crimes did not. Some felt the defendant should be taken directly from the courtroom to the waiting needle. No stopping to pass Go or collect two hundred dollars. But that was the other extreme. Execution was *final,* so "it required a level of scrutiny on both sides," Hembree said. Following the penalty phase of Winkler's trial, the defendant turned to the jury and *begged* for his life. The jury deliberated twelve hours before returning with thumbs-down.

* * *

Now Gregory Hembree was eager to return to room 3B in the Horry County Courthouse and prepare to handle the special difficulties trying Stephen Stanko a second time would entail. The first trial had only made Stanko more notorious. An extraordinarily large sample of jury summonses and questionnaires were sent out in hopes of finding sixteen impartial jurors. Four and a half years had passed since Stanko's violent rampage. That helped the jury pool forget the case's vivid details.

On the downside, there was the matter of Stanko's name. "He has a unique name," Hembree said. "It's one [that] people remember because it is so different. If his name was Smith, people may not remember, but with a name like Stanko, they don't forget—so that doesn't help us."

The solicitor was fairly certain that an impartial jury could be found. He was encouraged by the fact that Georgetown County had done it only one year after the crimes. If Georgetown County could do it then, Horry County could do it now.

Presiding over the preliminary hearings, as well as the trial, was Fifteenth Judicial Circuit Court judge Steven H. John, who grew up in North Augusta, South Carolina, and graduated in 1975 from the Citadel, with a degree in political science. He earned his law degree three years later at the University of South Carolina School of Law and began his legal career as a law clerk for a judge. In 1986, he opened his own practice in North Myrtle Beach, and from 1993 through 2001, he was the pro bono lawyer for the Horry County Disabilities and Special Needs agency. He married Susan Watts John, who was the director of Family Services for that agency. In 2001, he was elected as resident circuit judge of the Fifteenth Judicial Circuit, a position he'd held ever since.

Judge John was no stranger to big-time murder cases. During the spring of 2008, he presided over the double-homicide trial of Richard Gagnon. (Gregory Hembree was the prosecutor in that one, too.) Gagnon was originally arrested with his girlfriend, Bambi Bennett, and they were charged with the 2005 murders of Diane and Charles Parker Sr., Bennett's mother and stepfather. Diane was found in the bedroom, Charles in the bathroom, both shot, the scene a bloody mess. Gagnon and Bennett had been an item for two years when the murders took place, and the Parkers were Gagnon's employers. Bambi spent six months in jail, but she was released before the trial because of "lack of DNA evidence" against her. Suspicion at first was that Bambi had traded freedom for cooperation, but in the long run, she didn't testify at the trial for either side. The state hardly had an airtight case against Gagnon, one drop of victim blood on otherwise clean sneakers, and a claim by one interrogator that Gagnon had told him things that "only the killer could know." Kept intentionally vague, these things apparently involved blood evidence at the crime scene from a third unnamed individual. To boost its case, the prosecution hauled out a jailhouse snitch. Gagnon's big defense witness was also a caged canary, a cell mate who said he sure acted innocent when first thrown in the can. The trial was covered live by truTV, and resulted in a conviction. Judge John sentenced Gagnon to life in prison, without chance of parole.

Now, at Stephen Stanko's October 8, 2009, hearing, Judge John heard twenty-three motions by Gregory

Hembree and William Diggs, setting up the ground rules for the trial.

Stanko, during his court appearances, would not be in handcuffs or leg shackles, unless his behavior dictated otherwise. The jury would be sequestered during the trial and guarded by SLED agents.

On the day before Halloween, Stanko was transferred from his home on death row in Ridgeville, South Carolina, to the J. Reuben Long Detention Center in Conway, where he would be caged for the duration of his trial.

The Horry County Courthouse was on Third Avenue in the heart of Conway. The redbrick building, with white trim and pillars, was more than twice the size of its counterpart in Georgetown County. Several additions at the sides and back had been put on since the courthouse opened in 1908. (The courthouse before that, built in the 1820s, was still there, just down the street, and served as the Conway Town Hall.) The "new" courthouse came with a large front lawn, protected by mature shade trees, and a long driveway leading to the front entrance, giving it a plantation in the Old South feel. The building figured to be a busy place, if everything went as scheduled. Two noteworthy trials were slated to begin more or less simultaneously, the other being that of Miles Ferguson, from Ohio, who was charged with homicide via child abuse in connection with the death of his five-week-old daughter in July 2007 as the family vacationed in Myrtle Beach. Also on trial in the second week of November was Rodell Vereen, who faced buggery charges in connection with sexual activity with a horse.

* * *

On Wednesday, November 4, 2009, there was a short competency hearing during which Judge Steven John asked the defendant a series of questions to determine if he could assist in his own defense and if he could identify the roles to be played in the proceedings by the judge, prosecutors, defense attorneys, and the jury. Stephen Stanko answered all of the questions correctly.

Forensic psychiatry expert Pamela Crawford had a lengthy interview with Stanko on Wednesday morning and advised the judge that she found him competent to stand trial. Crawford performed the same function before Stanko's Georgetown County trial.

Voir dire would begin the following Monday, with a jury pool of three hundred peers.

The defense, of course, sought to keep any mention of the first trial out of this one, and for the most part, Judge John ruled that evidence regarding the Ling crimes would prejudice the jury. However, he ruled that there would be *exceptions*. Evidence from the first trial would be allowed in during the penalty phase of this trial, if there was one. Also, in some cases, the defendant's mental state, as testified to during the first trial, would be allowed in. The details of the Ling attacks, though, would not be heard by the jury.

During the Saturday evening of August 15, 2009, the Marion County coroner ID'd a body plucked out of the Pee Dee River as fifty-six-year-old Horry County true-crime author William Dale Hudson. According to Hudson's wife, her husband left their home in Conway at eight in the morning, on Wednesday, August 12, on a business trip. Three hours later, he called and told her he had a migraine and was planning to pull over to the side of the road to rest. On Friday, Horry police found Hudson's car in a Marion County woods. On Saturday morning, August 15, Hudson's body was discovered by fishermen in the Pee Dee, two miles south of the U.S. 76 bridge. Among Hudson's books was *Dance of Death,* about a Myrtle Beach housewife and mother who was secretly a stripper with a boyfriend, and who, with her boyfriend, conspired to kill her husband. The book was published in 2006 by Pinnacle True Crime. His other works included *An Hour to Kill, Kiss and Kill,* and *Die, Grandpa, Die.* A member of his family said Hudson was working on a book about Stephen Stanko (unrelated to this book) at the time of his death.

On November 8, 2009, on the eve of Stephen Stanko's second murder trial, the South Carolina Law Enforcement Victim Advocate Association (LEVA) presented the Solicitor of the Year Award to Gregory Hembree. In accepting the award, Hembree stated that all the people in his office, regardless of their title, were in the business of helping victims through the criminal justice system.

This was the second big award that Hembree had received in the past few months. During the summer of 2009, he was recognized by the Association of Government Attorneys in Capital Litigation (AGACL) for excellence in prosecuting death penalty cases. Hembree, who had successfully prosecuted eight death penalty cases, was one of only six prosecutors in the country to get their award.

For Hembree, the season had not been all sunny. He lost his dad, Dr. John Hembree, who was seventy-two. The solicitor's dad was the dean of the School of Dentistry at the University of Mississippi from 1987 to 1992.

His father had also served twenty-nine years of active and reserve duty in the U.S. Army, retiring as a colonel.

On Monday morning, November 9, 2009, the process known in South Carolina as "striking a jury" began. In South Carolina, this was done in two steps. First jurors had to qualify to be on the jury. Voir dire proceeded until maybe forty potential jurors had qualified. Out of that group, the actual jurors and alternates were chosen.

Outside the courthouse, it looked like a cattle call for movie extras. Potential jurors were brought into the courtroom five at a time, and each one could be questioned individually by the lawyers for up to a half hour. Fifteen members of the jury pool were qualified on the first day, leading to optimism that there might be opening statements by the end of the week. To save money, everyone would work right through the weekend.

Each potential juror was questioned by the prosecution as to his or her death penalty beliefs. Gregory Hembree called it "exploring their feeling." He saw to it that any citizen who rejected capital punishment out of hand didn't find a place on the jury.

William Diggs, his gray ponytail even longer than at the first trial, concentrated his questions on how much knowledge each potential juror had regarding his client's background and alleged bad acts. Diggs eliminated the plethora of potential jurors who already thought Stanko guilty and were eager to see him executed.

On Tuesday, another twenty-five potential panelists endured the qualification process, but only seven of them were not sent home. On Wednesday, the court remained open despite the fact that it was Veteran's Day. By Thursday evening, jury qualification was through, and those forty-five were whittled down to sixteen on

Friday—Friday the Thirteenth. Six men, six women. All four alternates were female. Judge Steven John told the jurors and alternates that his already-existing gag order applied to them, too. They were not allowed to talk with anyone about the case. Estimates were that they would be sequestered and without their families for seven or eight days. During that time, they'd be staying in a hotel, and they would not be allowed to watch the news, use the Internet, or read a newspaper. Jurors would be allowed brief phone calls and visits with their loved ones, but these encounters would be closely monitored by both the sheriff's office and SLED.

Sheriff Phillip Thompson, who was also the president of the South Carolina Sheriffs' Association, told A. J. Ross, of WMBF-TV, that they were being particularly careful to keep outside influences from interfering with the jury's work. High-profile case, life at stake—everything needed to be done properly.

In cases tried before a sequestered jury, both prosecution and defense felt pressure to be efficient, to stay focused on the job at hand, and do their jobs "in a timely fashion."

Bill Diggs moved that this jury should be "thrown out" and replaced by another, from somewhere other than Horry County. In Horry, he said, emotions ran hot, and it would be impossible to get a fair trial. Half these jurors had prior knowledge of the case, having been exposed to both electronic and print reports, Diggs argued.

Judge John denied the motion.

As with Stephen Stanko's first trial, the folks who were scheduled to testify were corraled into a room and kept from observing the testimony that preceded theirs. Unlike the first witness room, there wasn't much laughter, nervous or otherwise. All the jokes were spent, leaving just a "dust in the sunbeam" tension, a teeth-grinding atmosphere.

As the trial began, a major storm descended upon the area and the entire proceedings took place during what some South Carolinians called the *worst weather ever.* Security checks were given to folks still a little drippy from the dash to the courthouse door.

Opening statements began just after noon.

Gregory Hembree said, "I'd like for you, the jury, to please use your common sense and judgment that will reach a verdict that speaks the truth. Use your common everyday abilities, reasoning abilities, for making any decisions, for making *this* decision. Common sense and good judgment—bring it into this courtroom. That's why we have a jury of our peers. That's why we don't have a jury of judges, or a jury of lawyers, or a jury of something else. We have a jury of citizens because we want the good common sense."

William Diggs rebutted Hembree's argument by telling the jury to focus on Stephen Stanko's mental state: "I don't want to say this, and I know it's going to sound wrong to my client because he's a human being, but he's not healthy. Period. We can show you that he is not healthy. The activity here"—Diggs pointed to the front of his head—"shows that he is not healthy."

Anyone expecting a new slant on things from Stanko's defense was disappointed with Diggs's opening statement. He hadn't altered his strategy very much from the first trial.

Steve Stanko, he said, suffered from a brain disorder that kept him from "maintaining relationships, holding a job, and analyzing things." This didn't mean Steve wasn't smart. In fact, he had a very high intelligence quotient. That fact was irrelevant. His problem was behavioral, not intellectual.

Referring to Stephen Stanko and Henry Lee Turner, Diggs said, "The evidence is going to show these two men were friends. There's no need to kill your friend. Mr. Turner's death is senseless. It's terrible. It's a tragedy."

By two o'clock, the first witness was called. It was established that at 3:22 A.M. on April 8, 2005, a telephone registered to Laura Ling was used to call Henry Turner's home.

One of Turner's neighbors testified to seeing Ling's car outside Turner's home on Kimberly Drive later on the morning of April 8.

Horry County police sergeant Jeff Gause testified that his agency received a call from Turner's son stating that Henry Turner was missing. He had missed a family dinner that day, which meant something was wrong. Arriving at the scene, Gause noted Ling's car out front. They also noted that Turner's pickup truck, which should have been there, was missing. A police log indicated that Gause was the thirteenth official to enter the crime scene. The first was Officer Thomas McMillan, who discovered the body, quickly followed by EMT officer Walter Gable. Gause may not have been in the top ten to arrive, but his observations carried the most weight, as it had been he who'd thoroughly photographed the victim's mobile home and later drew the police schematic of Turner's entire living space, including the position of Turner's body on his bedroom floor, with his feet in the threshold to the bathroom.

In addition to Turner's body, shot once each from the front and back, Gause also observed a pillow with gun residue on one side and blood on the other.

Gause testified that it appeared Turner had been shaving when the shooting occurred, because an electric razor was found near the body. Turner's body was found with the pants pockets turned inside out.

To establish that Stephen Stanko had stolen Henry Lee Turner's pickup and driven to Columbia, South Carolina, on April 8, the night of Turner's murder, the prosecution called a man named Ryan Coleman.

"What do you do for a living, Mr. Coleman?"

"I am a bartender at the Blue Marlin," the witness answered.

"In what town is that bar located?"

"Columbia."

"And you were working in that capacity on April 8, 2005?"

"Yes, sir."

Yes, on that evening, the defendant had come into his bar, and he'd spent a good deal more than the average customer. His tab came to $180, Coleman said, because in addition to drinks for himself, he was purchasing rounds for others as well.

When the Blue Marlin closed and it came time for the defendant to leave, Coleman testified, he'd given him $300, which was the bill *plus* a $120 tip. *Very* generous.

The witness admitted that after closing up the Blue Marlin, he joined the defendant at another bar, also in Columbia. Asked if anything out of the ordinary had occurred at the second bar, Coleman said it had. Stanko had been bragging to his drinking buddies all night that he was a "successful businessman." Finally he ran into a bar patron who didn't believe him. "Bullshit," the guy said. This stuck in the defendant's craw, Coleman said.

"He became irate?"

"I think 'irate' would be an understatement," Coleman said. "He was red-in-the-face mad." Coleman heard the defendant threaten the man who'd accused him of lying.

All eyes were on Dana Putnam as she entered the courtroom and walked to the front, where she promised to tell the whole truth. Her black hair was still up, just as it had been on the night she met Stephen Stanko. Wearing a baby blue sleeveless blouse and hoop earrings, she took the stand and testified that she had met the defendant on April 9, the day after his spending spree in Columbia bars. She told Gregory Hembree that her initial impression of Stanko was very positive.

"He was a very charming, very attractive, very smart, well-read, respectable guy," she said. He was wearing a pullover Hooters shirt, and he was *very* popular.

Part of his appeal to the bar crowd was the size of his wallet, which seemed to hold an endless amount of cash. He took her and her friends out to dinner. He bought drinks. On Sunday morning, he even went to church with her.

When Putnam asked Stanko where all of that cash came from, he told her the yarn he'd been spinning all weekend. He owned eight and co-owned nine Hooters franchises throughout the Southeast.

If it had been any other time of year, she might have questioned the truth of his tale, but it was Masters weekend and Augusta was swimming with well-kempt affluence. "He was so charming and such a gentleman," she added.

Putnam told the story of Stanko spending the night at her home, and subsequently seeing Stanko's photo in the paper. She contacted Georgia authorities, and the defendant was apprehended without incident while exiting a shopping mall.

Still, she'd been duped, and she knew it. "I can't believe I fell for that. When I saw his picture in the paper, I just screamed and cried."

The witness with the biggest impact on the jury was Henry Lee Turner's daughter, Debbie Turner Gallogly, of Roswell, Georgia. She testified that two days after her father's twice-shot body was discovered by police, she and other relatives set about the difficult task of cleaning his home.

"What of note, if anything, did you find during that cleanup?" Gregory Hembree asked.

"We found a pool cue case, and inside the case was a business card."

"Did you read the card?"

"Yes."

"Could you tell the jury what was written on the business card?"

"It said, 'Stephen C. Stanko, paralegal and exotic dancer,'" Gallogly recalled.

The prosecution established on the first day that Stephen Stanko had spent Masters weekend with some sort of injury to his hand. How he hurt himself depended upon whom he spoke with. Rather than nailing down one lie, such as he had with the Hooters franchises, he told a variety of stories to explain his hand—punched his car, a guy hit on his date, etc.

Chris Powell, branch manager of the Murrells Inlet Bank of America, testified that seven hundred dollars in Laura Ling's account was withdrawn after her death. There was surveillance footage of the man who withdrew the money, and he resembled Stanko. Powell, however, said he could not positively ID Stanko from the somewhat blurry images. The jury saw those images, too. No matter what the witness said, it *was* Stephen Stanko.

On cross-examination, Powell noted that the man in the photos was making no effort to hide his identity or obstruct the camera.

In all, thirteen witnesses testified for the prosecution that Friday.

SATURDAY

No such thing as a weekend off when a jury is sequestered. On Saturday morning, November 14, 2009, the prosecution's first witness was Investigator James Gordon, of the Richmond County Sheriff's Office. He testified that it was he, after Stanko was apprehended, who processed Henry Lee Turner's stolen truck.

Gordon testified as to the items he discovered. These included a registration in the glove box indicating the truck belonged to Henry Lee Turner, a Goose Creek High School ring, Class of 1986, with STEVE engraved on the inside, a pullover Hooters shirt, a bag containing a loaded handgun, Turner's checkbook, and a receipt book belonging to Stephen Stanko. The evidence linked the truck to Stanko, and Stanko to the murder.

Dr. Kim Collins, who participated in the postmortem of both of Stephen Stanko's murder victims, determined that the decedent died because of two gunshot wounds, one in the right side of his chest, the other in the back. Both bullets, she testified, were found during the autopsy.

"Could you determine which wound came first, Dr. Collins?"

"Yes, the wound in the chest came first."

At 10:46, on the morning of the second day of testimony, after presenting precisely twenty witnesses, the prosecution rested its case.

"Mr. Diggs, is the defense ready to present its case?"

"We are, Your Honor."

Judge Steven John called an early lunch break. The defense would commence at one o'clock.

The defense presented a series of medical experts—some repeats from the first trial, some new—all of whom testified that Stephen Stanko's impulses were poorly controlled due to puny frontal lobes.

In order to make the medical testimony more credible to the Horry County jury, Bill Diggs took greater care this time establishing the chain of evidence for the PET scans.

Dr. Marc Einhorn, a self-employed neurophysiologist from Georgia, testified that he examined the defendant in 2006. The examination included both a PET scan of his brain and an intelligence test. Stanko's IQ was around one-forty, which put him in the "gifted area." Dr. Einhorn said the PET scans were made at the Medical University of South Carolina. Those images were sent to Dr. Joseph C. Wu, of the University of California at Irvine (UCI).

Dr. Einhorn was forced to admit on cross-examination that tests done while Stanko was in prison "came back fine."

Dr. Wu was an expert on psychiatric disorders and brain scanning, the associate professor in residence in the department of psychiatry and human behavior at the UCI Brain Imaging Center, and a leading expert in using PET scans to visualize brain function and/or activity. He'd published multiple articles on PET scans of neuropsychiatric conditions. He had received during the course of his career more than a million dollars in grants from the National Institutes of Health (NIH). In a leading book on psychiatry, *Kaplan & Sadock's Comprehensive Textbook of Psychiatry,* Dr. Wu wrote the chapter on functional brain imaging. He spoke with a thick Chinese accent and had a mustache.

With his expertise established, Dr. Wu told the jury about the sad shriveled state of the gray matter immediately behind the defendant's forehead.

Dr. Ruben Gur was a psychiatry professor and neurologist from the Univsrsity of Pennsylvania—a tall, bespectacled man, with a wild crop of curly gray hair. For his court appearance, he wore a brown jacket, with a blue shirt and tie.

As he testified, Dr. Gur stood and showed the jury a plastic model of the human brain. The model opened at its center and divided into two halves so Dr. Gur could show a cross-sectional view.

"Dr. Gur, during your examination, did you find that images of Steve's brain revealed a normal brain?" William Diggs asked.

"No, sir. Those images showed an abnormal brain," Dr. Gur replied. Abnormal in a way that could induce "malfunction in a very serious way."

Was it a common problem? No, Stephen Stanko's brain was rare.

Thank goodness, spectators thought, they were discussing the abnormal brain of a rare monster.

Dr. Gur characterized Steve's problem as a physical injury causing a personality disorder, the effect of which was that Steve had little regard for others. He treated other people like instruments. He was charming but had "no feeling beyond the external demeanor." People with the condition Stanko suffered from could be "super cool" yet glow hot in a flash.

"All of a sudden, they can attack," Dr. Gur testified.

Dr. James Thrasher, the South Carolina psychiatrist who examined Stephen Stanko not long after the murders, repeated his testimony that complications surrounding Steve's birth and a severe concussion as a teenager could have damaged his brain.

Thrasher explained that during his first interview with the defendant soon after the murders, Stanko had given him conflicting reasons why he'd driven to Henry Lee Turner's house after murdering Laura Ling. At first, he told Thrasher the same lie he'd told Turner, that his father had died and he needed consoling. (But that lie, Stanko must have realized, was destined to collapse when authorities discovered his dad was alive.) Later, Stanko told Thrasher he'd gone to see Turner because he was feeling suicidal and was thinking of turning himself in because he "might have" killed Laura.

At Turner's house, Stanko claimed, there had been an "altercation." Turner grabbed a gun and pointed it at Stanko. There was a struggle. During the desperate grapple, the gun went flying. Stanko dove and got to it first. He grabbed it and fired, all in one motion.

Taking it point by point, Gregory Hembree used masterful cross-examination technique to illustrate the ways Stephen Stanko's scenario differed from the evidence. Stanko's story, for example, did not account for the other two shots fired, or the hole in the pillow-turned-silencer.

"Did Stanko mention the second shot into the victim's torso with the .357 Magnum?"

"No."

"Did he mention the pillow?"

"No, he did not."

"Did he mention there was still an electric shaver near the victim's hand when he was found on the bathroom floor?"

"No, he didn't mention that detail during our interview," Dr. Thrasher replied.

SUNDAY

Even on the Lord's Day, the machinery of justice kept grinding, and the parade of defense witnesses continued. Brent E. Turvey testified that he currently was a senior partner at Forensic Solutions LLC, based in Alaska. He worked there in his capacity as a forensic scientist and criminal profiler. Turvey was a teacher, who in addition to studying and testifying about actual crime scenes, taught and researched crime scene analysis and criminal profiling. He'd earned his master's degree in forensic science at the University of New Haven in West Haven, Connecticut. Before that, he'd earned two Bachelor of Science degrees (history and psychology) from Portland State University in Oregon. He was an experienced expert witness and had testified for prosecution *and* defense alike all over the world in cases involving assault, fetish burglary, sexual assault, serial rape, domestic homicide, staged crime scenes, and sexual and serial homicide. He had testified in civil cases, as well, involving lawsuits stemming from crimes and autoerotic deaths.

Fetish burglary? Those were cases in which a serial burglar stole items that gave him a sexual thrill, sometimes alone and sometimes in conjunction with valuables. Those items might include items such as undergarments or high-heeled shoes.

Autoerotic deaths? These occurred when people accidentally killed themselves while using desperate and dangerous masturbatory techniques, such as hanging.

He'd coauthored several books: the *Rape Investigation Handbook, Crime Reconstruction,* and *Forensic Victimology.* By himself, he'd written *Criminal Profiling: An Introduction to Behavioral Evidence Analysis,* the third edition of which was published by Academic Press in 2008.

He narrated a slide show—projected onto a big screen at the front of the courtroom—of photos of the body, with its bullet holes and nearby razor.

Turvey showed the jury photographs of the gun that was used to kill Henry Lee Turner, a bloody suitcase, and Stephen Stanko's business cards in the truck he stole from Turner's home.

Turvey was asked his interpretation of the evidence. After looking at the big picture, how did he think the kill went down? Contradicting Dr. Collins's testimony that Turner was shot first in the chest, Turvey said he believed the defendant kicked down the bedroom door and shot Turner through the pillow in the back. The first shot was from behind and struck the victim in the back. Turner turned and began to walk toward the defendant, but he ran out of strength and dropped to his knees. The second shot was fired while facing the victim. The evidence showed that Turner had been struck on the right side of the head, and apparently at one point, the victim grabbed the shooter, because gun residue was found on the victim's hands.

"Mr. Turvey, would you say this was a skillful crime?" William Diggs asked.

"No."

"Did this crime exhibit foresight?"

"It did not."

"Precaution?"

"Hardly," the witness said, pointing out that the defendant left figurative bread crumbs for the police to follow. Hunting down Stanko was a simple matter of reading license plate numbers. He still had items that connected him to the crime scene. Every decision he made ensured he would be identified by witnesses, identified by law enforcement, and captured.

Brent Turvey was replaced on the stand by Dr. Bernard Albiniak, a bald and bespectacled physiological psychology professor from Carolina Coastal University, who testified to evidence that would eventually seem to the jury like a broken record. PET scan, frontal lobes, poor impulse control, complicated pregnancy, difficult birth, concussion as a teen . . .

Dr. Albiniak testified: "He is a psychopath."

MONDAY

On Monday morning, November 16, 2009, the fourth day of testimony, the defense rested its case. The prosecution put on a few rebuttal witnesses designed to poke holes in Stephen Stanko's insanity claim.

One was forensic psychologist Dr. Pamela Crawford, who had previously testified at Stanko's Horry and Georgetown County competency hearings. Dr. Crawford began her testimony with the jury out of the room. She described her conversation with Stanko and his account of the violence both in Murrells Inlet and in Conway. The defense believed all evidence regarding the Laura Ling case was irrelevant. Judge John listened carefully and decided to allow her to testify in front of the jury, but not about the Ling murder. This was a trial for the murder of Henry Lee Turner, and the judge wanted to keep it that way.

With the jury back, Dr. Crawford testified that she was a member of the American Academy of Psychiatry and the Law and the American Psychiatric Association, that she spent a total of seventeen hours examining the defendant.

"When were those interviews?" the prosecutor asked.

"[It was] 2006, and earlier this year."

She began to tell the jury Stanko's story of why he had shot Turner. Judge John interrupted Dr. Crawford's testimony, and again sent the jury out of the room. The judge asked Stanko point-blank why he shot Turner. Stephen Stanko said it was self-defense, that he was in fear for his life when he did it.

The judge called the jury back in and allowed Dr. Crawford to continue her testimony.

"At any time, did you discuss with the defendant what happened in Mr. Turner's home?" Hembree asked.

"Yes."

"Did he describe for you what happened?"

"Yes, he said the victim pulled a gun on him."

"Why did the victim do that?"

"According to the defendant, Turner learned that Laura Ling was dead, and the news angered him."

"What did the defendant say happened next?"

"He said they wrestled for the gun, and it went off twice, once striking him in the chest. He said the second bullet went off into the room somewhere."

The scenario was self-serving, of course, and, interestingly, it failed to account for the fact that the victim had been shot in the back, as well as for the fact that the body and the bullet hole in the wall were discovered in opposite ends of the home.

According to the defendant himself, Dr. Crawford testified, the death of Henry Lee Turner had nothing to do with a brain injury: "It's clear from what he told me that not only did he remember the events, but he was asserting that he was defending himself, which sort of rules out an insanity defense in the sense that he said that 'I remembered it. I did this because I was trying to protect myself,' and that's just pretty crucial."

"He knows right from wrong?"

"Absolutely," the witness replied. "He simply lacks a conscience. He lacks empathy."

"Why?"

"I don't think anybody can tell you why he doesn't have a conscience."

"Is he out of control?"

"No, he does not have a condition that would make him unable to control his conduct. In my opinion, the defendant has no condition that prevents him from conforming his conduct, and should be held criminally responsible under the laws of South Carolina."

Gregory Hembree paused to let that statement sink in. Then he shifted gears and asked if Dr. Crawford spoke to anyone other than the defendant during her investigation.

Dr. Crawford said she had. She had talked to members of his family, friends of his, and other people who knew him. They all described a charming but shallow personality, a man without empathy. They described a man perpetually in need of flattery, whose ego required frequent boosts of social support. His self-importance was inflated, and his need for admiration extreme. These were all aspects of a psychopathic personality, but not of insanity.

"And after those long examinations of the defendant, what was your conclusion regarding Stanko's psychological state?" Hembree asked.

She found him to be a highly narcissistic individual, totally stuck on himself, and every bit as sane as anyone in that courtroom—before, after, and including when he pulled the trigger twice and shot Henry Lee Turner dead.

If Dr. Crawford's testimony hadn't been damaging enough, the rebuttal continued with the testimony of Dr. William Brannon Jr. Dr. Brannon said he had closely examined Stanko's childhood medical records and

332   *Michael Benson*

found no evidence that there was anything wrong with
Stanko's brain at birth, that he did have jaundice as an
infant, but that frankly was not an abnormality, and
wouldn't cause a brain injury.

In response to the prosecution's damaging rebuttal witnesses, the defense put on a couple of rebuttal
witnesses of their own—but there were no new faces,
no new messages. Just familiar faces harping on the
same note.

The first was Dr. Ruben Gur. An encore performance
from Dr. Thomas Sachy followed, who was losing track
of the number of times he'd sat in a witness chair on
Stephen Stanko's behalf.

Dr. Sachy reiterated: damage to the frontal lobe, violent and psychopathic manner, PET scans, birth trauma.

Cross-examining Dr. Sachy, Gregory Hembree asked,
"Did Stanko know right from wrong during the time of
the killing?"

Dr. Sachy sputtered at first: "He didn't . . . He was
morally . . . How does the law say it? He didn't *appreciate*
the moral difference between right and wrong. Morals
are not something we think about. They are something
we appreciate. They are biologically determined by how
well your brain works."

Dr. Sachy's answers, because he was so highly educated, sometimes included a technical vocabulary and
complex syntax. His words could make a juror shrug, but
not in this case. Stanko knew the difference between
right and wrong—he just didn't care.

At one point on Monday morning, with the jury out
of the room, Judge Steven John asked the defendant if
he would be testifying on his own behalf. Stephen

Stanko quietly conferred with counsel for a moment and then told the judge he would not.

It was a few minutes before one o'clock when lawyers on both sides told Judge John that they had no more witnesses. The judge declared the lunch break.

Final arguments began at 2:30 P.M.

Delivering the prosecution's closing argument was Deputy Solicitor Fran Humphries, who reminded the jury that Henry Lee Turner had been shot twice. Once in the chest and *once in the back*.

Not only was the murder cowardly, it was premeditated as well. The defendant called ahead to let Turner know he was coming, and he arrived at Turner's home ready to kill.

"He's mean—and he likes himself that way," Humphries said. "He believes he's smarter than everyone else, and he just . . . doesn't . . . care."

The defendant was a man of excuses. It was always somebody else's fault.

He and his brain—to believe his defense—were seldom in the same room, seldom in the same building. While he was over here, minding his own business, his brain was over there, plotting evil.

Humphries said he knew the jury was plenty smart—certainly smart enough to see that Stephen Stanko's brain remained inside his head at all times, that he was a murderer.

The argument lasted a smidgen more than twenty minutes.

William Diggs took about twice that long, hammering away at the only point he had tried to make all along.

The guy had an injury. Maybe it happened at birth, maybe that blow to the head he took, maybe during some accident that they didn't even know about. But a lot of the electrical activity that would normally be occurring in the front of a normal brain was absent in Stephen Stanko's brain. He had a *deformity*—and that meant he was insane when he shot the poor victim.

"Sane people do not behave in the way Stephen Stanko did. Sane people do not do what Stephen Stanko did. He's got a personality disorder and it's caused by a defect. He's got areas in his brain that don't function," Diggs said.

Diggs showed the jury one more time the colorful slides of a normal brain next to Stanko's brain. He reminded them what a PET scan was, and what it revealed. He reminded the jury that he had kept the promise he'd made in his opening statement. He'd shown them what insanity *looked like*.

Law in South Carolina said insane meant not knowing the difference between right and wrong, and the ability to make that distinction lay right there in the frontal lobes, right where Steve had his defect. Plus, look at Steve's circumstances. He'd been in a tough place, just out of prison and trying to get by, and he attacked the man who befriended him, who was willing to help him? Made no sense at all. He had to be insane. Now Steve was in dire straits, with no one to watch his back. He didn't have friends. His family wouldn't support him. The reason the jury hadn't seen any Stanko supporters in the room was that there *weren't any*. Stanko was flying solo, and he needed their help.

"Every single member of his immediate family has given up on him," Diggs said. "Does anyone really believe Stephen Stanko is in this courtroom because of bad choices? That's incomprehensible."

Diggs was done. One reporter glanced at her watch. Three-thirty in the afternoon. There was a short break, and Judge Steven John gave the jurors their instructions:

They were to consider evidence, and evidence only. All evidence was to be weighed equally, whether it was from the first day of the trial or the last. If there were problems, they were to contact him immediately via a bailiff. A unanimous vote would be necessary to convict the defendant. He thanked them profusely. He understood how difficult it was to be a sequestered jury. It was like having a twenty-four-hour-a-day job.

They were to be commended for executing their public duty with such diligence. Then he ordered them to go to their room and begin their deliberations. The jury began its deliberations a little after four o'clock.

It took them only forty minutes. They were back. Reach a verdict? Yes, Your Honor. Of murder, guilty. Of armed robbery, guilty. Stephen Stanko again showed no emotion.

Bill Diggs moved that an immediate mistrial be declared. The jury had only been out for less than an hour. They could not have possibly gone about their deliberations in any kind of attention to detail. They had sworn to undertake a deliberate process, and there was no way they could do that in less than an hour! He said that he thought the first jury at Stanko's first trial in Georgetown County had been quick, and they had taken two hours. That was an eternity compared to the actions of *this* jury. This jury swore that they were to have no preconceived notions. It was a joke. He suspected that some of these jurors had made up their mind even before they were qualified. He cited at least one juror who had admitted during voir dire of having prior knowledge of Stephen Stanko and his alleged crimes.

* * *

Outside the courtroom, to reporters, Gregory Hembree explained that one of the reasons the jury was quick was that the questions most juries deliberate slowly over—whether or not the defendant committed the crime—were not a factor here. Stephen Stanko admitted that he shot Henry Turner. The only question was whether or not he was sane when he did it, and even the defense couldn't always get its witnesses to say he wasn't.

"It was ironclad as to Mr. Stanko's guilt. Their theory was rejected," Hembree said. *Simple as that.*

Hembree didn't want to talk about the speed of the jury's deliberations, however. He wanted the public to know, instead, about the relief Turner's family felt over the guilty verdict. That was the whole reason they were there, why this trial happened, why it wasn't redundant—the way some critics had said. This trial happened to give the family of Henry Lee Turner closure, and that had happened. Mission accomplished.

"You could see relief in their faces," Hembree said. "They want Stephen Stanko held accountable for the killing of their dad and family member."

Turner's sons, who witnessed the entire trial, gave reporters "the hand." There was still important business ahead and they would reserve comment.

Tuesday was a day off for the jury, the twenty-four-hour cooling-off period between the guilt and penalty phases of the trial.

Even though Stephen Stanko had chosen not to testify during the guilt phase, he still could—if he chose—testify during the penalty phase. He couldn't really plead for his life, because there was already a cell reserved for him on death row, but, in theory, the jury didn't know that.

WEDNESDAY

For the penalty phase of the trial, proceedings started a few minutes late that Wednesday because William Diggs was late in arrival.

Judge Steven John asked Diggs's co-counsel Brana Williams, "Didn't he understand that court started at eight-thirty?"

"According to my paralegal, he left the office at eight o'clock," Williams replied.

It was after nine o'clock before Diggs came in, apologizing profusely. But Judge John was not in a forgiving mood: "Why were you late?"

"Traffic, Your Honor."

Judge John said he would deal with his tardiness when the trial was over. He needed everyone there at eight-thirty so motions could be discussed *before* the jury was brought in.

Unfortunately for Diggs, he was already in the judge's doghouse by the time he made his first motion: all evidence regarding Laura Ling's murder be excluded from the prosecution's case.

"Denied."

The murder of Laura Ling wasn't relevant when it

came to deciding whether or not Stephen Stanko was guilty of Henry Lee Turner's murder. But when it came to life in prison or the death penalty, the events in Murrells Inlet were very relevant indeed.

The jury entered, and Judge John told them it was as if the trial was starting over. Both sides would give opening statements, each side would call witnesses, and both would give closing arguments.

The jury was to determine only one thing: should the convicted killer and rapist be executed. A unanimous vote was necessary, just as it had been during the guilt phase of the trial. If it wasn't unanimous, the verdict must be for life in prison without a chance of parole.

Fran Humphries delivered the prosecution's opening statement, apologizing to the jury up front for some of the things they were going to have to hear. "In this phase, we will be presenting evidence of the defendant's previous bad acts," Humphries said. Those acts, he warned, were offensive to a civilized mind. Stephen Stanko was not just a guy who exploded and committed all of his major crimes on the same day. His behavior had been potentially deadly for many years.

The jury was there to examine the "conduct and character of Stephen Stanko." The things jurors had already heard "didn't touch" the things they were about to hear. "It will be difficult and trying," Humphries said. "You will want to close your eyes and close your ears."

Brana Williams gave the defense's opening statement. She said that for once she agreed with the prosecution.

The jury was indeed going to hear things that would bring "tears to their eyes." They would hear things that "indeed, were shocking. I also think you are going to hear things that will make you say, 'I just don't understand. It just doesn't make sense.'" She reminded them, however, that there might be a big voice inside, or maybe even a small voice, saying that this man should not be put to death. She beseeched the twelve men and women to listen to that voice.

The prosecution's first witness was Elizabeth McLendon Buckner, whose job it was to tell the story of Stephen Stanko and the chemical-soaked cloth, one more time. She'd testified at the first trial, had an awful experience, and was back again—feeling sad. When she learned they wanted her to testify again, her first thought was "Uh-oh, not again." There was still a part of her that wanted Stephen to be saved. She wanted him to snap out of the evil trance he was in and become a nice guy again. But it wasn't going to happen. He could not be saved. She remembered how emotionally exhausting the first trial had been. But then she thought about the Turner family. They deserved justice. They had been so supportive of Liz during the first trial, and they needed closure and a process just as much as Laura Ling's loved ones had. The Turners had been so comforting when she needed it most, and she could not let them down. So she took a deep breath and did it.

Questioned by Fran Humphries, Liz testified for about a half hour, and several times had to wipe the tears away as she spoke. During the first trial, Liz had been somewhat rudely cross-examined by Diggs's second chair. This time, the cross was conducted by William Diggs himself.

The questioning was less ambitious than it had been at the Ling trial, and Diggs couldn't have been nicer, recognizing that Liz's victim status made her a sympathetic character to the jury.

Liz found the second trial to be a smaller, quicker, quieter version of the first. Although many of the witnesses were the same, their time on the stand was shorter. There were fewer spectators, and there was far less media. The first trial was just larger in general, covered exhaustively by a major TV network. There had been a murder, a rape, and a list of fraud charges that had to be proven. The second trial had one shooting, a stolen truck, flight—and that was about it.

Kelly Crolley then testified how she had been taken for $125 by Stephen Stanko, who claimed to be collecting for a children's cancer charity. Crolley later said testifying was no fun, but it was her duty. She wasn't completely sure how she felt about the death penalty, but she certainly had no problem in telling the truth.

There was a series of witnesses—all women—who each testified briefly to more or less the same thing: They met Stanko; he had told them he was a lawyer and offered various legal services for a fee. They'd paid the fee, the services were never rendered, and Stanko disappeared. If you put all of these witnesses together, they testified to Stanko scamming thousands of dollars.

The solicitor might have wanted Penny Ling to appear on the stand at the second trial, but it wasn't going to happen. Penny was done. She'd already told the story of losing her mother and being raped—once in court—and that was enough. It was horrific and she no longer cared to revisit it. She didn't want to be the victim anymore. She wanted to get on with the rest of her life. So Penny's dad, Chris Ling, provided the jury with the information the jury needed regarding what the defendant had done to his daughter.

The tough part for the jury came next. The prosecution played a recording of the 911 call Penny Ling had made after the Murrells Inlet attack.

As the tape began, Chris Ling, Penny's dad, got up and moved toward the exit.

"I just can't listen to it again," he said, as if an explanation were necessary.

And so the jury heard the little girl telling the dispatcher that she'd been raped and her mother was dead.

It was four-thirty on Wednesday afternoon when the prosecution called their final witness of the day, Henry Lee Turner's girlfriend, Cecilia Kotsipias. She told the jury that Turner called her his "brown-eyed lady." Whenever they were someplace where there was a deejay, Henry would get him to play "Brown Eyed Girl" by Van Morrison for Cecilia.

"How did you meet?"

They met in Myrtle Beach, and on their first date, they "danced and danced and danced." Theirs was a long-distance relationship. She lived in Charlotte, but they saw each other as often as they could, and the relationship had been going on for years. They liked to go fishing together. He was a military veteran, she testified, and he had a couple of pairs of red, white, and blue pants he liked to wear. She said that when she met him, he was like the Grinch and had never enjoyed decorating a Christmas tree. After he helped her decorate hers one year, he learned to love it. They talked on the phone all the time. Three or four times a day. He wanted to get married, but she didn't.

Then came that day. It started at four o'clock in the

morning when Turner called her and told her that he had Stanko in his house. "He told me Stephen's father had just died and he said he was going to take him in."

Turner ended that phone conversation by saying, "I love you, Brown Eyes." Those were the last words she ever heard him say. "We had a great life. Stephen Stanko ruined our lives. We should still be fishing and singing." When Charlotte police came to her door and told her Turner had been found murdered, the first words out of her mouth had been "Stephen Stanko."

At five minutes past five in the afternoon, the prosecution rested its case. Judge Steven John adjourned court for the day.

THURSDAY

On Thursday morning, November 19, 2009, Brana Williams presented nine pro-life witnesses, the first of which was Dr. James Thrasher. His testimony was concise. He'd examined Stephen Stanko in 2006 and found that he lacked the requisite capacity "as to moral right and wrong." He characterized Stanko's mental capacity at the time of his violent spree as "impaired."

One of Stanko's middle-school teachers, Barbara Boland, testified both about the Stanko she knew as a student, and, in her current capacity as Christian counselor, about the kind and gentle Stanko she spoke to in prison. She'd visited him in prison several times, most recently in 2008. Since his spree of violence, she felt, he'd experienced a spiritual reawakening, a rebirth.

"I can assure you that he is very remorseful for what he did," Boland said. "I believe he has turned his life around."

She added that she didn't think he had "jailhouse religion." She felt that he was legitimate, that he had actually "been saved."

* * *

From the witness stand, Frank Shealy identified himself as a chaplain at Lieber Correctional Institution in Ridgeville. Shealy was asked about Stephen Stanko's social behavior while incarcerated. The chaplain testified that Stanko always had a positive effect on the prison community he was in: "He is an exceptional inmate in the death row population. He steps *into* issues. When trouble starts brewing, he calms it down. He works as a peacemaker." Stanko could be a buffer between inmates and the prison administration. He was an intelligent negotiator who had a calming effect. "He is the leader on death row," Shealy said. Any prison population would be worse off without him.

Clarice Wenz, Wanda Brooks, and John H. Fulmer, from Goose Creek High, repeated their testimony that Stanko—once upon a time, a long time ago—was a "most likely to succeed" prospect.

At about quarter past eleven on Thursday morning, the defense called its final penalty phase witness: Dr. Evelyn Califf, a Myrtle Beach counselor, who at the request of the defense had done a study of Stephen Stanko's life by examining all of the family photos she could locate and by interviewing all of Stephen's relatives who were willing to cooperate.

"Did you base your report on any other sources?" Brana Williams asked.

"Yes," Dr. Califf replied, "I also used conversations I had with Mr. Stanko, doctors' reports I read, newspaper articles that had been written about him, and e-mails he'd received from one of his sisters."

"There were family members who did not cooperate?" Williams asked.

"Yes, his father and his sister Cynthia," the witness replied.

Dr. Califf shared with the jury some of the photos from Stanko's life. She pointed out how often the camera found him smiling when he was a young boy.

"But, by the time he was in high school, the smile disappeared," she commented. "By that time, his home life offered no safe haven. It was a home in which he could never feel safe."

THE PERFORMANCE

Judge Steven John asked Stephen Stanko if he planned to make a statement to the jury.

"I do, Your Honor," Stanko said.

"In that case, I must remind you that you must stick to subjects that have been covered during this portion of the trial. You were given a chance to testify during the guilt phase of the trial, and you turned it down. You may not say things now that you wished you had said then, because now the prosecution will not have an opportunity to cross-examine you. Is that understood?"

Stanko said he understood.

The judge called for the closing arguments. Gregory Hembree reminded the jury that they swore under oath that they could impose the death penalty, given the right evidence and the correct circumstances.

"This is the evidence, and these are the circumstances," Hembree said. The defense theory, he opined, could easily be shrunk down to a nutshell. "They say because I do bad things, I have a personality disorder and I am crazy, therefore I don't have to suffer the consequences for the things I do. Under that logic, *no one* should ever be held accountable. That's a great strategy for someone accused of murder," Hembree said. "I have another way of looking at Stanko's actions—He is just plain evil. He has something inside that makes him evil. He *likes* it and is very, very, very good at hiding it. When a person's conduct is so evil and brutal that person gives up the right to remain among us. This is *that* conduct."

Hembree warned the jury that they would be hearing from Stanko himself very soon, and he was a very good actor. "This will be *the* performance of his long, horrible career," Hembree said.

Stephen Stanko delivered that great performance. Nervously fidgeting behind the podium, voice soft yet tremulous, he began by apologizing to the Turner family.

"I don't know if it will do any good," he said. "I am sorry. I am. I hope someday they will accept it. I had to say that I did it, and I'm sorry you got put through it. I'm sorry to Rodney and Roger and Cecilia for what I put you through."

Stanko snuck a peek at the jury, to see how he was doing. Unfortunately, as far as he was concerned, the panel looked very much as they had before convicting him of murder.

There may have been a twenty-four-hour cooling-off period, but they were not cool.

Eyes again lowered, Stanko spoke of his victim. "Henry and I were friends. We were friends, and much more. We used to ride motorcycles together, and we played pool quite often. At a time when my dad and I were at terrible odds, he was there. He treated me like a son."

The speech started well, but it lost focus and eventually rambled. He tried to pick apart Gregory Hembree's case, but his points were sometimes dulled by his asides and rhetorical tangents. He skipped from a long discussion about the evolution of cell phones to his own family to the movie *Minority Report,* a Tom Cruise sci-fi picture, based on a Philip K. Dick short story, which depicted a world in which murders are prevented through the effects of a trio of mutants who can see the future.

Some might have noticed that his family was absent and that was okay by him. He didn't want his family there, or Turner's family there. He didn't want to hurt anyone else.

Then he got to the crux.

"To kill me would be to cheat science out of an opportunity," he said. Scientists were on his side. Why spoil an opportunity to study his brain and perhaps learn how to treat future people with frontal-lobe problem/difficulties?

Stanko figured his best defense was a good offense; so he matter-of-factly cast wild aspersions in the solicitor's direction. "Hembree has a four-and-a-half-inch knife right now. Talk about breaking the rules. And he has walked by me twenty-five or thirty times," Stanko said. Referring to the guilty verdict, he added, "You made a decision already and I think that is great. But you can't put me in an aggravating circumstance and say he is a lying, deceiving son of a gun and do the same thing."

He reminded them that his life was on the line, a statement that might've irritated some jurors. Did he think they were idiots? He begged the jury to give credence to the testimony of defense experts talking about his brain and his faulty frontal lobes and whatnot. They were sincere. "They were being honest about it," Stanko emphasized.

There was more fuzzy "insulting to the intelligence" logic. Two wrongs don't make a right, he argued. If they sentenced him to death, weren't they doing the same thing they thought he did?

He'd heard it said—so he knew the jury was aware—that he already had a cell on death row, ready and waiting for him. That was a bad, bad hotel. Room service sucked. You could check in, but . . .

It wasn't funny.

"You have an opportunity to change that," he said. It wasn't like he was asking to be set free. He knew that he would never walk among them again. "I am not going to get out of prison," Stanko reminded them. "My *best-case scenario* is life in prison."

He admitted that he had been criticized for pleading not guilty at this trial, that he was wasting everyone's time by again seeking justice for himself. He claimed to have done so with good reason.

"I didn't accept a plea because there would have been no opportunity to show the evidence again," he said. "There would be no opportunity to let twelve people *look* and *change the world*."

To Turner's family: "I hope the hate and anger they have can be cured with the memory of Henry. That wasn't right. It wasn't. I am sorry."

He showed the jury a leather brace he had been wearing throughout the trial, a brace that could be triggered by remote control to shock him into stupefaction, should he try to escape.

The judge gave the jury their final directions and then sent them to their deliberation, where once again they efficiently performed their solemn duty. In just longer than an hour, the jury was back.

Stephen Stanko hung his head as the verdict was read.

"'Today, November 19, 2009, we recommend that Stephen C. Stanko be sentenced to death.'"

Stanko's head nodded up and down a bit, and then was still.

JUSTICE DONE

Outside the courtroom, Henry Lee Turner's son Roger Turner spoke to reporters. "This has been a long time coming definitely, and so it's definitely closure for me, even though, you know, I don't have my father anymore."

Had he given any weight at all to the defense team's insanity case?

"No, he's of sound mind. He knows right from wrong. The insanity defense is just the last in a long line of con games he played. It's so outlandish, that it seems to me completely fabricated."

What questions still lingered in his mind?

"Why Dad? I mean, *dadgum,* he was seventy-four years old, eight days before his seventy-fifth birthday. I mean, come on, he befriended him!"

Roger thanked the members of the Ling family who attended the trial. He'd been there for every minute of every day, and he appreciated them "showing up."

Was he shocked by Stephen Stanko's apology?

"No, I expected it. I'm glad he did it. It doesn't take back what he did, but I accept it."

Where to, from here?

Roger Turner eloquently replied: "We breathe in and out, and make every day matter."

Outside, also doing press, Gregory Hembree thanked Brana Williams for doing such a great job. No, he wasn't surprised that the jury gave Stanko the thumbs-down. As long as the defendant stuck to the insanity defense, there could be no mercy. Yes, there was still an appellate process to endure. Stephen Stanko was out of appeals for the Laura Ling murder, but he could still appeal for Henry Turner.

The next stage in Stanko's legal process, Hembree noted, was the PCR, or post-conviction relief. At that hearing, Stanko would claim his lawyers were ineffective, and that their failure to defend him properly had denied him due process. That hearing would be handled by the South Carolina attorney general. Whatever decision was made at the PCR would then be appealed to the state supreme court, which was the end of the road.

Answering a hypothetical question, Hembree said it was feasible that Stanko would be executed for Laura Ling before he exhausted the legal process for Henry Lee Turner.

No, there was no way for him to predict how long the appeals process would last.

"They are two independent cases," he said. "They operate independently from one another."

"Did you ever have any doubts?"

"No."

"Were you ever worried that the jury would listen to the defense's frontal-lobe theory?"

Hembree said he'd seen that kind of defense before,

not just in the first Stephen Stanko trial but in other cases as well, and he felt it faulty at its base.

"It is a misapplication of science," Hembree said. "The science is valid, the application is invalid. The application is not generally accepted in the medical community."

Hembree called the testimony of the doctors Gur, Wu, and Thrasher, etc., a "dog and pony show." Dr. Thrasher was there because the defense needed a local doctor to confirm what the outsiders were saying. Some of the other doctors popped up testifying in cases around the country, Hembree said, and "their story is always the same." PET scans were valid and helpful in multiple ways, Hembree said, but he did not believe they could be used to determine if a person was insane.

Hembree was aware that, had he chosen to, he could have tried to get all of the PET scan evidence declared inadmissible because it wasn't accepted in the medical community. That might have worked. There had been cases in which that had occurred. Hembree recalled one recent trial in Texas in which a federal judge declared evidence inadmissible because the witnesses' application of science was unreliable.

The solicitor chose not to go that route with Stephen Stanko, but he did have an expert lined up—an *utmost authority*—who would testify that PET scans could not be used in the way the defense was trying to use them. Hembree, however, could tell the jury wasn't buying it, anyway, so he didn't bother to refute the testimony about the frontal lobe.

The best argument for not attacking the evidence was that it didn't create a big appellate issue. The argument for attacking was that there might be a juror or two who were easily swayed by anything that seemed scientific—

but Hembree knew the two juries that convicted Stanko were smarter than that.

Just because a man doesn't care about the difference between right and wrong does not mean that he lacks understanding of the distinction. A guy might believe his neighbors were aliens or Nazis and that he was saving the world by shooting them, and that guy might be legally insane.

But Stephen Stanko wasn't like that. He might have *liked* the fact that murder was wrong, but he knew it wasn't right. Stanko's flight into Georgia was evidence of that. The fact that he'd later claimed he killed Henry Turner in self-defense was evidence of that.

Psychiatrists said that he was *antisocial*. Well, all that meant was that Stanko didn't like to follow the rules. That not only *wasn't* an excuse, but it correctly described almost every criminal out there. Every defendant Hembree prosecuted had some form of antisocial disorder.

"It is a misleading diagnosis," Hembree opined. "They're admitting that he is not insane by South Carolina standards, yet arguing that he wasn't responsible for his actions, nonetheless—he's not insane, *but he is*." It was a desperate defense, and the Stanko juries rejected that whole line of reasoning out of hand. You could tell by the swiftness of deliberation at both trials.

The defense was allowed to present their PET scan testimony at both the guilt and penalty phases of both trials, and all four times it didn't help the defense one iota. Using the PET scans as part of the penalty phase was "really improper," Hembree said, "but we didn't care."

Again, the juries weren't buying, anyway, and ignoring it saved a potential appellate problem down the road. Once the jury rejected in the guilt phase the evidence about the frontal lobe, and Stanko's defense reintro-

duced the same stuff during the penalty phase, it had
no steam left at all.

What did he mean by "dog and pony show"?

Some of the defense's expert witnesses had testified
for a fee to almost identical data in other cases. Just a
couple of months before the second Stephen Stanko
trial, Dr. Joseph Wu testified in a Sarasota, Florida, court
that Michael King brutally murdered beautiful twenty-
one-year-old Denise Amber Lee because of his brain
injury. Wu examined PET scans of King's brain and
found that the frontal lobes weren't sparking normally,
probably because of a sledding accident King had had
when he was six. Jury didn't go for it.

In civil cases, Dr. Wu had had better luck. In 2008, between Stanko's trials, Dr. Wu successfully testified that a
Michigan bus driver whose bus was struck by a train
when he tried to drive around the lowered crossing
guards was not liable for damages because PET scans
showed that the lights in his frontal lobes had been
dimmed—in this case by post-traumatic stress disorder.

As recently as February 2010, Dr. Ruben Gur testified
that a Florida man, Kemar Johnston, should not receive
the death penalty for the murders of Alex and Jeffrey
Sosa because of malfunctioning frontal lobes.

Gur also testified in a Texas case that juveniles should
never be sentenced to death because their frontal lobes
were not yet fully developed, which was why teenagers
struggled with impulse control.

Gregory Hembree was right. There was a pattern.

Immediately following his second death sentence,
Stephen Stanko was moved from the jail in Horry
County back to death row at the Lieber Correctional
Institution, in the town of Ridgeville, Dorchester County,

where he was expected to stay until sometime in 2010, when he would be returned to Horry for his PCR hearing.·

As he was returned to death row, he was asked if he had any requests.

"I only need one thing," Stanko said. "A Bible."

Maybe the request was for cosmetic purposes. Or, maybe, like so many condemned men before him, he turned to the main source—and sought loopholes.

"CAN'T KILL HIM TWICE"

Many South Carolina taxpayers, who picked up the tab for the second trial, thought the whole thing a waste of time. Redundant, they said.

The man was already sentenced to death. A second death sentence? What the hell did that mean? Some thought that was why the county held the trial over a weekend, when it was least apt to be noticed by the public.

Some, with clenched jaw, wondered why the animal wasn't dead yet.

Yet, some said the trial *was* necessary. A second death sentence was valuable, like insurance—the very redundancy citizens complained about might stifle future mercy toward the chameleon killer, might guarantee or even *speed up* his execution.

On February 17, 2010, Graeme Moore, of News Channel 15 in Grand Strand, Pee Dee, and the Border Belt, reported that the accounting for Stephen Stanko's second murder trial was complete. The people of South

Carolina had shelled out $215,000 to convict an already-condemned man. Most of that was slated to go toward paying for Stephen Stanko's defense.

According to Hugh Ryan, at the South Carolina Commission on Indigent Defense, William Diggs and Brana Williams together charged $84,000 as their trial fee, and billed another nine grand for the expert witnesses they hired. The victim's family was also provided free room and board by the state.

Melanie Huggins, the Horry County clerk of court, said that her office had spent close to $30,000 on room and board for the jurors, as well as other "routine expenses."

The reporter interviewed Brana Williams, and she frankly blamed the solicitor's office for the hefty price tag. A plea deal would have been a bargain! She said, "Taxpayers could easily have been saved the cost of a second capital-murder trial if they had offered Stanko a life-without-parole opportunity." Williams complained that the prosecution refused to bargain at all. If Stephen Stanko accepted the lesser punishment, South Carolina would be two hundred grand richer.

The announced tab didn't include all of the expenses for the trial, which had been held on a weekend. It didn't count the overtime that had to be paid the court employees and the cost of operating the courthouse extra hours.

Gregory Hembree defended the trial. How could you take something as aggravating as a history of violence and turn it into a mitigating factor? What sort of justice would there be if Stephen Stanko's sentence was lessened from death to life without parole because he's committed a second murder in another county? Henry Turner's family deserved every bit as much closure as

Laura Ling's family had gotten—and that necessitated a trial and a conviction.

"If that's your father that's been killed, what's that worth to you?" Hembree said. "I mean, is it ten thousand dollars that you're willing to invest in that trial as a taxpayer? Is it fifty? Is it one hundred?"

EPILOGUE

Stephen Stanko's father passed away on November 12, 2010.

In April 2010, Stephen Stanko responded to the author's request for an interview with a three-page letter. He said that the author's letters to him were returned by the SCDC because on death row he wasn't allowed to receive stamps or self-addressed stamped envelopes. He appreciated the invitation to participate in this book, but was disappointed that the author was not seeking a full-fledged collaborator.

Stanko requested a copy of the book proposal and table of contents, and stated his expectations that the book would end up a "complete and honest finished work."

He informed the author that he remained a busy, busy guy, with five literary projects in various stages of completion. Three of his projects were about death row—two serious, one "comical." Other topics included sentencing reform and correctional psychology/sociology. There was a novel in the works, too. Since the end of his second murder trial, now three writers had contacted him regarding projects. He hadn't decided with whom to work, if anyone yet.

At the bottom of the first page—which was written in near-perfect printing, with minimal syntax or spelling errors, and no repetition—he wondered if the author was aware that he had hypergraphia (overwhelming urge to write, not a disorder but indicative of brain changes associated with epilepsy and mania).

Regarding this book, Stanko wrote that he would appreciate *a fair shake*. He understood that his life was *an incredible story*. He finally asked for money, assuring the author that any funds sent would be used toward the book, meaning the author's book, and not for his own personal needs. *Unless you have such a giving heart that you provide me some funds for that.* Adding, *Ha ha.*

Stanko opined that laughter was the absence of terror and terror was sadly the absence of laughter. He wrote that the past two years, since the passing of his mother, he had learned humility. These days he had a more *humble heart*—but added that he still had *far to go.*

As of 2011, Liz Buckner would like to have reported that the Stephen Stanko affair was completely behind her, but sadly that was never going to be the case. It would always be there, part of her fabric, who she was. She *worked* to prevent it from affecting her self-esteem and confidence, even after all these years.

For the most part, the battle had been a victorious one. She did not wallow in self-pity. At times, he came into her mind, but it was a fleeting moment, maybe caused by something familiar. Songs—like "One Night a Day" by Garth Brooks and "Someone Like You" by Van Morrison—would call up a flash of memory.

Sometimes a sound or a smell would trigger something, and a memory would momentarily jam her stream of consciousness. She still thought of Stephen every time she passed a Baskin-Robbins ice cream place. Bananas Foster was his favorite flavor.

When she did think extensively of Stephen Stanko, she did it on her own terms, while she worked daily on her own book about him, based on her personal experiences, a warning to women about the dangers of dating a psycho.

She realized that some of the damage caused by Stephen Stanko was permanent. He took her life away. She was no longer the trusting person she had been in 1992 when she met him. She was never going to be that person again. She was *guarded* now, wary of people. She worked, which involved a lot of travel, a lot of being in the spotlight. She was the creative mind behind a marketing consulting business. She traveled and met with new people every day. She shared nothing of her private life with her business acquaintances. She knew lots of people who didn't even know she had a son. When not working, she preferred solitude. Socially, there were walls up, protecting her against the theoretic strangers out there who would try to take advantage of her the way Stephen had. She didn't venture out. She was solitary.

Liz might have given up on her dreams of being an FBI profiler years before, but that did not mean her ambitions toward crime busting were completely stifled. By making public every detail she could recall about Stephen Stanko, she hoped to make her contribution to the great pool of knowledge, and hopefully give the FBI experts in Quantico, Virginia, an assist in figuring out what made killers tick.

Putting it all down on paper began not long after Stanko attacked her in 1996. She'd experienced anxiety after the attack and had sought psychological help. Her counselor suggested, as therapy, that she keep a journal, and she eventually filled up notebook after notebook. For a long time, she considered her journals private—ideas she was externalizing but nonetheless keeping private. The unrealistic goal back then was to make Stephen Stanko a part of her past and not a part of her future. Soon she realized there was no getting rid of it—no matter how many journals she filled.

The notion to try to publish her story developed after the murders, when Liz realized she had to do everything she could to educate women regarding men without consciences. If she could keep one potential victim safe, her labor would be worth it.

She didn't know why, but the Charleston area had grown more dangerous for women over the years. She didn't know where these women-haters were coming from, but it was frightening, because it wasn't always like that.

Her own conscience still troubled her sometimes. What if she had written her own book while Stephen was serving his eight-and-a-half-year prison sentence, maybe—just maybe—Laura Ling would have read it and it might have saved her life.

And not just Laura, but all of the gullible women in the world who love and trust too much, who love and trust bad men—she might have stopped it from happening again and again and again. It was sickening to watch the TV news, to see how many women were being victimized. There was too much of it. Much more than there used to be, although she didn't know why. It seemed like every day you turned on the news and there were more attacks on women and children.

During the stretch of 2005 to 2010, when Liz worked

most regularly on her book, she threw everything out and started over a couple of times as she refined and learned to better express her message. For a time, she planned on calling the book, *Four Years to Life*. Sometimes she thought of calling the work, *The Man Behind the Monster*, because so much of the media attention on Stephen had focused on the monster and she was one of the few who knew both sides of the story.

Bad men were clever, she emphasized. By the time the man revealed his monster within, it was too late for the victim to escape. Predatory men were not going to show their bad face until the victim was good and hooked; so it was important for women to recognize the early signs that she was dating a sociopath: the narcissistic behavior, the seemingly compulsive manipulation of others.

When she wrote, she still found her own honesty surprising her. She almost startled herself with the balance when she wrote about Stephen Stanko. He had caused her a lot of pain, but there had been a lot of laughter as well. It seemed almost bizarre to hear herself say it now, but he was . . . *fun-loving*, for the most part.

As long as she molded herself into *just* the girlfriend he wanted, and wasn't a problem or an obstruction to him, then he was very nice. Kind. Gentle.

Over the years, she had followed cases that reminded her of Stephen, cases like that Scott Peterson who killed his beautiful wife, Laci. He was another Stephen Stanko in Liz's eye. Then there was that couple from Utah, Mark and Lori Hacking. Before he killed her—when she was five weeks pregnant—he did nothing but lie to her. He planned to move her across the country based on the lie that he was going to medical school in North Carolina. He reported her missing and lied convincingly to the media for two weeks, until he was arrested. Stephen would have done that, too.

Stephen was always threatening to take Liz to other parts of the country, really anywhere: New York City . . . Seattle, Washington . . . Rochester, New York. He said it was because of business concerns, but knowing what she knew now, she suspected he just wanted to put some space between himself and the people he'd burned. Plus, he'd be taking her out of her element, to separate her from her support system so that she would be exclusively dependent on him. A dependent woman was the ultimate mark, malleable to the max when subjected to sophisticated psychological manipulation. That's the way these men were. They separated their women from their sources of information. Victims were forced to trust them and believe the things—the lies!—they said.

In her writing, Liz still questioned why she let Stephen back into her life, in the days before he tried to suffocate her with a chemical-drenched cloth. She fell for his tricks every time. He had to try to kill her before she caught on. She knew that Laura Ling, were she still around, would be kicking herself for the same reason.

Liz had spent too many hours contemplating that attack of fifteen years before. She looked at it alone and as part of the "big picture." She realized she was *practice* for Stephen Stanko. Hers was the incomplete murder, the one he used to help improve his technique. He learned that the chemical asphyxiation scenario was a Hollywood construct. Next time, he'd use a knife. He got his taste of violence, went to prison, did some research on how killers did it and the perverted fetishes they fulfilled, and then he went out and did it.

Liz didn't believe Stephen got his first taste of violence when he attacked her in 1996. She believed he had been thinking about hurting and killing people long before that. He'd already begun his research. Fortunately for her, he was using the cinema as his source, rather than a nonfiction source that might have sparked a more lethal game plan.

Another aspect of the case that still puzzled her was the sexual nature of Stephen's crimes against Penny Ling. She'd been with the man almost four years and it never occurred to her that he was a future rapist. Maybe it was something he picked up while researching serial killers, or maybe it was something that had been tickling around in his brain (or whatever) for years. The rape shocked Liz because Stephen had a niece whom he adored. He was very close to her, loving toward her, and supportive of her activities, like gymnastics. How could that same person who adored his niece like that rape a teenager?

At the time, Liz saw the events as linear, one thing after another, bad to worse, when it came to her killer ex-boyfriend; but with wisdom, she came to see his behavior as a cycle. The same events happened over and over again. Pick up a single mom; promise security; leech room, board, and money; fail at real life; replace it with a con game; become frustrated; outlive your welcome in the woman's home; become violent.

It had happened to her, and to Laura Ling, and it probably would have happened to Dana Putnam as well, if she hadn't seen Stanko's photo on page 5B. The Ling crime scene had a lot in common with the 1996 scene in her home. He used neckties to bind his victims. He dropped the chemicals and, instead, beat Ling in the face and head until she was semiconscious, then strangled her. It was a horrible way to look at it, but he'd *learned,* improved his technique.

Liz would never understand why she was still alive. Why had Stephen stopped and let her live? Why hadn't he finished her off? Did he run out of guts—so that he had to kill Laura Ling to prove to himself he was a real man? It was a sick thought, but he was a sick guy.

Liz didn't just write about the things she knew. She did research so she could approach, with some knowledge under her belt, the subject of abused women—and the men who abused them. She knew about sociopaths and psychopaths. She remembered reading the definition of narcissism and thinking how it fit Stanko to a tee. He was self-centered to a pathological degree, and self-aggrandizing. He needed to be the big man, bigger than life, the alpha male, and every ounce of his energy was dedicated toward making that so. He had to believe his own lies. He could not be honest with himself, because reality could never satisfy his ego the way his imagination could.

She thought about the "nature versus nurture" question. Not that she was a medical expert, but Liz didn't believe that Stephen was affected at all by a difficult birth or a concussion as a teenager. She did, however, think that Stephen's upbringing and his personality disorder were associated. Liz had had a conversation with one of Stephen's relatives once and had learned some insight into what life was like with a naval master chief in charge. It was stifling, she'd been told, almost despair inducing.

And in 2010, Liz still worked on her book every day. Maybe not three or four pages every day, but a few sentences; maybe a paragraph about a new idea that had struck her; maybe a full page, on an especially prolific day. Until recently, she hadn't had an awful lot of time. Lately she had been working at home, running her marketing consultant business, spending most of her day at the computer—so she had increased flexibility in her schedule, more time to dedicate to doing the things she wanted to do.

As far as getting her writing published, Liz hadn't gotten very far. She had taken some tentative steps to secure herself a literary agent, but without success.

She'd thought the Stephen Stanko name itself would be a door opener. She'd also spent time contemplating self-publishing, but she had decided she didn't want to go that route. She lacked the distribution capabilities to make such a venture efficient.

But she would never give up. She wanted to provide abused women with a voice. When in that situation, everyone needed to know that they weren't alone. All of those women who had crawled into their holes needed to know there was hope. And most of all, they should know that none of it was their fault—nothing was true *just because* their attacker said it was.

Liz became infuriated when she thought of it. She knew that Stanko, even on death row, was still promoting the notion that Laura Ling was in some way responsible for her own death.

Not all of Liz's writing was about Stephen Stanko. She also wrote poetry, some of which she had gotten published, and music as well. She was the sort of person who would get up in the middle of the night and sit with a light on in a quiet spot and just start writing.

"I don't want this to be my only book. I want this to be my first book," Liz said.

In 2010, Penny Ling was finishing her bachelor's degree at a prestigious private university in South Carolina. Like her parents, she was very intelligent and earned several scholarships.

Dana Putnam married George Burkhart during Christmas break, 2009, in Key West. They live in Georgia.

* * *

Dr. Kim A. Collins, the forensic pathologist on both the Laura Ling and Henry Turner cases, was the wife of federal judge David Norton and lived on Wadmalaw Island, with two dachshunds and three retired racing greyhounds. She would have loved to say that the Stanko case was the toughest of her career, but it wasn't even close. Once, nine firefighters, whom she considered her colleagues, were killed in a fire. "These were the people we were working with. Now your colleagues are your victims. Anytime you know the person, it is hard to fathom," she said. She insisted that all nine autopsies be conducted in one day, so that they could stay together as a team throughout the postmortem procedure. This allowed the city of Charleston to have an official police and firefighter escort of the bodies to the funeral homes the following day.

Sergeant Jeff Gause, the man who photographed the Turner murder scene, was slightly injured in a car chase in 2009. On a Saturday night, Steven Wayne Branham, wanted for the robbery of a Family Dollar Store in Little River, rammed Gause's car three times, causing him to spin out of control. Gause was flown by helicopter to New Hanover Regional Medical Center in Wilmington, North Carolina. He was treated overnight at a nearby hospital and released in the morning. The incident was only a prelude to the conclusion of the chase. After smashing into Gause's car, Branham crashed through a ditch, crossed a front yard, and eventually plowed several hundred feet into a cornfield. There, with cops in close pursuit, he shot and killed himself. Controversy briefly flared when police stated that a Horry County sergeant, not Gause, was seen, gun drawn, standing over the "dead at the scene" perp.

The story quieted quickly when forensics determined Branham actually had committed suicide.

Georgetown County investigator William Pierce, one of the first cops at the Laura Ling murder scene, was promoted to the rank of Enforcement Captain by Sheriff Lane Cribb on July 16, 2008. Captain Pierce's new duties included overseeing the Criminal Investigations Division, the Uniform Patrol Division, the Organized Crime Bureau, Courthouse Security, the Warrants Division, and Community Services.

At the end of December 2009, Horry County deputy solicitor Fran Humphries, who'd been involved in both of Stephen Stanko's death penalty trials, retired from the Fifteenth Judicial Circuit. After twenty years in prosecution, he said he was ready for "new adventures." He entered a private practice with the Monckton Law Firm, where he would be working both criminal injury and criminal defense cases. Calling the move "bittersweet," Humphries said he was proud to have worked all those years at Greg Hembree's side. "I am thankful that I had the honor of working under the finest prosecutor in this state, and a finer man," Humphries said.

Kelly Crolley was still working at her family's furniture store in Surfside Beach. She still wondered what Stephen Stanko had in mind when he entered the Owl-O-Rest in 2004. Did the con game go off as planned? Or, was he out to steal furniture?

Crolley couldn't help but feel a little guilty. If she

had been more tenacious when she first suspected Stanko was a crook, maybe he'd have gone to jail and he wouldn't have had an opportunity to kill those people.

Nonetheless, life for Crolley was good. Her daughter, who weighed less than two pounds when born, was a beautiful and healthy ten-year-old in 2010.

Clarice Wenz, Stephen Stanko's chemistry and physics teacher at Goose Creek High School, retired as a teacher and took a part-time job as a consultant for a science book publisher. She taught teachers how to operate the classroom equipment that accompanied the publisher's text.

Stephen Stanko's original coauthor, Dr. Gordon Crews, was "not trying to be a vulture," but still hoped the original manuscript for *After the Gavel Drops* would be published. They worked for years on it, and he'd like to share that effort with the world.

That manuscript, Crews said, was "much more realistic and gritty" than the one that was appropriate for high-school students. But Crews, who was in the spring of 2010 tenured as a full professor at Marshall University in West Virginia, could do nothing with the material he had until he got Stanko's permission. When Stanko finished his appeals process, Crews planned to get in touch to see if Stanko wanted to do another book.

Dr. Michael Braswell, who turned down an opportunity to coauthor Stephen Stanko's book (although he did write the foreword), believed that Stanko's time was running out. He was close to exhausting his legal options.

"His defense has become a caricature," Braswell opined.

With Stephen Stanko back in Lieber, there were fifty residents of South Carolina's death row. Three more condemned men lived at Gilliam Psychiatric, and a fourth was housed on death row in San Quentin, California, where he'd been convicted of another capital murder. Seniority went to Edward L. Elmore, twenty-eight years on death row. At fifty-one years old, Elmore had been there more than half of his life.

Even from a psychopath's point of view, there were elements of Stanko's behavior during his spree that were *not cool*. Raping an underage girl. Very uncool. Pedophiles were the lowest rung on the prison ladder, and were—whenever the opportunity arose—treated like toilet paper. And then there was getting caught. Also uncool. He had simply taken inadequate steps to evade capture. He was still driving the truck he stole from his final victim. Why not switch vehicles? Perhaps he only knew how to steal a car if he had the keys in his hand. Why hadn't he changed his appearance? A simple brush cut might have done the trick. Perhaps he was too vain to get rid of his hair.

And so Stephen Stanko sat on death row, facing a lengthy legal process to be followed by his execution. Even though he lived in a cage, his psychopathy raged on. He still believed himself to be someone he wasn't.

No longer the jailhouse lawyer who helped everyone with their paperwork, Stanko was isolated on death row, alone with his hopeless addiction to patting himself on the back. Was he a martyr? For a cause? Maybe the martyr for prison reform?

That would show the archaic corrections system! That would show them all what a great man Stanko was. Was he a future inductee into the "Killer Hall of Fame" because he was so cool in the hours after he killed two people, he was able to make friends, even begin a relationship with a woman, while on the run for his life? That was ultracool, the stuff of which movies were made. Did he wonder who would play him in the movie?

Maybe years on death row would one day burrow—like a rodent—a hole in his delusion, causing him to see himself with a clear, unaffected eye. Inside his head, he would hear his echoing name—*Stanko, Stanko, Stanko*—the very name that everyone remembered, everyone had a joke about, the name that might have caused a fair share of sadness in his childhood in Goose Creek.

He was lonely. Unable to manipulate others, clock ticking, needle waiting, perhaps one day he would only be able to manipulate himself into a writhing case of the horrors.

BIBLIOGRAPHY

Jones, Mark R., *Palmetto Predators: Monsters Among Us,* Charleston, S.C.: The History Press, 2007.

Stanko, Stephen, Wayne Gillespie, and Gordon A. Crews, *Living in Prison: A History of the Correctional System with an Insider's View,* Westport, Ct.: Greenwood Press, 2004.